THE BOOK OF
MYLOR

A Cornish Creekside Village and Harbour

MYLOR LOCAL HISTORY GROUP

HALSGROVE

First published in Great Britain in 2004

Title page: *The village street before 1904, when the ash tree was felled and Ash Villa was built.*

British Library Cataloguing-in-Publication Data.
A CIP record for this title is available from the British Library.

ISBN 1 84114 326 X

HALSGROVE

Halsgrove House
Lower Moor Way
Tiverton, Devon EX16 6SS
Tel: 01884 243242
Fax: 01884 243325
email: sales@halsgrove.com
website: www.halsgrove.com

Printed and bound in Great Britain by CPI Bath.

Christopher Perkins.

FOREWORD

Having been associated with Mylor for 30 years, it is a great honour to be asked to write this foreword. The village and dockyard could not have been more delightful places to live and work during those years. My wife, Sarita, and I started and built up our yacht-charter business from the perfect base of Mylor Harbour and we have enjoyed living in Mylor for many years, firstly at Little Tregew, then Six Turnings and more recently at Porloe.

Mylor is fortunate in that, unlike many other villages in Cornwall, it has retained a strong sense of traditional values and local pride in its community. As the splendid selection of photographs in this book shows, huge changes in the way people live, travel and communicate have occurred over the years; but despite all this, the village has retained its essential elements – its local characters, pubs, shops, churches and local businesses. The village remains the focus for those involved in work on both land and sea, although the pace of life has changed so dramatically, of course.

Many congratulations to those who have been involved in the production of this superb volume. I know that it will be a great success and will become a treasured addition to many local bookcases, as well as a useful reference work. Those who peruse and enjoy the contents will be grateful, as I am, to the contributors and editors who have produced such a fascinating insight into the past of this very special village.

Christopher Perkins
High Sheriff of Cornwall 2003/4
January 2004
Porloe

KEY
● ● ● = Parish Boundary

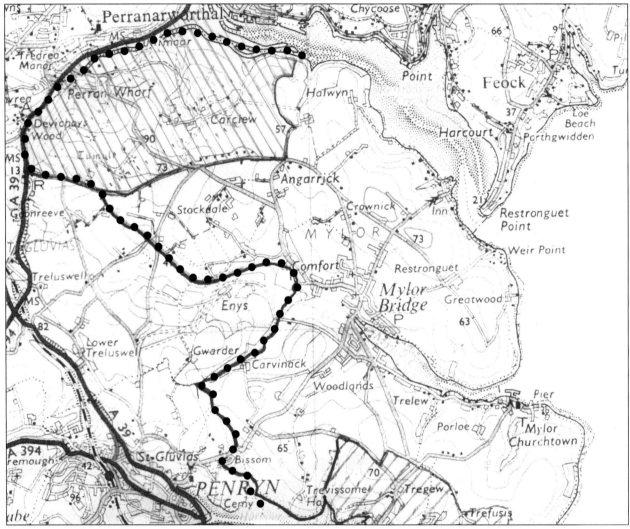

Map showing Mylor parish boundary, 1979. Cross hatching indicates Carclew (top left) and Flushing (bottom right).

(REPRODUCED BY KIND PERMISSION OF ORDNANCE SURVEY © CROWN COPYRIGHT NC/2004/29911)

Children on the playing field, 1950s.

ACKNOWLEDGEMENTS

Joan West, working with Janet Mosedale and Val Jeans-Jakobsson as a team to draw together the wealth of material for this book, would like to thank others in the Mylor Local History Group for their research and writing, including Althea Bailey, Felicity Collins, Kate Crombie and Wendy Potter. Thanks are also due to: Dorothy White who typed for many hours, working from our contributors' handwritten notes; Michael Jeans-Jakobsson who provided valuable computer expertise to produce the final version of the book; and Phil Jones (CATS, computer services) who was involved in the early stages, transforming numerous typed articles to computer disk.

Many others (past and present) have written articles or helped with recording memories:
John Bramley, Becky Bunny, Betty Butterworth, Jean Calvert, Nancy Chamberlin, Doreen Christmas, Nora Coleman, Bruce Collier, John Collins, Dorothy Congdon, Frank Curnow, Mary Dale, Rosemary and Oliver Dale, Phil Davey, Joan Davis, Stan Evans, Eileen Ferris, Bernice Gay, Roger Graffy, Eric Gray, Eric Gunton, Maureen Harmer, James Hawke, Martin and Janet Heard, George Hearle, Fred Ingram, Revd Charles James, Heather Johns, Ken and Ann Keast, Percy Lobb, Mary Martin, Minnie May, Jackie Meyers, Vera Moore, Harry Moore, Elliot Nicholls, Eric Nicholls, Phyllis Nichols, Ken Norcross, Christopher Perkins, Eileen Prout, Sue Prout, Sandra Redwood, Arthur and Barbara Rickard, Barbara Roach, Glynis Robinson, Rose Rogers, Elsie Rowe, Derek and Penny Rowe, Ada Stead, Morwenna Stephens, David Thomas, James Thomas, Alan Townend, Daphne Train, John Treneer, Frank Vinnicombe, Pixie Wells, Christopher Whiteley, Nan Williams and Mary Young.

Others have loaned precious photographs, including:
Our churches and chapel, Mylor village school, Mylor Yacht Harbour, Tony and Ruth Andrew and the Parish Council, clubs and societies, Yvonne Andrew, Molly Bowers, Andrew Campbell, Ruth Chamberlain, Irene Champion, Barbara Cowling, Ann Craig, Peter Gilson, Carolyn Harman, Colin and Joan Heard, Ann Langford, Daphne Neale, William Rickard, Elsie Rowe, Len and Margaret Simpson, Runa Spring, Peter Watson and Paul Willis.

Artwork has been provided by Peter Clark and Jean Clapham (line drawings), Bruce Collier (cartoons), Wendy Jones (photography), and Margaret Simpson (paintings). Watercolours are reproduced by kind permission of the artist, M.W. Cockell.

Others, who have helped in various ways, include:
Angela Broom, Courtney Library, RIC, Prue Evans, Peter Ashworth, National Maritime Museum Greenwich, staff at Falmouth and Truro Libraries, Record Office – Cornwall, Department of Cornish Studies – Redruth, Commonwealth War Graves Commission, Royal Naval Museum Portsmouth, and Bob Harwood – the Ganges Association, the late N.G. Treseder and Moira Tangye whose history classes inspired us to start writing.

Many thanks to all the above, and apologies to anyone we may have missed out.

EXTRACTS FROM *ALL THE DAY LONG* BY HOWARD SPRING ARE REPRODUCED BY KIND PERMISSION OF THE PUBLISHER STRATUS.
EXTRACTS FROM *MEMORIES AND GARDENS* BY MARION HOWARD SPRING ARE REPRODUCED BY KIND PERMISSION OF HARPER COLLINS.

An aerial view of Mylor Creek with the Yacht Harbour in the foreground and the village of Mylor Bridge at the top of the picture, 2002.

The passenger vessel Alexandra *steaming out of Mylor Creek soon after 1900.*

CONTENTS

Aerial photograph of Mylor Bridge, 2000.

(BY KIND PERMISSION OF WENDY JONES)

INTRODUCTION

Mylor Local History Group was formed three years ago under the leadership of Joan West, a local historian, after a number of us attended a series of WEA local history classes in the village. Each member had an interest in history and a desire to carry out research into Mylor's fascinating past. Each chose to write about an aspect of village life with which they felt a particular connection, sometimes through earlier experiences. Thus 'farming', 'the harbour', 'churches' and 'schools' etc. began to form natural sections and the project grew rapidly. In January 2003 we linked up with Halsgrove aiming to produce a book in line with others in their Community Histories Series.

During our studies and following an appeal for additional information about the village, we have been overwhelmed by the number of photographs, newspaper cuttings and written material received. For all these we are most grateful. We added them to the vast quantity of material already collected by Joan West over more than 30 years. Joan has been our inspiration and her tenacious pursuit of historical academic evidence has introduced us to many local stories of tragedy, humour, mystery and intrigue!

We feel privileged to have been able to undertake the creation of this book, which is the first comprehensive study of Mylor since Dr Olivey of Albion House wrote his book in 1907. Numerous references have been made to his work which has been a valuable resource. Although Mylor and Flushing are part of the same parish, we have limited our study to Mylor and as you will see there is more than enough material for this book from our village, which has always been a thriving and varied community.

It has been a hard task for us to decide which items should be included, and which should be set aside, maybe for the next generation to compile a volume II or maybe even a volume III! We apologise to all those donors whose information is not included in this book and thank them for their help and interest. Perhaps we shall be able to find a suitable place in the village to store these precious archives? Possibly a small area in a newly-refurbished Tremayne Hall might become a reality in the future – we can certainly hope!

No doubt we have made mistakes and, as with any historical events, there are different versions and accounts – memories can be remarkably varied and unreliable! Also, the spelling of local names has changed over the years and this too can be confusing. For all this we apologise in advance and trust that the book will give you some of the pleasure that we have experienced in its compilation. How lucky we are to live in this beautiful, sheltered, creekside village, tucked away on the south coast of West Cornwall!

Val Jeans-Jakobsson
Secretary of Mylor Local History Group

Aerial photograph of Mylor Churchtown, 2000.

Chapter 1

Carclew

In the Beginning, The Bonythons, William Lemon, The Third William Lemon, Sir Charles Lemon, Land Clearance, Early Photography, Lieutenant Colonel Arthur Tremayne, Memories of Carclew, William Francis Tremayne, The Fire, The Bonythons Return, A Quaker Presence.

How Many Miles to Mylor?

*How many miles to Mylor
By frost and candle-light:
How long before I arrive there,
This mild December night?*

*As I mounted the hill to Mylor
Through the thick woods of Carclew,
A clock struck the three-quarters,
And suddenly a cock crew.*

*At the cross-roads on the hill-top
The snow lay on the ground,
In the quick air and the stillness,
No movement and no sound.*

*'How is it?' said a voice from the bushes
Beneath the rowan tree;
'Who is it?' my mouth re-echoed,
My heart went out of me.*

*I cannot tell what queerness
There lay around Carclew;
Nor whatever stirred in the hedges
When an owl replied 'Who-whoo?'*

*A lamp in a lone cottage,
A face in a window-frame,
Above the snow a wicket;
A house without a name.*

*How many miles to Mylor
This dark December night;
And shall I ever arrive there
By frost or candlelight?*

In his book *Cornwall: A Journey through Cornwall's Past and Present*, published in 1988, A.L. Rowse tells how he came to write his poem about Mylor. He 'walked up through the lovely woods and down to lovely Mylor.' He recalls going up the hill one dark, snowy night on his way, unromantically, to a political meeting. He was alone and a little afraid. 'So fear prevailed in the poem that formed itself as I went', though when originally published it had the prosaic title 'Walking to the Meeting'.

In the Beginning

Although Mylor was not considered worthy of the name of 'village' until the seventeenth century, its history is long. We know that the area was inhabited in the Iron Age, about 600BC, for there are the mounds of earth called barrows at Carclew. These are unexcavated burial places – in fact, the name Carclew derives from the Cornish language: Cruc (a barrow) and Clu (a ditch or fence).

A panel, representing prehistoric times, from the Tregellas Tapestry, conceived and researched by the late Rita Tregellas Pope, a Cornish Bard whose home was in Mylor. It was completed in 1996.

(REPRODUCED BY KIND PERMISSION OF HER DAUGHTER, KATE CROMBIE)

A circular earth fortification – an earthwork – between Mylor Church and Trefusis dates from the same time and in Devichoys Wood there are the remains of a round or homestead site of the late Iron Age, about 100BC. The round enclosure bank would most likely have been topped by a wooden palisade. The following extract from a letter from the Department of the Environment (6.8.74) confirms this:

... part of a circular enclosure exists on the south side of Devichoys Wood. If this circular enclosure belongs to the large class of monument in Cornwall known as 'rounds', it represents the visible remains of a homestead site of the late Iron Age, approx. 100 BC. The round enclosure bank would have probably originally been topped by a wooden palisade. No excavation has taken place on the site and we can say little more. The site is mentioned in the late

Mrs E. Dawson's checklist for the purist publisher in the periodical, Cornish Archaeology.

Later came people seeking metal. The Carnon Valley nearby was very rich in tin, so merchants of many lands, including Romans, were attracted to the area. Tin, extracted by streaming, would have been carried by boat to Restronguet and thence down the Fal for export. In the museum at Truro there is a large tin ingot weighing 160lb which was dredged up off St Mawes, and the shape relates to the copper talent of Crete.

The history of Cornwall is the history of tin. This unique tin ingot was dredged up off St Mawes and is in the Royal Cornwall Museum.

At the time of Christ's birth, Cornwall was inhabited by predominantly Celtic stock, originating in south-eastern France and swept before the expanding Roman Empire across the south of England bringing its culture and language. The Romans seem to have had little impact on Cornwall but when they left there were organised groups of Christians here.

Among the travellers of the fifth and sixth centuries were missionaries coming to reinforce the faith. One from Brittany was St Milor, an abbot-bishop, who is our patron saint. Over the next two centuries trading developed in the sheltered Mylor creek and small settlements began to form, the basic unit being the farmstead clustered around by huts for animals and serfs. In 823, Egbert, Saxon king of Wessex, laid claim to all land west of the Tamar. He did little with it, but there are Saxon place-names to prove that they were here – for example, Carsawsen means 'camp of the Saxons' and is a local farm.

In 1066 the Normans invaded Britain. King William I seems to have inspired faithful forces. He had excellent soldiers and administrators, who were confident that rich rewards would result from supporting him. His half-brother, Robert de Mortain, was the King's right-hand man, and for his loyalty and efficiency he was rewarded with almost 300 manors scattered throughout the county, some of which he sublet to friends.

Mylor comprised three manors: the manor of Mylor, centred on the church, Trefusis manor and the manor of Restronguet. In 1290 we know that the last named was held by the Bodrugan family and Carclew emerges as the Barton or chief farm of Restronguet, the tenancy of which was granted to Richard D'Angers, a Norman baron, for one silver mark and an annual rent of half a mark.

The Bonythons

A century or so later, a descendant of the Norman baron died, leaving a daughter, married to Richard Bonython, to inherit. Henry Bodrugan then gave Carclew to the couple 'free of any dependence on Restronguet'. When the War of the Roses started, the Bonythons, being staunch Lancastrians, rebelled against King Richard III when he seized the throne. James, the owner of Carclew at that time, was forced to flee the country and all his possessions were confiscated. However, when the victorious Lancastrian, Henry VII, became king, the Bonythons were reinstated with honour and considerable compensation.

The family continued as owners of the Barton and when James Bonython died in 1697 he made several bequests, including £100 to be given at Christmas yearly for the relief of Mylor's poor, and £10 for erecting an almshouse for the poor elderly. We do not know what happened to the Christmas gifts but the almshouse was built and stands still at Tregatreath, the boatyard home of Martin and Janet Heard. Clearly, this is a very old house, having a two-storey part for tenants, and a right-hand portion added later for animals, when it became Tregatreath Farm. The present front was originally the back, the windows and doorway facing south, so that the almshouse tenants could sit before their house and watch the play on the adjacent bowling-green.

James Bonython's heir was a daughter, Jane, who at the time of her inheritance was married to one Samuel Kemp, a well-to-do merchant of Penryn and an ambitious man who dreamed of a great new mansion with vast ornamental gardens. Unhappily, he did not have the money to make the dream a complete reality and he died in 1728, leaving no children and his widow greatly in debt. On her death, Carclew was bequeathed to her cousin, John Bonython of Grampound, and ten years later the estate was bought in its entirety by William Lemon for £3,300.

William Lemon

The 'Great Mr Lemon' was born in Gulval in 1695 in humble circumstances. He started out as a working tin miner but by natural ability and hard work became the most eminent Cornish industrialist of his time. He amassed great wealth, owning both tin mines and the Calenick smelting works. Already he had built the largest and most impressive house in Truro, Princes House, which can still be seen in 2004. The house was the work of a self-educated architect, Thomas Edwards, who was responsible for designing many other Cornish buildings, including Trewithen, Trelowarren, Tehidy and Helston Parish Church.

William Lemon was a powerful man but much admired and respected, men doffing their caps and women curtseying as he approached. Davies Gilbert, the Cornish writer and philosopher, writes in his *Parish History,* 'The people of Truro drew back from their doors as he passed,' and the Revd Samuel Waller exhorted the children to be circumspect in the presence of Almighty God, adding 'Only think, my dear children, how careful you would be if Mr Lemon were looking upon you.' But that great man was ever aware of his lack of formal education and in his later years employed a master from Truro Grammar School to teach him Latin and Greek.

William Lemon wanted to build a really grand house and, once more, Thomas Edwards was sought. The mansion of Carclew was completed in the classical style and around it, Mr Lemon established 230 acres of parkland with 150 fallow deer, laid out fine gardens and planted extensive woodlands. A record of the time shows the following list of the many rooms at Carclew in 1760:

Garret
Mr Lemon's room
Master Jacky Lemon's room
Garland Room
Master Lemon's room
Chinese room
Green room
Best room
Best staircase
Back staircase
Study
Common Parlour
Tapestry room
India Paper room
Saloon
Hall
Lobby
Housekeeper's room
Kitchen
Servants' Hall
Steward's room
Buttery and Pantry
Laundry
Scullery
Wash-house
Brew house
Maid's chamber
Shepherd's chamber
Coach-house and chambers
Wood Chamber
Gardener's room
Hind's house

The Third William Lemon

The first William Lemon died in 1760, having served twice as Mayor of Truro and as High Sheriff in 1712.

His son and heir, also William, pre-deceased him by three years so it was his grandson, yet another William, who became master of Carclew and the first baronet in 1774.

He was well versed in estate management and soon saw a chance to increase his holding by purchasing the ailing Restronguet Manor, so the two estates were once more united, with Carclew owning all the land between Mylor and Restronguet creeks. Properties in Kea, Feock, Stithians and other villages were also purchased. In 1770, he was elected MP for Penryn and Falmouth and continued as a Whig member for 50 years. Although often absent in London, he still played an active part in Mylor affairs and was seen as a father figure in the village.

After Sir William's death in 1824, his one remaining son, Charles, succeeded. He had married Charlotte Fox Strangways by whom he had three children: Charles, who died at three weeks; another Charles, named after his dead brother; and a daughter, Charlotte Augusta. The latter died in Switzerland aged nine and, less than a year later, Charles, his heir, drowned in the swimming-pool of his school, Harrow. Three weeks later, the mother, Lady Charlotte herself died of a broken heart.

The pall of tragedy hung over Carclew for some considerable time, but Sir Charles' niece, Louisa Hart Dyke, came to live there, acting as chatelaine and companion to her uncle.

Sir Charles Lemon

Sir Charles again took up his public life. He was Member of Parliament for Penryn in 1830 and later for Truro. His interests in Mylor were social welfare and education, being also active in the Cornwall Polytechnic Society for the Promotion of Science and the Arts and was its first president. The gardens of the mansion were further extended and many rare and beautiful plants introduced, including valuable specimens brought back from the Americas and Far East by the famous plant hunters, William and Thomas Lobb, who had come to work at Carclew as

Engraving of Carclew House on stone by J.R. Jobbins, dating from the mid-nineteenth century, from a sketch by T. Sopwith.
(By kind permission of Courtney Library, RIC)

Map of Mylor and Restronguet Creeks drawn by Baptista Boazio in 1597, showing Cariklewe (Carclew) and Mr Bonithon's (Bonython) land.

Above: *Carclew House in the mid-nineteenth century, the main residence of the 'Great Mr Lemon' who engaged Thomas Edwards of Greenwich to complete it in the classical style.*

Left: *William Lemon, in an engraving by J.H. Meyer, b.1696. Lemon built Prince's House, Truro, in c.1737, was Sheriff of Cornwall in 1742 and died in 1760.*

Sir Charles Lemon, Baronet of Carclew, c.1850.

Engraving of Carclew House made for William Lemon by Wm Borlase in 1758. Wm Borlase was vicar of Ludgvan from 1696 to 1772 and an eminent Cornish antiquarian, naturalist and Fellow of the Royal Society.

(BY KIND PERMISSION OF COURTNEY LIBRARY, RIC)

young garden boys. Noting their talent, Sir Charles had encouraged them to study plant cultivation and botany. The house now became an outstanding centre of intellectual and cultural life in the county. The rich, distinguished and famous were entertained in an atmosphere of progressive ideas. Carlyle, Tennyson and Davies Gilbert, the Cornish writer and philosopher, and many others are recorded as visiting in *The Journals and Letters of Caroline Fox of Penjerrick*.

Sir Charles Lemon, in advanced age, sitting below the terrace with his niece. He was president of the Royal Polytechnic Society, giving encouragement to science and invention and championing mining education. He died in 1868.

In 1837, the village inn, first known as the Griffin and then the Red Lion, was rebuilt, enlarged and renamed the Lemon Arms. Tenants would come there on quarter day to pay their dues, then go upstairs and enjoy a cut of roast beef and a pint of ale; a great social occasion.

The poorhouse occupants were transferred to the Union at Budock in 1845. Sir Charles bought the building and its extension (now Old School House) for £145 and a school was set up to accommodate more than 100 girls and boys. This he maintained out of his own pocket until his death. An Italianate clock tower and bell ensured that the children were not late for school.

Land Clearance

Among a number of cuttings from old newspapers on display at an exhibition marking the hundredth anniversary of Mylor Parish Council was one from 1919. It is a letter from John Pascoe Treneer, son of

Robert Treneer of St Gluvias, born 3 February 1853, then 81 years of age and a resident of Kingston, Ontario, Canada. Mr Treneer recalls the days when Sir Charles Lemon resided at Carclew:

As a boy, I went to Mrs Enys' School in Broads Lane, where the teacher was Mrs Harvey. When I became too big for a woman's school, I went to Mylor School, conducted by Mr Ashton, schoolmaster.

Then I went to work at Carclew, the estate of Sir Charles Lemon, Bart, where my father was teamster for 25 years, except seeding time and harvest. Then we sowed the grain by hand and carried the seed in, mowing with the help of 15 men. In those days, they got no extra money but there was 16 gallons of local-brewed beer a day, a gallon a day for each man.

My father did not drink. The land steward was Mr Sanders, a Scotsman, and one day he asked my father why he did not drink his share. But my father was a class teacher and trustee of the Bible Christian Church and staunch temperance supporter.

As a boy, Mr Treneer drove horses in an all-wrought-iron plough with his father at the handles. They ploughed up Mylor Downs, which ran from near Carclew Lodge to Mrs Enys' school (56 acres). It was the first time this land was ever broken and it was a hard job. He saw his father thrown from the plough onto ploughed land with great force when they struck the large spar boulders in the ground. They took 13 weeks to rip up the downs and had to carry a pick with them. After that was completed, he went to the cow and poultry yard at Carclew, carrying the milk and cream to the house twice a day.

A friend, Mr Hodge, a grocer in Kingston, passed the Falmouth local paper to him and there he read of the death of Alec George whose father was a shepherd at Carclew. Alec helped his father and also worked in the carpenter's shop. In those days, William Copeland was blacksmith; William Bullen and George Hall, masons; Mr Bailey, coachman; and Thomas Rogers and John Pearce, hand sawyers. At Sir Charles Lemon's death in 1868, the men on the farm got £1, the boys ten shillings and the servants in the house two years' wages.

Early Photography

In August 1841, (William) Henry Fox Talbot, pioneer of photography and eminent scientist, visited Carclew House and took photographs of the house for the first time. Sir Charles Lemon was the uncle by marriage of Fox Talbot and it is thought that the photographs he took there were among the earliest taken in Cornwall.

Fox Talbot had been developing his process during the 1830s. He took out a patent in 1841 for his Talbotype technique, but he made it clear that he intended the use of it to be free to the scientific world. Everyone was excited and impressed by the new process and Sir Charles Lemon identified the advances in optics and chemistry which had made the images clearer and the margins more distinct. At that time Sir Charles was President of the Royal Cornwall Polytechnic Society.

Henry became a Fellow of the Royal Society in 1831. His certificate of recommendation was signed by seven fellows including Michael Faraday, as well as his uncles, Sir Charles Lemon and William Thomas Fox-Strangways. Henry was also elected MP for Chippenham in 1832 and was welcomed to Westminster by friends and relatives already there, including Sir Charles.

The Talbotypes of Carclew included the main elevation and also a group of four people posing in front of the house. Reference is made to a third image, a view of the chapel, by Sir Charles in a letter to Henry Fox Talbot.

Lieutenant Colonel Arthur Tremayne

Sir Charles Lemon died in 1868 at the age of 84 and was succeeded by his nephew, Arthur Tremayne, the son of Sir Charles' sister, Carolyn, and John Hearle Tremayne of Heligan. He had been commissioned in the 13th Light Dragoons and served in Ireland and the Crimea, where he was one of the gallant 600 who took part in the Charge of the Light Brigade. During the charge, his horse was shot from under him, as was the heel of one boot – 'An ordinary incident of war', remarked this gallant gentleman.

Shown below is the 1881 census entry for those then living at Carclew, which gives an idea of the kind of household that Arthur Tremayne maintained.

Memories of Carclew

Mr Harry Moore of Waterings Road, Mylor, who died many years ago, recorded some memories of his childhood. He spoke of Carclew and the cricket club, its colours of blue and gold stripes after the racing colours of the Tremayne family. After the matches, both teams were entertained to tea at the mansion, the old Lieutenant Colonel sitting at the head of the long table, whilst footmen and serving girls waited on the players. In the early years of this century there were two kinds of cricket; the country-house variety and the village game. Country-house cricket is now largely a thing of the past, its heyday being the Edwardian era. It owed its existence to the enthusiasm of the squires and landowners, who fostered the game on their private grounds, giving tenants a chance to play and watch amateur cricket at its best. The social side was important too and there have been many descriptions of the

NAME	RELATION TO HEAD OF FAMILY	MARITAL STATUS	AGE	GENDER	PROFESSION	WHERE BORN
Arthur Tremayne	Head	M	53	M	Lt Col Cavalry (retired)	London, Middlesex
Emma Tremayne	Wife	M	38	F		Gwennap, Cornwall
Arthur E. Tremayne	Son		8	M	Scholar	Mylor, Cornwall
Alice Opie Tremayne	Daughter		6	F	Scholar	Mylor, Cornwall
Kate Scarlett	Governess	U	24	F	Governess	Taunton, Somerset
Mary Yestrim	Servant	M	37	F	Cook Domestic	Worcester
Elizabeth Oliver	Servant	U	33	F	Lady's Maid	St Erth, Cornwall
Annie Roberts	Servant	U	27	F	Housemaid	St Keverne, Cornwall
Alice Rowe	Servant	U	18	F	Housemaid	St Keverne, Cornwall
Alice Baily	Servant	U	20	F	Nursery Maid	Mylor, Cornwall
Louisa Williams	Servant	U	26	F	Laundry Maid	Veryan, Cornwall
Bessie Harnell	Servant	U	22	F	Laundry Maid	Feock, Cornwall
Emma Howe	Servant	U	20	F	Still room Maid	Kingsbridge, Somerset
Margaret Collick	Servant	U	25	F	Kitchen Maid	Knackers Knowle, Devon
Elizabeth Normington	Servant	U	19	F	Scullery Maid	Redruth, Cornwall
Jeremiah Patrick	Servant	U	53	M	Butler, Dom. Servant	Norfolk
Albert Sanders	Servant	U	21	M	Footman	Lostwithiel, Cornwall
Lewis Johnson	Servant	U	20	M	Footman	Northumberland
Edward Pope	Servant	U	20	M	Groom	Perranarworthal, Cornwall
Robert Rogers	Servant	U	19	M	Helper in Stables	St Gluvias, Cornwall

Above: *This drawing by Peter Clark is a representation of one of the first photographs of Carclew House taken by Henry Fox Talbot in 1841. Sir Charles is thought to be the figure on the left with his sister, Lady de Dunstanville and his niece, Louisa Hart Dyke. The other man may be Mr Bunbury who was visiting at that time. Copies of these photographs are kept in the Science Museum, London.*

Right: *The clock tower, erected in 1845, outside the Tremayne Hall (once the village poorhouse and later the village school). This sketch appeared in the Mylor newsletter of 1979.*

Far right: *Lieutenant Colonel Arthur Tremayne pictured at High Cross in Truro in the late-nineteenth century; one of the gallant 600 who survived the Charge of the Light Brigade.*

Housemaids and a gardener at Carclew, pre-1900.

Footmen and indoor staff at Carclew, pre-1900.

house parties and dances that went with Cricket Week. The Cornish Choughs were formed in 1906 as a result of an after-match dinner at Trevarno, Helston. Captain William Tremayne of Carclew (son of Lieutenant Colonel Arthur Tremayne) was one of 57 original members of the Choughs invited by circular to join the club. All were well-known Cornish families. In 1908, there was a two-day match at Carclew in which the Choughs drew with Captain Tremayne's eleven.

When Mr Moore left school he was given a Testament by the Lieutenant Colonel. He was ushered into the study and in came the old gentleman, tall, stately, white-haired and with a big white beard. He noticed the boy looking curiously at the mementoes hanging on the wall – swords, sabres, pistols and a pair of cavalry boots with one heel missing. The Lieutenant Colonel wrote in the Testament and escorted Harry Moore to the steps at the front door, shook his hand and wished him good fortune.

Each year the children of the school were conveyed to Carclew in wagons for the annual tea. There were games and races and tea-treat buns. Finally, the ladies of the families came and stood on the balcony and showered the children with sweets. Although at times Lieutenant Colonel Tremayne's manner was brusque – ever the old military officer – he was at heart the kindest of men.

In addition to being a prominent landlord he was a very influential member of the community. He died in 1905, beloved by many. In his memory in Truro Cathedral there is a marble plaque, which reads:

To The Glory of God
And in Memory of Arthur Tremayne of Carclew
Late Lieutenant Colonel, 13th Light Dragoons
One of the First Members of the Truro Diocesan
Conference and of the Building Committee of this
Cathedral Church
Born May 15th 1827
Died November 14th 1905
Aged 78

William Francis Tremayne

Arthur's eldest surviving son, William Francis Tremayne, succeeded him. Like his father, William had an Army career. He married whilst serving in Ireland and there were four children. He suffered repeated illness but, nevertheless, when he took up residence at Carclew, he played a full part in Cornish affairs for more than 20 years, as County Councillor, JP, and President of the Royal Cornwall Agricultural Association. In fact, public work took precedence over his widespread estates. When war broke out in 1914, Captain Tremayne became Recruiting Officer in Truro and concerned himself with service charities. Mrs Tremayne did charitable work nearer home: she ran a paying-in club from a hut on Mill Quay where, once a week, the more needy wives and mothers of Mylor

would come and buy lengths of cloth from large bolts bought by Mrs Tremayne. It was quite an occasion, the women enjoying a cup of tea and a chat as they waited.

Shortly after the end of the First World War, Captain Tremayne decided to reduce his land holdings in Cornwall substantially. In five days in June 1920, 5,904 acres in 15 parishes were disposed of and little remained in the possession of the family apart from the house, farm and park.

When Captain William Tremayne died in 1930 his death had little impact. Many Mylor villagers now owned their own houses. Far and wide the power and influence of landowners had all but evaporated – they were relics of a bygone age.

However, Captain Tremayne was buried with full military honours at Mylor Parish Church and was the last person to be buried in the Lemon vault. His son and heir was Captain Charles Henry Tremayne. Both he and his wife had mixed feelings about moving to Carclew, for they were living in a pleasantly compact villa in Wiltshire and were happily settled. They did, however, take up residence and the Captain played a part in local affairs, being a member of the County Council and President of the Royal Cornwall Agricultural Association in 1932, but Mrs Tremayne was seldom seen.

The Fire

On 6 April 1934 there occurred the last tragic event in the history of the great house of Carclew. During the evening of the previous day, Captain Charles Tremayne had collected a house guest, Mrs Swinton, from the last London train at Truro and on her arrival an evening meal had been served. It was a cold night and there was a good fire in the library. The house was practically empty, only Captain Tremayne, his wife and two daughters, the butler and one housemaid were living in and everything seemed to be in order when, at about midnight, everyone went to bed.

At about 2a.m. the Captain was woken by an unusual noise and found the central block of the building well alight. The main hall and staircase were impassable and the external telephone was already dead. Happily, the parlour-maid, Miss Lennard, in the servants' quarters, awoke about the same time and roused the butler. By a miracle, the house telephone system was still intact and she was able to speak to the Captain and tell him that the rear staircase was clear. All the family and staff were taken out by this route and no one was seriously affected, but Mrs Swinton could not be released from the second floor of the main block until estate workers had produced a long ladder for the purpose. She, also, was unharmed.

In the meantime, a car had been sent to Perranwharf to the telephone exchange and a general fire alarm was raised. Both Falmouth and Penryn Brigades attended and arrived shortly after 2.30a.m. Their efforts were directed at preventing the rapid

The fireplace in the hall at Carclew House was adorned with flourishing scrolls and possessed a fine fire grate with Adams style decoration. The eighteenth-century lantern and the lattice-back Chippendale chairs were charming contemporary additions to the room. It is seen here prior to the 1934 fire.

Above: *Carclew House was destroyed by fire in April 1934. This picture of the ruins was taken in 1959.*

Left: *The hall and staircase of Carclew House were each divided by a colonnaded screen and decorated with rich plasterwork.*

A cricket match at Carclew, played against Old Probians in 1902. Left to right, back row: ? Donaldson, W.J. Rees, G. Pike, ? Massy, ? Donaldson; front: I. Parker, ? Hosken, Captain W. Tremayne (captain of team), ? Fanshaw, ? Murphy, ? Cookson. Sitting is Charlie Tremayne, son of the captain. After the match, tea was served by servant girls in the charge of footmen who wore tailcoats and powdered wigs.

Shooting party at Carclew before the First World War with Lieutenant Colonel Tremayne centre front.

spread of the flames. Some family effects, including valuable heirlooms and china, were saved, principally from the dining-room area. The fire burnt fiercely throughout the following day – it had obviously started in the library and very little of the main block escaped major structural damage. Much of the family silver was melted by the blaze. All the furnishings, including a number of Chippendale items, and many of the fine paintings, including masterpieces by Reubens, Romney and Canaletto, were destroyed. By a strange freak of fortune, a portrait of the great Mr Lemon, the founder of the estate in its final form, was rescued practically unharmed.

Carclew was a smouldering wreck. Its ruins still stood but Mylor had lost one of the finest country houses in the West Country.

The Bonythons Return

When John Bonython of Grampound sold the Carclew estate to William Lemon in 1738, the family's 300-year connection with Mylor was severed. Descendants of James Bonython made their home in Australia.

A book was published in 1966 by Eric Glenie Bonython – *The History of the Families of Bonython and Bonython of Carclew* – in which he relates that in 1897, Lavington Bonython came from Australia to visit Lieutenant Colonel Tremayne at Carclew. In conversation, he remarked that he would love to own a Cornish estate. The Lieutenant Colonel firmly discouraged him: 'Carclew will belong to the Tremaynes for ever.' The mansion burned down in 1934 and in the following year, Sir Langdon Bonython wrote from Australia offering to buy the estate, but after assessing the cost of rebuilding – and believing the prospects for English landowners difficult with such heavy burdens of taxation – he withdrew.

Five years later, Mr and Mrs Glenie Bonython visited Carclew to find the house and lands sold, the unburned part of the ruins being used to house refugees from Hitler's tyranny. They returned in 1954 and were distressed to find the ruins more derelict. They moved on to Mylor Church, but where was the Bonython Memorial? The familiar aisle had been sealed off by a screen dedicated to two members of a family killed in the Second World War and behind this was the vestry.

When they gained access, they found the monument among those of the Lemons and Tremaynes, for this was the Carclew aisle. The new vicar said that the monument could not be removed without the consent of the highest authorities. Permission given, an architect was found and the great monument was moved with great fear and trepidation. In 2004 it is in the south aisle of the church.

A Quaker Presence

In 1939, after the fire and the sale of the Carclew estate, the remains of the disused mansion, together with over 100 acres of land, were put at the disposal of the Society of Friends by one of their number, Arthur Pearse Jenkin, who was a property auctioneer. His vision was that Carclew might offer to the many refugees who were already in England in great numbers:

A place of rest and a home in exile. Working in co-operation, they could grow garden produce and help provide useful service for others. Families of very limited means might also have holidays in healthy, peaceful surroundings.

Serving others and simple living would strengthen the Quaker spirit in Cornwall. But first the building had to be restored to some degree to provide for a large number of people. New floors were laid, doors renewed, walls repainted and drains put in good order. A gardening programme was begun and an appeal went out for furniture, bedding, kitchen utensils and so on. When war began in September, Falmouth High School Guides were invited and went along on a regular basis to help with the work. One of these was a Mylor resident, Mrs Nora Coleman, living in Penoweth, Mylor at the time of writing, who remembers:

In 1938, we were asked by our school to knit squares to be made into blankets for refugees from the Spanish Civil War who were arriving at Carclew. Help was also needed with the task of making the semi-basement kitchens habitable after the fire four years previously and with starting a vegetable garden to help feed themselves.

Armed with trowels and paintbrushes, we cycled to Carclew on Saturday afternoons – not from a sense of duty, I'm afraid, but because it was fun! Later came refugees from Hitler's tyranny.

During the war, American troops stationed nearby used the remains of the old house for various purposes, mainly storage, but since then there has been no attempt to revive the ruin and its dereliction has continued until the time of writing. However, Jack and Daphne Neale, in the adjacent property, have created a beautiful garden and woodland setting for the ruin which gives it a dignified atmosphere and retains its sense of history.

Chapter 2

Memories of Village Life

*The Street, Bridge and Leat, The Village Pump, Shops, The Bakehouse, Sewing, Household Memories,
Childhood in the Village.*

The Street

Mylor Bridge, 100 years or so ago, was a very different place. Harry Moore, born in 1881, remembered the village street:

Many of the houses were thatched and lime-washed with small windows. There was a narrow pebbled walk separating the houses from the main road, but some houses had a small flower bed with snowdrops, jilly flowers, hollyhocks and crocuses in spring and odorous chrysanthemums (maroon and bronze) in autumn with windows filled with pot plants, geraniums, pelargoniums and musk. Some had little latticed porches. Each side were little shops, with bottles of sweets in the windows. There were Christmas decorations, dates, currants, raisins, prunes and figs in boxes. Inside were lucky bags, turnovers and seasonal fruits.

I remember the dogs lying in the sun outside the houses, the cats on the doorsteps and the ducks in the leat. It was a self-contained village. The principal means of locomotion was by walking or donkey cart. The 'Penny Farthing' bicycles were only for those who could afford them. Later there was a two-horse bus between Mylor and Flushing, connecting with the ferry rowing-boats. Afterwards came the four-horse Jersey cars for longer trips.

Everything was made in the village. There were, for instance, five cobblers who either worked full-time or else part-time to help the family income. The roads were very rough, being paved with two-inch stones that were either brought in from the fields or broken up at road corners by stone-crackers wearing goggles and using a long-handled hammer. There were no steam rollers, so the stones were trodden down by pedestrians and horse traffic – hence all the cobblers.

As a small boy, Harry used to have his boots (with water-tight tongues) made by Mr William Hocking, whose shop is now the village stores.

On the left side was his boot business, on the other were the groceries. He had a bright green container for treacle. The customer's basin was placed in one pan of the scales and weighed against some pebbles. Then the basin was taken to the container and back to the scales to be

weighed. The drips were saved by a small tin hanging under the tap. There were bladders of lard hung up to the beams, with flasks of olive oil protected by plaited straw covers. In the boot-repairing room were hung the wooden lasts, sharing the beams with the spiders' webs.

I can see the old man with his spectacles on the tip of his nose, and I can smell the leather.

Another cobbler was Bobby Pearce who lived at Tregatreath. His father owned a ketch called the Anna Mary. Old Captain Joe Pearce also ran the coal store at Mill Quay. Bobby was deaf and dumb and he was courting a lady who was also deaf and dumb. Her name was Fanny Sara. John May was also a cobbler who lived in New Row in a neat little cottage with a walled garden. It was on the site of the car park. John was a Balaclava soldier and was a tall upright gentleman. He wore a frock coat, a black beaver hat and a Gladstone collar and tie. His wife was a large buxom woman with hair parted in the centre. She wore a tight-fitting black bodice with a white starched front and a cameo brooch (common with ladies in those days).

His brother Walter May was the stone-cracker and he was also a militia man. He married a widow – a smartly dressed lady, a Mrs Buckingham called Mrs Buckram because she was so starchy and they looked a smart couple on Sundays – top hat, swallow tail coat, striped trousers, silver topped cane and she in a satin coat – 'oh the frou frou!' Another cobbler was Mark Tallack whose shop was at the top of the village facing down the road. He was also a musician – he played a violin and flute.

In the latter part of the nineteenth century, a welcome sight was Thomas Clemence, a one-armed pensioner, who served the Flushing, Mylor and Restronguet area as postman for 10s.6d. a week. In those days, Flushing had only one post a week.

Bridge and Leat

The leat was a very important facet of life in the village. Water was fetched from the leat if there was not enough in the barrel from the launders (gutters) for the weekly wash. Many preferred the soft water of the leat to that from the pump. There were no detergents in those days. Even in the 1940s on a Sunday night, buckets and a large bath would be filled from the leat

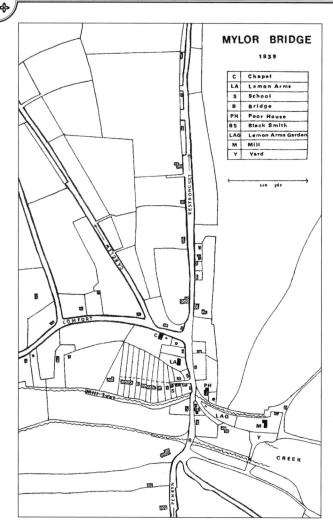

MYLOR BRIDGE

1839

C	Chapel
LA	Lemon Arms
S	School
B	Bridge
PH	Poor House
BS	Black Smith
LAG	Lemon Arms Garden
M	Mill
Y	Yard

110 yds

Left: *A sketch map of the centre of the village taken from the tithe map of 1840/1 showing how few houses there were then.*

Below: *Mylor Bridge before it was widened in 1950. Before that it was only wide enough for one vehicle. Originally built in 1590, it formed part of the main route from Truro to Penryn.*

Below: *'Village Life' as painted by Margaret Simpson in the 1970s, showing Ash View Supply Stores with Robert Bullock outside.*

for the next day's wash. The water was heated in a copper or large iron boiler on the range, with 'scaps' of Puritan soap, lots of common soda and Reckitt's Blue being used in the wooden washtub. Mondays were washdays usually, but there was definitely no washing done on a Sunday, not even babies' napkins. There were also the superstitions, 'No blankets were washed in May nor any garment on the first.' An old local saying was – 'Wash in May, wash friends away!'

Once washed, the clothes were put through the mangle. If you did not own one then there was a Miss Thomas in New Row who would put your wash through hers for a penny. Everyone in New Row had her own stone slab onto the leat from where to collect water and some had clothes-lines on the bank. Others had long lines through the garden. When the clothes were dry, then began the mammoth task of ironing with flat irons heated on the range.

The pump next to the Lemon Arms was used by all those living in the centre of the village as well as being very convenient when beer was brewed. It is seen here in the 1930s.

For some, Friday nights were bath nights with rain-water from the tank heated in the copper. If water was needed at other times, then most young people were willing to fetch water from the pump, as it was an excuse to get out in the evenings to see anyone for a chat – but you had to be in by nine o'clock. Another

place for gathering was around the old oak tree by the bridge over the Mill Leat. Even back in the late 1800s Henrietta Hankins remembered playing round the oak tree each evening with three kittens in her pinny.

The famous Mylor Oak Tree next to the leat in the early 1900s. Cut down in c.1960, it was a favourite meeting-place for young and old.

For many years it was a common sight to see young men sitting on the walls to watch the girls go by. Small children would catch tadpoles in the leat and take them home in a jar. Fred Ingram recalls: 'We were allowed to keep them until they had legs – mother didn't want frogs around the house.' Even in the 1950s, there were small trout and tadpoles in the leat. Ducks owned by residents were let out to swim on the leat. The banks of the leat had cut grass along the New Row side, and the leat itself was cleared regularly to keep the mill-wheel turning efficiently and to ensure clean washing water. Mr Rees, the father of the blacksmith, used to carry out this service before the war, for which he was paid. The Fire Service was the last to perform this duty, as the leat provided an emergency water-supply.

The famous Mylor Oak was felled in about 1960 without the use of power tools. It was found to be hollow inside and full of water. An old ring was found in the trunk, the remains of an old washing line.

The Village Pump

The pump in Lemon Hill was donated to the village by the Cornish philosopher Davies Gilbert. He was a man of great scientific attainments, becoming President of the Royal Society. He discovered Sir Humphrey Davy and recorded the history, legends, folklore and language of his native Cornwall. He was Squire of Trelissick and related by marriage to the Enys family.

Harry Moore remembers:

The village pump stands resplendent in the old farm colours of red and blue. These were colours of the wagon wheels in days gone by, the rims were painted blue and the spokes red. Up to 1944 the pump supplied water to all the houses from the bridge to the top of the village, and it was a familiar sight to see people going to and fro with their pitchers. In the evenings, the man of the house would go to the pump for water for the following day and nip in at the Lemon for his daily pint. And in the days when beer was brewed at the Lemon Arms the old pump proved a most useful servant.

Rose Rogers (born in 1910) also tells of the days before mains water:

In the early days there was no water-supply. People either had a well in the garden or fetched their water from various pumps or wells. There was the village pump and others at Passage Hill, Comfort, Rose Hill, Church Road, Cranwell and Tregatreath Beach. Springs were at Hackett, Church Road – weir and surface wells – and Bellair. Streams were used at the bottom of Brick Hill, Waterings, Salt Box, and the leat in the centre of the village.

Shops

The two carpenter's shops in Harry Moore's time were both run by the Tresise family. One shop was where our present butcher's shop stands.

I remember father and son working there. George, the father, a tall white-haired man and his son John. It was a busy place with two or three apprentices. I remember carts and wagons being built, also wheels and ladders made. There was a saw pit too. The other shop was where the entrance to the Playing Field is now. It was owned by Mr James Tresise, a brother of George.

Rose Rogers recalls that there were seven shops in her day. Among them were:

Miss Thomas in New Row (she who had the mangle) and Miss Rowe had a shop in Angarrack. At the top of the village there was Mr Moore and in the centre Mr Frost (now our grocery store). Mr Down had a shop where the car park is now (it was bombed in the war). All the shops put up shutters at night. There were now three boot and shoe repairers – Mr Hollingsworth at Clinton Terrace (afterwards Bells Hill), Mr Rowe in Passage Hill and Bobby Pearce at Tregatreath. Bobby was deaf and dumb so customers wrote their requirements on a slate. Our butcher, Mr Rollason, had no shop but delivered the meat from a covered wagon. Customers could go to the killing house most mornings, this was where Mr Rollason lived in Bells Hill. Butchers from other villages also came with their carts. A fish and chip shop was run by Harold Rollason. Billie Ferris (Billie Rum) sold hot pies for 2d. and for an extra penny provided a tune on a gramophone. This was in the cottage which used to be the Bakehouse. A travelling medicine man, Mr Penrose, whom we called Bilkey Man because he sold pills by that name, came on a push-bike.

Eric Gray, who writes about the period between 1925 and 1963 also has something to say about the shops:

The village was catered for by only three general stores for many years, suitably distanced in the main street. Inez Tresise was responsible for the lower shop. The middle shop was run by the Frost sisters and later taken over by the Curnows (of the Lemon Arms). The top shop, with good living quarters, was bought by Bert Williams, having come from Bideford and marrying local girl Iney Gray, my Aunt. Some of his house deliveries to outlying districts were made by car – still an unusual sight in the middle 1930s. The bread was brought by Stanley and Noel Thomas from their Penryn bakery and then re-delivered locally. Sometimes a visit was made to the bakery when I would be hooked on the smell of newly baked bread. I was allowed this privilege as I helped to take bread, duly balanced in baskets on my bicycle handlebars, to houses in the village as a small wage earner on Saturdays and during school holidays.

It was just as well mothers were home most of the time as so many of the everyday necessities were delivered to the doorstep. Milk would be ladled from large containers to personal jugs, and as refrigerators were non-existent, the milk would be kept in a pantry usually on a stone slab or in Summer outside on the north-facing side of the house. Most people ordered their coal for delivery in the Summer, when the prices were lower. There would be regular callers who sold brushes and similar wares and exotic looking brown men in turbans who opened suitcases full of bright silk garments and accessories. Gypsies came selling pegs and posies of lucky heather and French men with their bicycles strung with onions. How vibrant it all was, no one could complain of being lonely. The village was alive with callers, not cluttered as now with parked cars and a stream of passing traffic.

According to Eileen Ferris, a big bag of flour would be delivered frequently for baking from Brimacombe's in Penryn. The old man came round to take orders early in the week for delivery on Friday. If her mother forgot anything then the girls would think nothing of walking into Penryn for it. In the 1930s and '40s the shop there had more selection than the village shops, but 'you wouldn't have starved'.

Miss Tresise's shop was described as 'drab and dark' and there were the Misses Frost who also sold newspapers. At one time there was a fruit and vegetable shop at the entrance to New Row, owned by Mr Downe, who was also at one time the postman. At various times there were other small shops in New Row. Lizzie Connor sold home-made nettle beer for a ha'penny, mutton pies for two pence and marinated pilchards. Miss Thomas also had a small shop. Mrs Murdoch used to sell sweets to the children and cook chips on a primus, which was also used for heating tongs for hairdressing!

The village pump was a gift to the village by Squire Gilbert of Trelissick in 1852. He was related by marriage to the Enys family.

Top: This is the earliest known photograph of the village, taken c.1880.

Above: Eric Gray, secretary of the chapel, speaking at the Chapel Fête on the playing fields, c.1960.

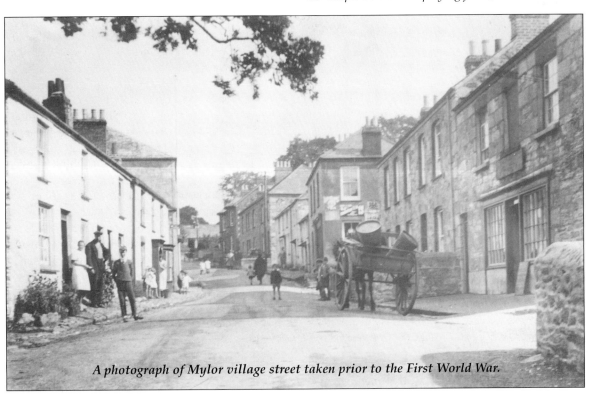

A photograph of Mylor village street taken prior to the First World War.

James Thomas, writing about the 1941–48 period, noted that:

Our milk was delivered by a gentleman called Jefford as I recall, and he used to tour the area in a pony cart, with two or three large churns of milk sitting in the back. The milk therein would be dispensed by means of polished steel measures on long hooked handles into a jug that the customer had to provide. These hung around the rim of one of the churns and carried certification from Weights and Measures. We had a pair of jugs in blue and white ceramic, covered with muslin fly guards, held in position by a fringe of glass beads. There was always a sense of form following function: milk was kept in china jugs, while drinking water was stored in brown earthenware pitchers.

Mr Eddie Rollason was for many years the butcher for Mylor and Flushing, with his faithful horse Dobbin pulling the butcher's cart. When Dobbin retired aged 25, a motor van took her place. This picture was taken in 1930.

Our peripatetic butcher was Mr Rollason [also mentioned by Rose Rogers] whose mobile shop looked like an old stage coach to us children. It most closely resembled a summerhouse on four wheels; it was painted black with a yellow lining and was drawn by an elderly shire horse. I believe that he kept two in a paddock and stable behind his butchery. His wares were hung from a *rail inside the vehicle and were dispensed as required from a scrubbed bench at the rear. I used to be fascinated by the way the horse's reins were routed through two small holes over the top of the front window of the cart, and Mr Rollason would stand in the body of the vehicle and control the horse and brake without being submitted to the vagaries of the weather.*

Many people have recalled Mr Rollason and the killing house on Bells Hill. The shed had a dirt floor – not a hygienic tile in sight – and a large Great Dane roamed around keeping his eye on proceedings. Some considered that the meat was very close to the horse's tail but nevertheless Mr Rollason was a popular figure and as a useful sideline he was not averse to putting down stray dogs if required!

One of his horses, called Dobbin, enjoyed her weekly tour through the village with quite a few stops for tit-bits, like an apple or a nicely buttered crust, from the customers. When later required to go on the Flushing round she was not enamoured of this idea and if Eddie left her unattended she would whip round and start off for Mylor! No doubt she objected to the long climb up Flushing Hill.

The Bakehouse

Very few houses had the means of cooking cakes and bread, so every village had its bakehouse. 'My great aunt, Mary Moore, kept the Mylor Bakehouse' says Harry Moore. It was on the site of Ash Villa, and she lived with her brother Mr Thomas Moore who managed the shop later occupied by Eskett Williams:

I often called to see my great aunt. I can still smell the nutty smell of new bread, the savoury smell of dinners and pasties and still more of the smell of the rich Christmas cakes.

Rose recalls:

After the Second World War, Willie Prout had another bakehouse, behind the village pump. Cottages there have been demolished. Bread was delivered by Mr Beer of Flushing, also by Mr Trudgeon and Mr Tripp from Penryn. Newspapers were fetched by Mr John Frost, who also had a taxi. During the summer when butter was cheap you could take your buzza (earthenware pot) to the farm to have it filled. Pot butter and a slice of Mr Beer's bread was something to be enjoyed! Milk had to be sold as liquid or scalded and sold as cream or made into butter. There were tea gardens at Lawithick, near the church, with rustic tables and seats. These were open in the summer and catered for people walking to and from Flushing mainly.

Jam and cream teas were also sold by Mrs Andrew, Mrs Ashwin, Mrs Curnow and Mrs Hooper at Tregatreath, Miss Engell at Penarrow, Mrs Andrew at the entrance to New Row and Mrs Willie Copeland at Mylor Downs. Dressmakers were Mrs Collins and Miss Frost of Passage Hill and Miss Trott of New Row. The barber was Dick Ralph, on Fridays and Saturday evenings. He had a cottage at Chapel Terrace, near the entrance to Bonython Close. There was also Stanley Prout, near the pump.

Sewing

Mr Copeland ran his tailoring business in the garden shed of Fir Hill, Mylor Downs. He alone used a sewing machine; hand sewing was done by five or six local women. He met the needs of the whole village and many farms in the district. Even though he was so busy, he also found time to play in the Mylor Band.

Household Memories

Pride of place in any Cornish cottage was the range in the kitchen and Mylor was no exception. Several examples are still in existence, if not in use. The brass work was cleaned once a week with Brasso and the iron blackleaded. The boys may have collected the water but cleaning the range was women's work. The ranges had good ovens and some believe it the only way to cook a true pasty. The oven was the part that was often replaced. These were made and repaired at the Smithy.

> INSTRUCTIONS *for cleaning a range:*
> *Rake out all ashes and dust; remove all flue doors; pull out dampers; take off the tops and rounds. Brush off soot, sweep flues with brush; brush top of oven; rake out soot from oven dustpan. Do the same on boiler side of range; replace tops and rounds. Wash oven with strong soda water; wash top of range and remove grease. Allow to dry! Then black lead range with black lead brush and rub off with another. Polish with a third. Rub all steel parts with emery paper. Polish taps or brass with brass polish or brick dust and oil.*

The range was used to cook everything, the daily meal, bread and cakes. The dough for bread was placed above the hob to rise. Eileen Ferris said her mother never bought a cake but made them all – rainbow, fruit, coconut cakes and jam sponges. Also that they had the same main meal each day of each week – roast, cottage pie, stew, etc. Days were also set apart for different household jobs. She remembers Wednesdays and Saturdays were pasty days. Sometimes toast was made in front of the fire bars. On Friday nights, bread and saffron bread were left to prove on the lower rack and baked on Saturday morning at five o'clock so they had fresh bread by seven.

Apart from the range, constantly alight in the kitchen, most other rooms had open grates which were lit when necessary. Bedroom fires were lit only when people were ill, otherwise a stone hot-water bottle was the main way to warm the bed. Fires were mostly of wood as coal was expensive. The wood was gathered locally, but never on a Sunday. When there was enough money for coal it was collected from the quay, having been brought there by barge. One could borrow a wheelbarrow to transport the fuel home.

Oil-lamps and candles provided light. It was necessary not to turn the lamp up too high as the delicate mantle would smoke. After the First World War, Prout's garage sold paraffin for lamps and methylated spirit for the primus stove.

Mains electricity was brought to the village between 1925 and 1930, but the outlying districts had to wait many more years. Some houses had their own generators. Usually three lights and one socket were provided, with every extra socket costing one pound. Small rooms were not lit. Consequently appliances were often plugged into a light socket. Fred Ingram recalls that 'Flex from the ceiling hung down and the iron was plugged into an adaptor. When Mother was ironing the shadow went to and fro. It never would be allowed now.'

Mains drainage did not arrive in the village until 1964, so until then there were no indoor toilets: 'It was a trip down the garden to the shed with its newspaper on a string and then a bucket indoors, just in case!'

Cesspits were emptied by a man with a horse and cart, who lived in Flea Alley. These were old cottages at the entrance to Bonython, known then as Chapel Terrace. Many of the cottages were whitewashed and limewash was used in yards and outhouses to kill germs. Damp was always a problem and wallpaper quickly deteriorated and had to be replaced at regular intervals. The road outside was edged with spar stones and drainage channels into which all waste water was poured. The cottages in the centre of the village were small but usually full of children.

Childhood in the Village

Fred Ingram recalls:

You had plenty of freedom. You could go anywhere. Someone would be after 'e for pinching apples or something like that. We never took them away, only one in the pocket like, only to eat.

The creek was cleaner then and was a favourite place to swim. Fred used to think how clever his mother was; she always knew where he had been playing. How was that? She could tell by how he smelt when he came home, whether he had been to the farm, the creek, or the dump – a favourite place to play, even if it had its dangers. It was where the playing field is at the time of writing. It also had an old oak tree that the majority of lads could climb without too much trouble. Although children had more freedom to wander, there was more discipline and more respect. The village policeman would say 'I know your father' and he only had to make a pretext of writing your name in his book

These cottages behind the pump were demolished in the late 1980s. They are seen here in the 1970s.

Looking down Lemon Hill in a painting by Margaret Simpson completed in the 1980s.

A fine example of a typical Cornish range, as it still looks today. Several are known to exist in the village, but this one is in Ash Villa, the home of Minnie May. The house was built for her grandfather and celebrated its 100th birthday in 2004.

Above: *Mylor Creek, photographed by Wendy Jones in 2000.*

Left: *Len and Margaret Simpson outside their home Cob Cottage on Lemon Hill, 2000. They have been deeply involved in many aspects of village life and Margaret's paintings feature on several pages of this book.*

'Ash View Supply Stores' painted by Margaret Simpson. The picture reveals how the store looked in the mid-nineteenth century.

and you were on tenterhooks waiting for your father to say something. It had the desired effect and you respected him. All adults used to dispense a certain amount of discipline to anyone found misbehaving. Before the war Fred remembers a new master at the school who arranged for a selection of books to be brought from the county library and that there was always a squabble amongst the boys for the Percy F. Westerman tales of cadets on merchant ships.

Minnie May and Jean Calvert also remember a happy childhood in the village. Jean talks of her friends who joined her to become a gang who called themselves The Five Rats. They were Mary Rollason, Eleanor Vinnicombe, Hazel Grey and Pat Burley. She remembers one incident when they were looking after some babies in prams. They pushed them to the church and, finding a wedding taking place, decided to watch the proceedings from the back. (It was Fred Tresise's wedding.) On the way home they saw a big fire at Rose Hill – an eventful afternoon for the baby-minders!

Minnie's grandfather owned the general stores next to Ash Villa and it had belonged to his father before him. Mr Moore ran it for 50 years with Minnie's mother, Lilian, and supplied groceries to HMS *Ganges*. Minnie's father was also a wheelwright and the village undertaker. He often took wheels to be finished off at the forge, a favourite meeting-place for young people. Coffins were made at the back of the butcher's shop, and Minnie recalls 'If we heard banging in the back of the shop we knew someone had died!' The bier was made by Dr Olivey of Albion House and kept underneath the carpenter's shop.

They both remember playing by the creek in the fields known as Black-gate, Red-gate, Quarry and Vatten Vane, before Greatwood quay. 'We could swim quite early. We swam all day long,' recalls Jean. There

did not seem to be the worries about letting children go off to play as there are in the twenty-first century. 'We used to play on the coal barge, too, that used to come to the quay,' says Minnie.

Eric Gray has many happy memories of carefree childhood days:

The bridge itself was ideal for playing Pooh sticks with twigs and leaves, but sometimes cigarette cards were dropped on one side. Then we would rush to the other side to see who was the winner. The stream coming under the bridge widens at this point and was ideal for youngsters trying to catch eels from under the stones. Another so-called sport was Tob fighting – the collection of turfs from the nearby fields and dipping them in water to throw at each other.

Before cars invaded the countryside, we were able to use Rose Hill as a race track, sitting precariously on our home-made four-wheeled carts. We would race down the road, stopping only when the level surface of the bridge was reached, or bad driving ended in catastrophe. Guiding them with a piece of rope tied to a set of pram wheels required a developed skill, especially into the turn at the bottom, feet often being used as brakes.

Springtime for boys almost certainly meant bird-nesting and catching tadpoles. Everyone played marbles. Green glass and the large colourful ones (the taws), were used to knock the small ones out of the circle. Hopscotch was popular and another craze was yo-yo throwing. Skipping kept you on your toes, especially when a long rope was used, as several children, by running in at an angle, could join in the fun. 'Salt, Mustard, Vinegar, Pepper' was the cry as the action speeded up.

Winter seemed to pass quickly as the weather was never too severe; board games, cards and jigsaw puzzles were regularly enjoyed by families. The gramophone was accorded the same pride of place as the television occupies today, and playing records at a speed of 78rpm, the needles required changing quite frequently. Dance band leaders became big names such as Ambrose, Geraldo, Jack Hylton, Jack Payne and Henry Hall. We had a magic lantern and would gasp as coloured slides were projected on a wall or cloth. The coming of the wireless set brought up-to-date world news into our homes for the first time and also music that could be enjoyed by all and sundry. The first sets needed an accumulator or liquid battery to operate them. These required charging up at Prout's garage when they began to run down. Once electricity was installed, there was less crackling and whistling in the sets and a varied choice was available from Pye, Philco and Ekco. On Saturday afternoons men would sit with their pens prepared to take down the football results as they were relayed on Sports Report in the hope that a small fortune was on the way – few hopes were ever realised.

George Hearle tells of:

Boys who raided the local rubbish tip for bottles which they stuck on sticks, firmly embedded in the mud of the creek – then pelted them with stones. When toys were scarce, syrup tins with strings were used to walk on, like stilts, and old inner tubes were rolled along instead of hoops. Whips and tops would appear from nowhere and the patterns merge and disappear as speed built up. Iron hoops, guided by metal hooked rods, were raced downhill through the village, with no concerns for people or traffic. There seemed to be a lot more walls in those days, which were regularly used for ball games or handstands. The ways you could throw a ball seemed endless, under the leg, behind the back, bounce and toss, and so on; you could make up your own sequence. The more dangerous games were in the use of peashooters on people, catapults against birds and the unlawful smashing of the porcelain cups on telegraph poles with stones.

James Thomas recalls:

Small groups of us would decamp for Carclew woods with egg sandwiches and bottles of water – then not be seen until teatime. Another favourite area was an inlet along Mylor Creek where an old stone-barge was rotting away. Although the hull was in a poor state, the deck would support weight and the mast and some of the rigging still existed. We used to swing aboard using a rope from the mast head and the vessel became our pirate ship for the day. There was also a Blondin or steel wire rope from one side of the quarry to the other from which was suspended a large wooden container to carry loads. Adventurous boys would ride in this box!

Rose Rogers tells of the day she was threatened with hobnailed boots:

I had joined my cousin Jack and other children, mud-larking in the creek (trying to catch fish when the tide was out). I had on a pair of Jack's short trousers and

his boots. Mother couldn't find me when it was time for bed. Someone said they could hear children talking in the creek. 'Not my Rose,' said Mother, but when I was found I had to have a bath. The smell of the mud was awful! I was told, 'Tomorrow I shall go to Falmouth and get you a pair of hobnailed boots.' I couldn't sleep that night, but it was forgotten the next day. No more mud-larking!

Children also knew where to find the first primroses, violets and later bluebells. The fields alongside Bells Hill were a favourite haunt for young children around Easter time to pick primroses (without permission, needless to say) which were then tied in small bunches and sold to relatives and friends.

Apples were always a temptation and any excuse was found to pass near an orchard. Blackberries were picked, put into greaseproof bags and sold for pocket money. A penny or two could also be made from selling the skins of rabbits which father caught. Also, a man with a pony cart would wait outside the school to collect jam jars for a factory in Truro: three jars for a toy windmill. Running errands usually meant some money to be spent on sweets or comics. Many remember sherbet dabs, aniseed balls, dolly mixtures, sweet cigarettes, locusts and liquorice laces. Boys bought 2d. weekly books and swapped them with each other.

Eric Gray remembers:

Pastimes included the craze for collecting cigarette cards; to possess a large collection was a status symbol. A pictorial encyclopaedia could be mustered, a galaxy of stars from the sporting scene, radio celebrities, wild flowers, flags of different countries and so on; they came free to us young collectors. They could be procured in several ways: by worrying someone who smoked, checking on discarded packets; by exchanging cards when duplicates occurred; by winning them in games where flicking the cards the furthest was important, or from members of the family or friends. I was unfortunate as my dad smoked a pipe! Comics such as 'Rainbow', 'Knock-Out', 'Tiger Tim' and 'Chips', with all their wonderful characters were around for years.

During autumn, we would collect horse chestnuts, bake them in the oven to make them tougher and be ready for a good old conker contest. On Guy Fawkes night, most houses with children had their own bonfire in the back garden, each with a small supply of sparklers, Catherine-wheels, bangers, roman candles, golden showers, silver rain and rockets. Some were balanced on walls or laid on the ground, while rockets were usually put into jam jars. Many minor accidents occurred, especially in the case of those that failed to ignite first time.

George Hearle also has a tale to tell about an occasion close to Bonfire Night:

Four of the lads were out for an evening stroll when they happened on a cottager hanging out her milk can in

The head of Mylor Creek, before the walls were built around the playing field creekside, c.1950s.

Resident swans and family in Mylor Creek.

readiness for the local dairyman to fill on his round. One of the boys had just bought some fireworks so he put a penny banger inside the can, ignited it and jammed the lid firmly back on. They all retired a few paces, standing well back to watch the fun, and didn't have long to wait. The explosion was so intense it blew the bottom from the can and they all legged it back up the lane – straight into the path of the village bobby. In consequence, they were all brought up before the local Bench and fined the sum of ten shillings each; rather a lot for young boys to find in those days. The magistrate, Beecher Johns, who had hitherto been on quite amicable terms with the injured parties, made an unfortunate remark: 'Oh well, boys will be boys.' After that, the cottagers refused to speak to him ever again.

Another anecdote of George's is known as 'The Rat' story.
In conclusion here is an account of the incident in his own words:

Freddy Tresise's father was the village undertaker and his demeanour befitted his trade. I suspect his son was a sore trial to him for above all else he loved to play the fool. The carpenter's shop had a problem with rats, which he caught in a wire trap. He would usually drown his victim in the leat that flowed alongside. On one occasion he hit upon a more exciting way of destroying his unhappy victim. Now this was a more robust age and your susceptibilities may perhaps be offended by the story I shall now relate. But here goes. At noon the school let out its pupils for lunch. They streamed through the village to see Freddy waving his rat cage aloft. 'Git your dogs, boys!' Boys and girls dispersed like magic to reappear in a minute or two with a dog, not necessarily their own. At this time there was a large dog population, all on free range. Most boys, with or without a dog, came back armed with a stick. Within minutes Freddy had his audience assembled. Yelling boys, screaming girls, snarling dogs fighting amongst themselves as they leaped at the rat, held aloft in its cage. Adults from nearby houses and passers-by completed the crowd. Among the adults watching the spectacle was Daddy Marshall who lived in the pebble-dashed house, nearest to the leat. He was a dapper little man who had once been a 'Gentleman's gentleman'. Always well dressed, he walked with a silver-mounted cane and was very bow-legged. Standing in his doorway he had a good view of proceedings. With the cage held high Freddy pulled the lever, decanting the rat in the middle of the road. Amid flailing sticks and snapping jaws the rat dashed down towards Trevellan Road. After running part of the way up the wall of what we know as Cornovi Cottage, it made it across the road, up Mr Marshall's path, between his legs and into his house. In hot pursuit was a procession of dogs. Three or four took the same route, through Mr Marshall's legs into the passage. The next animal in the pack was some sort of greyhound and its additional bulk carried Mr Marshall off his feet, allowing the rest of the motley pack to trample him underfoot. Some responsible adults helped Mr Marshall to his feet. Fortunately he had suffered no injury and equally fortunately his back door had been open. The boys who had dashed up the lane between the path and the leat reported that the rat had been dispatched in his back garden. So we went home to our lunches.

This cartoon drawn by Bruce Collier in 2003 charmingly illustrates 'The Rat' story, a Mylor legend.

Chapter 3

Roads and Houses

The First Roads, The Pattern of Settlement, Church Road, Old Almshouse at Tregatreath, The History of New Row, East Coast Connections, Greatwood House, The Vicarage, Porloe, Woodlands, Albion House, Lawithick.

Hugh Olivey writing in his book *Notes on the Village of Mylor*, states:

Ancient Mylor Churchtown stood on the top of the hill, some considerable distance south-east of Mylor Church and its north end is easily identified by living evidence, although all the buildings have been razed and no Mylor Churchtown now exists on this spot.

The First Roads

There is little documentary evidence concerning the roads in our parish until modern times, but the physical evidence can still be seen and tells of times gone by.

The geography and geology determine the routes followed by the roads. Mylor parish consists of two peninsulas, defined by three streams and estuaries – Penryn River, Mylor Creek and Restronguet Creek. Less than a mile of the boundary with St Gluvias does not follow a watercourse. The geology of Mylor is similar throughout the parish, for everywhere the underlying rock is a mudstone, shown on the map as Mylor Series Shales. Earth movements have contorted the once-level strata, especially the Carnmenellis granite massif, which reaches to Penryn and Mabe. The pressure and heat turned the mudstone to rather inferior building stone. On top of the shale is a capping of broken stone and clay, called head. It is the product of glacial outwash from an ancient Ice Age. This in time becomes a reasonably fertile soil.

It is lucky that Mylor does not lie between two major centres of population, so no main roads pass through our parish. There was, however, a time when the Penryn–Truro road followed the short stretch

Kerrier Hundred map by John Norden, surveyed in 1584.

between the junction with Irish Woman's Hill and Barras Moor. This was pre-1815 when the turnpike was built. All our roads serve local needs, although these have changed over the centuries.

Some roads have been improved, some remain as footpaths and a few have disappeared. There are footpaths running around our tidal and coastal areas. These will always have existed, although the earliest ones have disappeared into the water. There are barrows on high ground at Carclew and our prehistoric ancestors found food at the margins of the sea – especially shellfish. A beautiful axe head was reputed to have come from the 'head' at Penarrow, but its provenance was not verifiable.

Ancient roads are often well below the level of the surrounding country. We find this most often in steep paths running down to the waters such as Weir, Pandora and Hooper's Hill. This shows in such places as Mill Lane, Saltbox Corner and elsewhere where the bedrock is exposed. Another indication of antiquity used by archaeologists is the number of species of woody plants found in a 100-yard stretch of road. A total of 14 have been counted in Mill Lane, which runs between the village and Restronguet.

Before a more detailed examination of roads in 2004, one must turn to what has been the most important road over the centuries – the creek. Tracks will serve for traffic on foot, or even by horse, but are impractical for bulk and heavy goods. Consider for the moment the great Celtic cross at our Parish Church. It is of moor-stone, surface granite, and weighs several tons. The nearest outcrop of this stone lay at the headwaters of the Penryn River, near Mabe. The only way to move it in the fifteenth century, when it marked the Church of St Mylor, was by water. The effort that went into its fashioning, transport and erection is astonishing. In recent times, heavy materials such as limestone and coal, up to the 1930s, came by water.

The Pattern of Settlement

Before considering existing roads, a brief historical review of the pattern of settlement must be considered. There is no evidence of open-field strip cultivation in Mylor parish. The Domesday record shows most of the land being the manor of Cosawes, but by the nineteenth century it was in the hands of two landowners. The north side of the creek was Carclew land and the south side Trefusis, with a boundary against Enys property – most of whose holding was in St Gluvias. Probably the earliest settlement was the long-lost manor of St Mylor near the Parish Church – all that remains is Lawithick Farm. There were two cottages opposite Porloe gate until about 1940. Any buildings nearer the coast were replaced in 1800 by the Admiralty buildings of the Naval Dockyard. There was an unpaved road from the old house down past the naval reservoir to the foreshore, used by Harry Beer's bread van in the 1930s.

It is worth noting that the widespread farmsteads in the parish all have Cornish names, indicative of pre-seventeenth-century settlements. The present farmhouses were almost all built between 1750 and 1815. This was a period of almost constant war, when farming became more profitable. The old cob-built farmhouses were either abandoned, as at Crownick and Rose Hill farms, or used to shelter animals.

Corn prices remained high until 1850 and there was considerable reclamation of wasteland. The high ground which surrounded the village came under the plough, with much larger fields than the older settlements. It helped that local landowners had profitable mining interests and were not dependent on rents to finance capital expenditure.

Improved farming practices soon turned the downs into relatively productive corn land. However, the ploughing produced vast quantities of feldspar stones, and picking these small rocks, more of which appeared with every ploughing, gave occupation to children throughout the nineteenth and into the twentieth centuries. The spar proved ideal for the foundation of roads throughout the parish.

It will be noticed, even in 2004, that there are 'wastrels' (patches of land used as allotments by farm workers and locals until recently) alongside the roads, especially between Angarrack and Restronguet, and on the roads to Flushing. Even more extensive patches existed alongside Passage and Bells Hills, but from the first metalling, houses and gardens filled the waste space – continuing to our own time.

Celia Fiennes rode side-saddle through Cornwall in the 1690s and recorded in her journal that 'there is no wheeled transport here'. Many historians have quoted this observation since, which is generally thought to be true. In the saddle or on foot a traveller can pick his way, but with wheels, a firm road is necessary. In the eighteenth and nineteenth centuries, sporadic improvements were made using stone gathered off the land. In granite areas much more suitable stone was readily available.

An example of how roads developed is the road from Mylor to Flushing, in 1800. Leave the village by Rose Hill, turn left at Saltbox (previously Salt Box) to Four (now Six) Turnings, then up Pillars Hill to Tregew and down the hill to Flushing. Flushing Hill and Waterings Road are nineteenth-century improvements. To Penryn there was a road of equally ancient antiquity; it was a narrow and twisting track, not extensively improved until after the Second World War.

In the early-nineteenth century there was a rationalisation of boundaries between the Trefusis and Enys estates. The road that formed its boundaries was narrow and twisting as Landerio (the church enclosure of the oak trees) and Tregeweth farms had long been reclaimed and were relatively fertile land.

In the Carclew area, many new roads were constructed in the time of the Lemon dynasty. The only old road ran down to Perran Wharf – thence through Perranwell to Truro or Redruth and the mining district. Earth banks faced with spar stones – difficult to build with, but erected with such skill that they have lasted 150–200 years – flank the new or improved Carclew roads. Look at the fine example at Balaclava Cottage, built at the time of the Crimean War in 1853. Another early-nineteenth-century road connects with Enys Hill, which was built to link with the old Truro road at Enys Lodge.

Comfort is likely to be at least as old as the village proper. Indeed, the original form of the name Cwmford, a strange hybrid of Cornish and English, means 'the ford by the woods'. In this area, there were two economic products up to the mid-nineteenth century. There was a willow moor, giving an annual crop of withies for lobster-pots and baskets, and of much more importance was a large deposit of clay that gave rise to a brickworks. Most of the production was used locally for the chimneys of cob or stone-built houses. Itinerant brickmakers probably used the original methods and the product of many months' work would be stacked in a long tunnel-like run. This was covered with brushwood during summer and fired during a dry autumn spell. The bricks made this way varied in quality and were not frost-proof. Later a kiln was built, fired by coppice wood from Dowstall Bottoms. These later cheese-cut bricks were of better quality, but not as good as coal-fired bricks from 'up-country'.

When the sewage farm was developed in the 1960s, the trench on the little hill revealed at least four feet depth of clean clay, but elsewhere the clay was contaminated with feldspar crystals.

While the brickworks was in production the swamp at Belair (Cornish for watercress) was filled in with waste from the brickworks and Comfort Road afforded a more direct route to Angarrack and Carclew.

Church Road

Older inhabitants of Mylor knew this as the Under Road: it is the way from the village to the church along the south side of the creek. At Porloe it becomes Wayfield Road and is only a footpath at the time of writing. Carts could avoid the hill to the dockyard by going on the beach when the tide was sufficiently low – that is, before the New Quay was built in the 1960s. The village funeral bier required two extra men to push it up over the hill.

From the road there are three free council access points to the shore: between Nos 4 and 5, opposite No. 33a and at Porloe. These give an indication of the importance of the road for reaching the water. There are many connections with marine activity, past and current. Today one of the attractions of creekside property is for leisure boating. There are very few houses along the road where the inhabitants have no interest in the sea other than as a view. Householders on that side can obtain a foreshore licence from the Truro Harbour Office at a minimum annual rental of £67.50 for a boat of up to 50 feet. It is important for house-sellers that viewers of a property should come three hours either side of high water. Acres of mud provide satisfactory part-afloat moorings but are not inviting to the eye unless for bird-watching.

When the earlier houses were put up much of the materials came by sea. Nos 1 and 2 were the last houses to be built of stone from the quarry opposite. Restronguet or Ruan sand could also be delivered by sea and transported to sites by horse and cart. In 1925 the *Amazon* brought Plymouth bricks for No. 37. Nowadays all deliveries are by large lorries, to the detriment of banks and walls. Little notice is taken of signs 'Unsuitable for wide vehicles' at Six Turnings and Trelew Dip, or the faded old notice, 'Unsuitable for Motor Vehicles'!

Many of the early inhabitants had connections with the sea, retiring after a life served in the Royal or Merchant Navies or at the Admiralty dockyard and Falmouth Docks. Boats have been built and repaired on the foreshore on land now enclosed by quays and garden walls and also on the inland side of the road. At high water there was a footpath round the head of the creek via the farm lane, coming out where the land has been cut away above Cartref.

To some, Trelew was known as Captain Billy's Creek. He was a retired master mariner and lived in Nantrelew. Many people had shares in the coasting ships that came to berths in Trelew Creek. William Moore could remember their crews being paid off from tables there with piles of gold sovereigns.

There has been much infill house building and many new owners make alterations to existing properties. In the 1950s, the houses were known by name or by inhabitant. Since then numbers have been used. When they were first numbered there were 41, and in 2004 there are 51 and two in Wayfield Road. Sixteen of the houses are not continuously lived in, being either holiday homes or bought for ultimate retirement. Latterly there have been a great many changes of ownership, but it seems always to have been the case that people came for a short while, left and then the village traders sometimes found their bills unpaid – hence the informal name Mystery Road.

Many interesting people have lived along Church Road. Bobby Pearce, a deaf and dumb man, was a cobbler and lived with his deaf and dumb wife, Fanny, in a now-demolished cottage at Trenarren. Tommy Vincent, whose family still live in the village in 2004, was born in Sunningdale, another cottage beside the shore, since pulled down. With him were his parents, grandmother and nine siblings. Four of the little girls died of TB through undernourishment, as the father did not support the family well. He had been born in Beach Cottage, now also gone, at Porloe where the grandfather was a Coastguard on the look-out for rum runners. A Mr Ferris who supplied bread to HMS *Ganges* once occupied Beach Cottage. It was situated in the garden of the New House, which was hit by the

A view of Mylor Creek at low tide, looking across to Church Road on the southern shore, 2004.

Left: *Comfort, Mylor, c.1910. In the late 1800s Comfort (or Comford) was recorded as a separate community in the census returns. It was a collection of cottages and smallholdings and many of the people living there worked on the Carclew estate as gardeners, grooms, masons, seamstresses and domestic servants.*

Below: *Looking across Mylor Creek to houses along Church Road, 2004.*

second of a stick of German bombs in the Second World War; the first fell in the creek, the third in the field behind and the fourth up the Porloe valley. No one was killed or injured by these bombs. Marion Spring, who lived at Hooper's Hill in Wayfield Road, describes this incident in her book *Memories and Gardens*. Captain Pearce, who designed the current King Harry Ferry, occupied the new New House that replaced the bombed one and is now called Chynoweth.

View from the beach at Porloe in the 1930s with the merchant ships laid up between the wars in the distance. The oyster boat Ellen *in the centre is rigged with a short mast for trawling.*

Stanley Opie, an authority on Cornish tin, lived at Trelew Dip in the hut with the wooden extension, which Colonel Trefusis had added for the Scouts. This building was known as Tommy Lang's Sunday School and Tommy Vincent remembered going there. The house caught fire one Sunday morning and was afterwards abandoned. Stanley Opie suffered from asbestos dust in his lungs after working on insulating tankers in the docks.

A coasting ketch called *Penryn* had been used in Falmouth Harbour in the Second World War to tether a barrage balloon. She was taken up the coast in 1944 at the time of the Flying Bombs and was brought back by Bart Moore in 1947 and beached by the cut. Mr Crossley, of the Lynher Riverboat family, was a teacher at Mylor School and lived on board with his wife who had a baby there delivered by Dr Timmins. An old photograph shows a row of three windows inserted in the sides of the *Penryn*. After they left swallows nested on board. She was eventually broken up for scrap iron and firewood by the Tripconeys. For a long time after, it was possible to find her small pebble ballast and fastenings on the beach.

Mains water was not connected until the mid-1950s. Until then each house had a well or access to one. There is a public pump at Cartref painted like the ones in the village and there was another near the entrance to Trelew Farm lane. Tom Rowe and his sons dug many of the wells and some were no use as the salt water infiltrated. 'Grandpa' Curnow was a water diviner. The mains sewerage only exists as far as Carrick Cottage and houses beyond and below the road have septic tanks, or nothing.

There are various unsolved mysteries. A baby was found in the well at Trelew, which was thought to be that of a maidservant at the house. At Trevamo the owner went missing and was eventually found drowned in the large rainwater tank. A young Mylor girl earned a few pence from the postmaster that day taking a telegram to the house and is still horrified at the thought of what she then did not know had happened. There was another suicide at No. 1 where a retired Sergeant-Major cut his throat. At least one of these incidents is reputed to be on an account of a local *belle dame sans merci*!

Not only have houses been altered but also gardens. The older houses in the road had interesting plants like some of those still found at the Helford Fox gardens, Trebah and Glendurgan, but many have been lost. All the old gardens had their orchards, many with local Cornish varieties like the Pig's Snout. These age, but little has been done to replace them.

Some well-known people have lived here. Katherine Mansfield rented No. 17, now Quibo, during the First World War. She had escaped from the fraught household of D.H. and Frieda Lawrence at Zennor, but they followed her to Mylor. Howard Spring of Hooper's Hill wrote his sad novel *All the Day Long*, featuring Carclew and Mylor Creek. The house he describes as Little-in-Sight was either Quibo or Nantrelew opposite. This book was the fulfilment of a promise to Jane Kelly, daughter of Captain Kelly, the immediate post-Second-World-War principal of Falmouth Technical School. Mrs Batt, who lived at Trelew Vean, had been a Gaiety Girl and her nephew, Rolf Harris, used to visit her. The artist, Percy Thurburn, bought the land between Folieu and Morwenna and built himself a studio cabin. He had several yachts built at Porthleven, including the *Golden Vanity*, and later moved to Frenchman's Creek.

Colonel Ord-Statter lived at Trelew for many years and was a great benefactor of the village. He paid for the public conveniences on the playing fields and also provided the Ord-Statter Pavilion, besides giving much personal help to individuals and young people.

Church Road is still a good place to live. The lower end is particularly beautiful in spring when the hazel coppice on the landward side is awash with bluebells, scenting the lane on a calm day. In summer there is continuous activity on the water and on the farm opposite. The autumn colours of the oak trees, which brush the water, are glorious on a sunny day. All the springs on the south hillside overflow in the winter, streaming across the road to make a leafy mush at the sides, ideal for blackbirds or redwings in severe weather. There are many wading birds in winter with frequent calls from curlew, oystercatcher and red shank until they leave to breed in March. Mallards quack loudly all year round and egrets are regular visitors.

Old Almshouse at Tregatreath

The will of Richard Bonython of Carclew was proved

in the Consistorial Court of Exeter in 1698. Among other items bequeathed were:

... one hundred pounds to be disposed of by 'the Vicar and overseers of the poore of the parish [of Mylor]... with the advice and consent of some of the most substantial house holders of the said parish... may at Xmas yearly for ever be given... for the relief of the poore... an augmentation of the glebe land by one field of four acres called Blisco be surrounded by land belonging to Sir Peter Killigrew and part of the Manor of Mylor. Tenn pounds for erecting an almshouse for the poore of the parish of Mylor...

This information is taken from Dr Hugh Olivey's *Notes on the Parish of Mylor,* in which he comments:

The Vicar still has the field called Blisco as part of the glebe, but what has become of the Christmas gifts to the poor and the almshouse? No one knows anything about them and no records can be found.

Research revealed a 1767 estate map showing that augmentation of the glebe had indeed been made and stands far removed from the rest, being named on the map Carclew Field. Further west is the Almshouse at Tregatreath which still stands and is the boatyard home of Martin and Janet Heard. Clearly this is a very old house, built sometime after 1745 – the date of the will of Jane Kemp, daughter of Richard Bonython. She wrote:

I have in my hands Ten pounds given by my Father's Will towards erecting an Alms House... I hereby direct my Executor to pay the said ten pounds to the Overseer of the Poor with a further £10 in lieu of interest.

The building section of the Cornish Archaeological Unit at County Hall has shown interest in Mylor's Almshouse. From a photograph, it can be seen that the house is in two parts. It seems likely that the two-storey part was for the householder and the right-hand portion (probably added later) was for animals. Within living memory, and until Mr Terry Heard started his boatyard in the 1960s, the house was known as Tregatreath Farm and was farmed in turn by the Rickard, Porter and Hooper families, the latter having a milk round.

Cardew Barnicoat, who lived nearby, remembers as a boy that between the farmhouse and the creek there was a flat area of grass where the boys of the village played cricket and football. The buttress on the extreme left of the building was built about 1900 by Mr Barnicoat's father. In front of it is a large anchor which Martin Heard says was brought in by fishermen from the Manacles. It is over 200 years old.

Mylor had a bowling-green on the area behind the Almshouse (see map on page 41). Bowling-greens were frequently found where men had to pass the time in watching and waiting for the arrival of sea-going vessels. In more recent times, the bowling club moved to a new site in Passage Hill.

The History of New Row

New Row is a small lane leading directly off the main street in the centre of Mylor Bridge, between the Lemon Arms and its car park. It has mainly terraced cottages along the south side and around a square at the far end.

In 1800 there were no buildings there at all, only a track running between fields and parallel to the Mill Leat. At that time, the village was fairly small and the houses spread out. All the land to the north of the creek was in the ownership of the Lemon family of Carclew. In 1805, land was purchased for a naval dockyard at Mylor Churchtown and this was the start of the influence that the Royal Navy was to have on the village for more than a century. Over the years, houses were needed to accommodate the personnel and their families and an ideal site was in the centre of the village close to the Mill Leat.

The leat began at a small dam and weir to the west of the village on the edge of the Enys estate, where the stream was diverted along the leat to power the mill. It ran on higher ground and under the main street to a small pond north of the mill by the quay. The leat was broad and shallow, making it an ideal place from which to collect water, and this was an important factor when choosing a site on which to build.

Leases were granted by Sir Charles Lemon, usually of 99 years or on three lives, allowing the building of houses. Some leases insisted that properties were to be built of stone with slate roofs, suggesting that previous dwellings were of lesser materials, probably cob and thatch. The stone used in the buildings came from the quarry on the north side of the creek. The walls were constructed of roughly squared stones of almost the same size and filled with rubble and clay. Bricks used could have come from the brickyard in Comfort Road, with sand being brought from the beach for mortar. Any granite quoins would have been delivered by sea from further along the coast.

Over the years, some of the cottages have had so many coats of limewash that it is difficult to tell which are cob and which are stone. Cottages were often only one room deep as this made roofing easier. In the nineteenth century thatch was thought to be inferior and, as slates were then being split by machine, they became less expensive and more common.

The tithe map and associated list of 1840–41 give details of all the properties in the village together with the names of the lessees and tenants. It can be seen that each house appears to have land on each side of the access lane. In 1830 part of the lane was called Trenance Row and later it became known as Navy Row due to the number of naval personnel living there. The name New Row was first documented in 1901.

The first lease to be granted was in 1816 for a plot adjacent to the public house, then known as the Griffin Inn. The lessee was Thomas Tregenza and the next year he leased another plot to the south. Both plots

The Old Almshouse at Tregatreath, later a farmhouse and in 2004 the home of Martin and Janet Heard, owners of Tregatreath Boatyard. It is pictured here towards the end of the twentieth century.

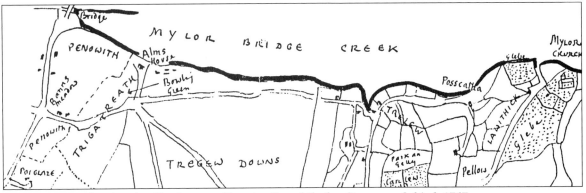

An estate map, showing the Almshouse at Tregatreath and the bowling-green behind, 1767.

This view of the end of New Row, taken in the early 1900s, features the famous Mylor Oak next to the mill leat.

were on what is now the Lemon Arms' car park. Mr Tregenza also leased the Square and is described as a farmer. The next lease was granted in 1824 to Thomas Porter with permission to build one or two houses. Two were built, now Nos 1 and 2. A direct descendant of Mr Porter, Mr F. Ingram, still lives in the Row at the time of writing. More leases were granted in the 1830s and by 1840 there were buildings on all the sites along the lane. One of the most important of these was a school erected by Sir Charles Lemon with a house next door for the schoolmaster, John Mitchell. The school is now Nos 5, 6 and 7, and the schoolhouse No. 8.

As all the houses were tenanted until 1920, and many until after the Second World War, there were a lot of changes in occupation. As families grew, houses were combined and then subdivided again when the family became smaller or moved on. It is difficult to trace where each family lived but there are names which appear over the years, such as May, Jarvis or Barwis, Pearce, Tallack, Drew and Tregenza, and it is interesting to trace the growth of these families.

Between 1851 and 1891 people with the following occupations were living in the Row: mariners, Greenwich naval pensioners, master mariners, superannuated gunner, engineers, roper, shipwrights, boatswain, sawyers, Coastguard and revenue mate, as well as sailors and mates from the Merchant Service. There were also small shops, shoemakers, laundresses, seamstresses, agricultural labourers and carpenters amongst others.

In June 1920, Captain William Francis Tremayne, owner of the Carclew estate, auctioned off an amazing amount of property, not only in Mylor parish, but also in Stithians, Kenwyn, Kea, Feock and St Gluvias. The whole of New Row was up for sale and in the auction particulars each house is listed, together with the tenants and the rent paid in 1919. Most properties were very much as they are today, in terms of size and

Frank Vinnicombe recalls a 'real witch' who lived along New Row and who taught him a secret method to charm away warts. She did not like people walking past her house though and would sometimes throw dirty water over them!

(CARTOON BY BRUCE COLLIER, 2003)

land attached. They had two or three bedrooms, maybe a boxroom, one or two sitting-rooms, kitchens or back kitchens, many had wash-houses and, very importantly, closets, mostly across the lane. However, for one cottage, until a separate closet was built, the occupiers had the right to use the one next door! All the properties had gardens, either adjacent to the south or across the lane to the north. Some had both. There were sheds, outhouses, stores, coal houses, one with a loft, a pigs' house, a greenhouse and one house contained a shop.

Perhaps because a lot of the cottages were in poor repair and had sitting tenants, very few were sold at the auction. Some had previously been sold to tenants but on the fourth day of the sale No. 3 was sold to Mr Rowe for £170 and No. 4 to Mr Keverne for £275. Some houses further down the Row were also sold for £85 or £90.

The cottages at the end of New Row facing Lemon Hill, c.1910. These were destroyed by a bomb in 1941 and the site is now the car park for the Lemon Arms.

The Second World War brought many changes to the scene, as described in Chapter 12. After the war, because of the destruction of the first two houses in the Row, all the properties were re-numbered and one bungalow was built on the north side to replace the house destroyed there. Water had been laid on to the village during the war and electricity connections were becoming more common. The houses were gradually modernised, with sewerage arriving in the 1960s. This updating continues today with the building of garages and outhouses, and New Row has become a very popular and convenient place to live.

East Coast Connections

According to the 1871 census records, there were many people living in Mylor parish who were born in coastal towns outside Cornwall. It is interesting to see that quite a few of these residents were born in Essex, and in particular West Mersea. Mersea Island is situated in the Blackwater estuary and is connected to the mainland by a causeway that is flooded at high spring tides. The main settlement is West Mersea, but there is also a smaller hamlet of East Mersea. In 1871 West Mersea had a population of about 900, when it was little more than a fishing village.

The two areas were very similar in that the main occupations were farming and fishing, but in particular the estuaries of both were very suitable for the growth of oysters. The oysters are dredged from the estuary bed and two-year-old or 'brood' ones are laid in beds to mature. Young oysters are often transferred from one part of the country to another to increase the local stocks.

This trade in oysters meant that people travelled by sea between the two areas in the nineteenth and twentieth centuries and many surnames are common to both. Large stocks were brought down to the area in the early 1800s when there was a series of severe winters on the East Coast. Several families from Mersea and the surrounding area settled in Flushing and Mylor. Another group came around 1900. In 1871 there were Banks, Gentry, Pearce, Wyatt and Woolf families amongst others in Mylor parish and there are people of these names still living in Mersea at the time of writing.

One member of the Banks family, Henry, returned to West Mersea at the turn of the century and bought a piece of land. The Mersea firm of oyster merchants, Banks Bros, were buying oysters for re-laying until the introduction of a disease which was thought to have originated from Falmouth.

Greatwood House

Greatwood House has had many occupants since its building in the 1840s by Philip Daniel of the Daniel family of Trelissick. He was the eighth son of Ralph Allen Daniel, a Truro merchant and smelter. The

Parc Vean, the home of Squire Daniel and his family who once lived at Greatwood. This photograph dates from 1970.

house he constructed faced east to the shoreline, instead of south-south-east, as did the old Wood Cottage whose site it occupied.

Philip Daniel did not live in the house for long, moving to Little Park (Parc Vean) on the Mylor to Flushing road where his son Ralph had built a house of similar style to Greatwood at that time. Philip died in 1859 and is buried in Mylor churchyard, as also is his son Ralph, their wives and children. His two granddaughters lived to age 90 and 91, dying in 1958 – the family grave thus spanning 100 years and three generations.

Edmund Harvey, who held the lease for 10 years, and was a relation of the Tresidder family, extended Greatwood House in the 1870s. It was considerably extended to the east and south in Victorian style, the turret being added then or later. At the time there were stables and coach-houses with gardens and orchard and about 19 acres of fields, mostly around the coast. This was the old Upton's tenement, later Wood tenement, which in the mid-1700s had been occupied by Richard Tresidder and his descendants.

The lease changed hands again to Captain Joseph Hinds. He was at one time churchwarden at Mylor Church, had a large grown-up family and, according to the 1881 census, kept a cook, housemaid, nurse and parlour-maid. By comparison, in the census of 1861 we learn that the resident landed proprietor, Benjamin Sampson, widower, had a staff of eight, including a housekeeper and valet.

The most long-standing tenant arrived in 1895. He was John Gregory Bond who came from London but, once settled at Greatwood, remained for 36 years. He developed market gardening there, and several people were employed by him. Mr Bond died in 1931 as a bachelor who had two faithful servants, one of whom inherited his lease, while the other honoured his name by a gift to the repair of the church tower.

Another family acquired the lease in 1931. Major Edward Pendarves Dorrien-Smith moved in and was able later in 1936 to purchase the property from the Tremayne estate. Sadly, his family encountered tragedy when first his daughter died in a motoring accident and then two of his sons were killed in action during the Second World War. His sons are commemorated on the Mylor war memorial and also with their three cousins in St Nicholas Church, Tresco.

Major Dorrien-Smith had a renowned garden, with shrubs, a tennis-court and peacocks. He also grew daffodils for the London market. After his death Captain and Mrs N.E. Gore-Langton kept a small herd of Channel Island cattle on the land, until they emigrated to Canada in 1961.

Greatwood was then taken over by a Mr Rainbird, who ran it as a hotel. It entered the most dramatic and tragic day of its history on 31 July 1966, with the sinking of the day-tripper boat the *Darlwyne*. Returning from Fowey with hotel guests and local people, the boat encountered a storm in St Austell Bay and went down. All 31 men, women and children were drowned. There is a memorial screen to them in the church. For Greatwood, the sad result was that the hotel closed and when, much later in 1973, it was recovered by the Gore-Langtons, following a lawsuit, it remained empty. Although bought by a property company, the house was neglected through the '70s and there was serious vandalism. Alan Townend, who lived at Greatwood later, graphically describes the state of the house:

The main staircase was taken away by water, squatters and the wind and rain resulted in the house being virtually a roofless shell by 1976. Floors too, had fallen in or been taken. The garden was completely overgrown and the water was not visible from the house.

Fortunately, Greatwood House and surrounds were rescued and restored by Frank Atherley and John Millan. Seven flats were created and occupied by 1979 and the stable block and rest of the estate were sold. It is now a fine house again with its commanding position and splendid views over the water.

The Vicarage

In the Cornish fashion, the front of the house is that with the most spectacular view. It has nothing to do with the approach from the road. The upstairs windows have elegant little balconies and one visualises generations of delighted visitors gazing out at the splendour of Mylor Harbour and, beyond, the Roseland Peninsula.

The present house was built by the Revd Edward Hoblyn, vicar of Mylor from 1823 to 1868. On his arrival in the parish, he found that the living was a vicarage with a net yearly value of £271, including 14 acres of glebe. Mylor Old Vicarage House had stood at the top of the churchyard and was built of stone, roofed partly of slate, partly of reed thatch. Inside were a parlour, hall, kitchen, dairy and two cellars. There were also a barn and stable nearby. The building was in a state of extreme decay. Promptly, the new incumbent had it pulled down and another built further up the hill to command the finest view. This was to be the commodious residence necessary to accommodate a large nineteenth-century family with 12 children.

Edward Hoblyn was a stern and autocratic parish priest – to give an example, when Mary Ann Quarme, innkeeper of the Clinton Arms opposite the church (at the time of writing a private residence called Lawithick) applied to renew her licence in 1840, Mr Hoblyn persuaded the magistrates not to comply – too many of his parishioners were turning left into the inn instead of right into the church on Sundays. In fairness to Mr Hoblyn, one has to remember that drinking was the social evil of the time and that the inn in question was undoubtedly of some importance in the smuggling trade.

In 1868, Mr Hoblyn died and the Revd J.W. Murray took up residence in the Vicarage. It was during his time in Mylor that a mighty movement of church building and restoration swept the country as a result of Victorian prosperity and values. A great deal of damage was done to ancient buildings and St Mylor was no exception. In the course of work begun in 1870 and completed in 1879, a fourteenth-century wagon-roof, Purbeck sandstone paving and oak pews with fine carving were removed and frescoes blotted out.

But much was done to enhance the church. The grey granite parish cross was reinstated; the pillar piscine unearthed in removing the foundations of the Old Vicarage House was placed on the south wall; and pieces of the fifteenth-century oak rood-screen were located and reassembled in or near its original position. Mr Murray took a keen interest in the work as it progressed and, when he died in 1888, the three bells in the detached belfry were recast in his memory.

It was in 1924 that a vicar affectionately known in the locality as the 'Sporting Vicar', the Revd Gilbert Young, moved into the living with his wife and daughter, Mary. This was a time when the house was alive with activity. High days of summer were the garden parties and fêtes with croquet on the lawn, tennis, country dancing and a two-tier system of afternoon tea – a standard one set out on the gravel drive and a special cream one in the Vicarage drawing-room. Sports days, in which the vicar played a leading part, were held on a field belonging to Rosehill Farm. Footballers had a decided handicap for there was a hump in the middle of the pitch and when one team stood near its goal, the goal posts of the other could scarcely be seen!

Shortly after 1930, due to the Depression, many merchant ships were laid up in Falmouth Harbour. Fourteen of them were in Mylor Basin. The crews always received a warm welcome at the Vicarage, where they could enjoy a meal, a game of billiards and pick up their mail. In 1934, *The Cornish Guardian* reported a Good Friday service, when almost every man and woman on board these ships attended.

At about this time, the state of the Vicarage roof was causing concern. All the bowls and buckets in

Above: *Greatwood House in the 1970s when it was unoccupied and semi-derelict.*

Left: *Greatwood House after its restoration, 1997.*

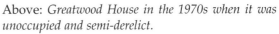

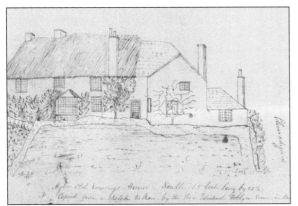

Above: *Sketch of the Old Vicarage House by the Revd Edward Hoblyn, vicar, in March 1824.*

Right: *Revd and Mrs Hoblyn outside St Mylor Church. Vicar from 1823–68, Revd Hoblyn had a new vicarage built to replace the old dilapidated one.*

Mrs Young's kitchen were placed strategically when rain fell. The opinion was expressed that the cost of the upkeep of such a large old building was not justified – it should be pulled down and a smaller, modern dwelling built. Such was the outcry in the parish, however, that in 1936, under the Revd Valentine Wagner, a plan was evolved to reduce the size of the building and five or six rooms, including the dairy and one upstairs used for receptions, were removed, leaving the more compact Vicarage of today.

The Vicarage as it is in 2004.

Porloe

Many of Mylor's farms stand on ancient settlement sites, their origin being recognisable from their Celtic names – for example, Crownick, the 'dwelling at the crossroads' and Halwyn, 'white hall or court'. These sites were ideally situated at least part way up a hill, well sheltered from rough weather. It was desirable that they should be fairly high for, the sea being the main highway in earlier times, a watch had to be kept for pirates and other sea-borne invaders. So, a favourable site having been found early in history, it is natural that when the original building was no longer weatherproof, a new one should occupy it incorporating material from the earlier building.

Such a farm is Porloe, the 'port or harbour by the pool' which has also been known as Portloe (1754), Purloe and Pellow. A lease records that it was run by a Mr Lawrence, who paid 10d. in rates per annum. In an Enys deed of 1788, the property was 'set to farm with messuage' – that is a dwelling house with outbuildings and land – lately erected by Thomas Patrickson Braithwaite, and known as Porloe Tenement.

In the middle gable there is a circular niche in which an alabaster statue of St George and the Dragon once stood. Much later in time, it is said that a young Flushing boy carrying pasties to Porloe took out his catapult and, with skilful aim, damaged one of the legs of the horse. This mischief was reported to the then vicar of Flushing, Canon Savage, who was an antiquarian. Examining the figure, he found it to be of foreign origin and of a kind bought to display in sixteenth- and seventeenth-century houses. He brought it to his church, St Peter's, where it can be seen to this day on the right-hand side of the entrance porch.

Porloe land runs down to Mylor Creek and a right of way exists by which seaweed and sand could be brought from around the coast for use on the land. Below ground there was also activity as, by simply lifting the carpet and a few floorboards in the living-room, an eight-foot-square room was revealed from which an underground passage led to Mylor Creek at Polscatha, the bay of little boats. This was not unusual in an area where smuggling was once rife. For example, a brick-lined tunnel runs from Trefusis to a gazonne or gulley at Penarrow. How easy it must have been to run a boat into the inlet, up Porloe Slip – and all under the eye of the Coastguard living nearby at Beach Cottage!

Beach Cottage at Porloe Slip, at one time the home of the local Coastguard, seen here in the early 1900s.

Thomas Patrickson Braithwaite, who built Porloe, served under Lord Howe as Flag Lieutenant in the Seven Years War (1755–63). Later, he obtained command of a Falmouth Post Office packet ship and was comfortably off, receiving £78 a year – seamen were paid only £15. But, like other packet captains, his main income was from the sale of goods illicitly imported. In 1785, this sum was £4,000! Brought to court, he was found guilty of being engaged in compromising transactions with Brazil. However, he seems to have escaped severe punishment for by 1788, a new packet ship, *The Howe*, was brought into service and Thomas was its captain. But shortly after he took over his new command, signs of financial difficulty began to surface. We hear of Lord Wodehouse selling the lease of Porloe and the land going to Joanna Hobbs of Mount Stewart.

The dairy school held in the Tremayne Institute in January 1927. Left to right, back row: V. Carlyon, F. Tregenza, A. Rawling, R. Dunstan, J. Lawry; front: Bertha Thomas, Ethel Gray, C. Rosevearne, Miss Nicholas (instructress), M. Dunstan, B. Thomas.

Captain T.P. Braithwaite retired in 1794 and died the same year, being buried in Mylor churchyard. His wife, left in straightened circumstances, obtained the post of Matron at Greenwich Hospital. In 1799, John Loudon Macadam, victualler to the Navy in the Western Ports, rented Porloe for three years, remaining until the Peace of Amiens, a treaty with France, was signed. Then he left for Bristol, where he was shortly made Surveyor of Roads and, together with Telford, revolutionised the highways of Britain within 20 years, so that coaches could drive safely and fast throughout the land.

In 1839 John Rowe, yeoman, obtained a lease on the property from Lord Wodehouse. According to a history published by the *Cornish Echo* in 1904, John Rowe of Porloe supplied HM ships with beef and on killing days the village bought offal cheaply at the farm.

John Rowe was succeeded by his son, John Reed Rowe, and later tenants included George Dunstan and George Richard Dunstan in 1893. The latter took over the farm on his father's death. G.R. Dunstan was a distinguished pioneer of clean milk and created a model dairy at Porloe. This attracted a great deal of publicity and an account in the *Cornish Echo* (1928) reported that milk was produced under the very best of hygienic conditions:

The up-to-date milking shed was scrupulously clean, the mechanical milking nothing short of miraculous as was the sterilising of the milk and the cleansing of the mechanical equipment.

The whole milking process was under the supervision of Mrs Dunstan, England's champion butter-maker. She was said to have worked in the dairy of Windsor Castle. In 1928, a letter to the *Falmouth Packet* newspaper paid tribute to Porloe Dairy – the methods of milking employed, the general cleanliness, the sterilisation. It was signed H.W. Rose, Captain, Army School of Hygiene, Aldershot.

In 1930, G.R. Dunstan died and was followed by Francis Jefford and, later, by his son, George, who continued to work the farm and dairy until the end of the Second World War. It was a busy, self-supporting farm, but in time the animals gave way to potatoes and cauliflowers. When George and Jean Jefford retired from farming in 1992, the Trefusis estate sold Porloe, the valley leading to Mylor Creek at Polscatha and the fields around the house to John Bonython, whose forebears had owned the Carclew estate in the eighteenth century.

After starting renovation work on the house, Mr Bonython had a change of plan, selling the house to Christopher and Sarita Perkins, who completed the restoration and enjoy Porloe as a small farm and family country house at the time of writing. Porloe Farm has now returned to much the same acreage as the Jeffords farmed in the 1980s, due to the acquisition of a further 80 acres in 1997. The Perkins family breed event horses and fatten cattle and sheep on the 20 acres around Porloe, the other 80 acres being farmed on a share basis with Matthew and Paul Dale of Restronguet Barton.

For the year March 2003–04, Christopher Perkins held the office of High Sheriff of Cornwall, so Porloe was a delightful and friendly base for the entertainment of both the High Court Judges during their visits on circuit to Truro Crown Court and for many friends. Also welcomed at Porloe have been prominent figures in the judiciary, the armed forces, the police and the Cornish business, civic and charity worlds.

Quite probably, in Porloe's early days 250 years ago, Captain Thomas Braithwaite would have been entertaining similar local and county personalities. Porloe has certainly responded by welcoming all. Christopher and Sarita Perkins think that Captain Braithwaite would approve of the enjoyment that the house he built has given, both lately and over the years!

Porloe Farmhouse as it is in 2004, fully restored.

Woodlands

On the outskirts of Mylor lies Woodlands, built on the foundations of a small farm shown on a map dated 1700 in the Record Office in Truro. Possibly, even earlier houses had stood there for it has long been the custom to reutilise proven favourable conditions – this spot was sheltered from the south-westerly gales. An earlier house would have been sited lengthways into the hill, the ground having been cut away to provide a well-drained platform. In such a situation, farmsteads have been built in Cornwall from medieval times. Woodlands was earlier known as Polglaze. An entry in the Assize Record of 1362 gives the name 'Polglas juxta Lyndirriomur' which translates as 'the green (or blue) pool near Landerio' – the latter being an adjacent farm.

Admiral Bartholomew James leased the property on his retirement from the Navy in 1801 and built a more substantial house in the Georgian style. A grassy slope ran gently down to a large pond, created, it is believed, by the damming of a portion of the stream joining several earlier ponds on adjoining land, which provided fish for Glasney Collegiate Church in Penryn which was dissolved at the Reformation.

Several years ago, an extension to Admiral James' building was to be made. A bulldozer broke into the rising bank and a passage was revealed. A few metres into the hill, the roof rose to form a circular chamber in which three or four people might stand upright. For what purpose could such a passage have been designed? In Cornwall, smuggling springs to mind. Or could religious or political offenders have escaped through its narrow confines? Since it was not brick-lined like the tunnel running from Trefusis to Penarrow, it was considered too dangerous to explore. This is fortunate, for one night, a month or so later, there was a sharp frost and the walls crumpled and fell

in. Another portion of the hill was sliced off and a new stone wall closed in the unsolved mystery.

We learn from the *Royal Cornwall Gazette* (1896) that Admiral James had been a person of genial temper with a penchant for eccentric festivity. At the jubilee of George III in 1809, his rejoicing took the form of a 'dinner to the poor of the neighbourhood' at which he himself presided, when:

... an enormous sea pie, weighing about 200 pounds flanked by good old Sirloin, etc. was followed by ample cans of strong beer, till the hearts of the poor people sang with joy.

He liked to celebrate his birthday with gusto, even in the most trying circumstances. Once, he recorded in his journal, a very severe gale sprang up when sailing near Gibraltar. The ship's company assembled to partake of a rich banquet, fearing to offend by their absence:

The dread of not pleasing me by their sitting and eating added to the ship's motion, produced a scene truly laughable... some of us were thrown from our seats to leeward!

It is evident that Admiral James had great personal charm. During the American War of Independence, he was in charge of an expedition of 2,000 troops to Hampton, Virginia. The object was to pillage the town and take as prisoners the leading citizens. Bartholomew, however, was so distressed at the fear of the ladies of one household that he 'sat down in friendly manner and relieved them of the fears our visit had thrown them into.' Later, he withdrew from the town 'loaded with presents from Mrs Jones and her amiable daughters'!

He seems to have been a great success with the ladies. At a reception in Naples, he met Lady Hamilton, mistress of his friend, Lord Horatio Nelson:

... that exquisite and charming, lovely woman... in the ecstasy of singing God Save the King... she tore her fan to pieces and threw herself into such bewitching attitudes that no mortal soul could refrain from believing her to be an enthusiastic angel from heaven, purposely sent down to celebrate this pleasant, happy festival.

Above: *Woodlands, the Georgian-style house built by Admiral Bartholomew James in c.1801.*

Right: *Woodlands, seen here in the early 1900s, when it was home to the Pike family. Harry Pike was a market gardener and employed local ladies to pick daffodils, anemones and violets which were sold locally in Falmouth and also sent to Covent Garden along with tomatoes, which were grown under glass.*

Albion House in the 1970s, once the home of Dr Olivey, author of Notes on the Parish of Mylor.

The Admiral was a distinguished sailor, but in money matters he was 'all at sea'. He had been unfortunate in inheriting his father's considerable debts. But he, too, thanks to unsound investment and unscrupulous friends, was scarcely ever out of debt.

In 1794, one difficulty had followed another so quickly that, as he wrote:

I had no time to breath between them; no sooner out of one jail than into another – even into that blessed receptacle of filth, Bridewell, was my poor carcase conveyed; so that I was enabled almost to say that there was scarcely a lock-up house from the pump at Aldgate to Charing Cross but what I had been honoured with knowledge of.

Much of Admiral James' service in the Navy had been the harassment of shipping in wars with America, France and Spain. At one point he collected enough prize money to clear all his debts, leaving him sufficient to build Woodlands. Ten years later, however, he was once more so heavily in debt that he was forced to lease his house and move with his wife to Flushing, where he died in 1828.

Albion House

The property we know as Albion House in Bells Hill was built in the late-eighteenth century and extended at either side by wings as deep as the original house in the mid-nineteenth century. The whole house was then attractively slate hung.

In 1812 the house was advertised in the *Sherborne Mercury* newspaper to be disposed of by Joseph Lawrence, together with a stables, outhouses, farmyard and about eight acres of good arable land, all held under the yearly rent of £1.1s. and 'comprising a neat,

comfortable tenement in every respect adapted for a gentleman's country residence.'

For a time, the Bell family of Falmouth came to live there. George Bell had been a packet-ship agent in the eighteenth century and his eldest son followed suit. Another son was a packet commander and yet another a naval officer who fought under Lord Exmouth and later commanded the frigate *Medusa*. Albion would be an apt choice of name for a family home with such close naval connections. It is possible that Bells Hill takes its name from this family.

Another distinguished resident of Albion House was Hugh Pengilly Olivey, a surgeon who was born in 1833. He had married Harriet Vincent in 1859 and they had one son, Hugh, who died at only 14 minutes old in North Curry, Somerset. From conversations recorded with elderly local people, it seems that Dr Olivey was often seen riding his horses through the village. He was a kindly though private person. Mrs Olivey died in 1890 and Dr Olivey in 1918. At the disposal of Carclew land and property in 1920, Albion House was put up for sale, described as 'a Residence, Farm Buildings and Land now in the occupation of Mrs Doble, the estimated Rental value being £100 per annum and consisting of 11 acres.' Mrs Doble was the former Margaret Olivey, sister of Hugh, who had married Matthew Doble, a farmer of 190 acres.

During his time in Mylor, Dr Olivey compiled the book *Notes on the Parish of Mylor,* published in 1907. This does not purport to be a history of the parish but of some of its more notable buildings and people. From old authorities, he records customs, institutions and anecdotes which otherwise would not have been available to the Mylor Local History Group who now pay tribute to this valuable volume.

Lawithick

In the days before the coming of Christianity to our creek, it is said that a chieftain gave to the pagan populace a grant of land for the burial of their dead. Rituals surrounding burial were very important to them. This land was named Lan-wythek, from lann (enclosed cemetery) and gwythek (holy place among the trees). It is a reminder of the ancient Christian background of the area which can be traced for over 1,500 years.

About AD411 a Celtic abbot-bishop named Milor sailed from Brittany, perhaps with a small group of monks, and landed about where our present church-yard rises from the shore. He built his first church of wattle, which was the tradition.

In 1066, the Normans invaded England and began a great church-building movement, employing stone-masons brought over from Normandy. Our church was one of these.

The house opposite, recorded as being existent in 1227, is thought to have been built to meet the need for accommodation for builders and was called Lawithick. It then became a farm and there are leases from the time of George III held in the County Records Office, Truro.

In *Notes on the Parish of Mylor* by H.P. Olivey, the Revd J.M. Murray, vicar from 1868–74, is recorded as saying:

I have been informed by Mr Thomas [Parish Clerk in 1873] that the house he now occupies near the church used to be an Inn called the Clinton Arms. Its last occupier was Mary Ann Quarme. The Revd Edward Hoblyn [vicar from 1823–68] persuaded the magistrates to refuse a licence to her because people went into the inn in preference to the church opposite. She left in March 1840 and Lawithick reverted to a farm.

The passenger launch Ibis, *owned by Mr Bell, ran trips from Falmouth to the Lawithick tea garden. In 1906 she was thought to be the first passenger vessel on the Fal estuary to have an internal combustion engine.*

In 1931, Mr and Mrs Curnow and their children, Bernice and Jim, moved into the house and farmed six fields on the Cregoes beyond the church. Crops included corn and potatoes with some grazing and a coppice. When the slump came between the wars and boats were laid up in Mylor Pool, Ye Olde Tea Garden in their pretty front garden became very popular, a launch called *Ibis* running regular trips to it from Falmouth.

War came and Mrs Curnow took in six evacuees from Highgate, London, who were so happy they stayed in touch and became firm family friends. In 1943, a party of about 25 US Navy personnel arrived and lived in two Nissen huts in the Curnow's orchard on the other side of the lane. Their assignment was to repair landing-craft on the slip in readiness for the departure on D-Day.

At the time of writing, Lawithick is a private residence, beautifully restored.

Lawithick, once an inn known as the Clinton Arms, is shown here as the Old Tea House in the early 1900s.

Chapter 4
❖
Some Local Trades

The Blacksmith, Road Improvements and Transport, Farm Vehicles, Steam Power, Bicycles, Motor Cars,
Motor Buses, Commercial Vehicles Between the Wars, The Lemon Arms, The Foundry – A Noise-Filled Valley,
Mylor Quay and the Mill, The Brickworks, The Wood Yard, Flower Growing, Treseder's Nursery.

The Blacksmith

In the nineteenth century the Mylor smithy was run by Michael Oates and his son William. In 1841 they were aged 55 and 25 respectively. William eventually took over the business and by 1841 he lived there with his wife Mary and their two sons, William, who was then 22 and John, 19. William's unmarried sister also lived with them. In the latter part of the century, David Rees rented the smithy from William Oates and travelled daily from his home in Flushing to Mylor with his son William James. When William married Hester Cantell in 1893 he rented the house next door. This was at one time called Jessamine Cottage but was later renamed Lemon Cottage when the main village

street became known as Lemon Hill. Father and son continued to run the business together until David died in 1906.

William and Hester had 16 children – seven boys and nine girls. All but one survived to adulthood. The eldest sons assisted their father with the work, but when the First World War began they went into active service and Marjorie helped her father from the age of 13. Two days a week were spent working up at Carclew and Marjorie was to be seen riding a large cumbersome bicycle, known as an 'Iron Gate', up the steep hill, carrying all the necessary heavy tools. She also helped her mother with the sending out of bills for the work done and this was generally carried out every six months.

Mylor's main street, c.1919. On the right is the blacksmith William Rees outside the blacksmith's shop. The boy with the bucket is David Rees and the little girl is his sister Linda. The lady on the left is Mrs Richards and the gentleman in the middle of the road is Captain Lewarne. The Tremayne Institute on the left, once a mission and Sunday school, is a snooker club in 2004.

Sadly, the two eldest boys died in the war: Charles Wesley at the Battle of Jutland and Stanley on the Somme in 1918. After the war, the next two sons, William Clifton and David James, joined their father once again and these two continued to operate the smithy until 1985. The smithy was a favourite place for villagers to congregate, both young and old. Children coming home from school would stop to watch the horses being shod and James Thomas, writing about life just after the Second World War, remembers the butcher's horse being taken to be shod:

An AA sign, as recalled by Eric Gray. It is yellow with black lettering and set into a wall in Comfort Road.

As children we used to try to be present when the horse was led down, because Mr Rollason would allow one, or sometimes two of us to sit on the horse's back during the walk to and from the smith. I can still remember the width of that horse's back, we sat on rather than astride, and I suppose such an adventure would be banned on grounds of safety today, but we did not, as far as I know, suffer any accidents. In retrospect, I feel that we had more pleasure in our daily lives than the young folk of today.

The children were fascinated by the bellows and the distinctive smell of the blacksmith's shop would never be forgotten. Harry Moore remembers:

It was the Mecca of small boys at shoeing time. I can hear the sound of the hammers, see the light of the fires at dusk

in winter and see the sparks. I can smell the burning of the hooves and the smell of hot iron. I can hear the gossip of the boys waiting for horses to be shod and their jokes, and I remember the sky-larking. On one occasion one of the village boys wanted to join the Navy as a stoker and some of the other boys challenged him to sit by the forge and endure the sparks as they blew the fire. He did until his clothes began to burn and then water was thrown over him. He joined the Navy and was on board the Camperdown *when she rammed the* Victoria *on naval manoeuvres in the Mediterranean.*

Marjorie Rees, aged about 14, assisting her father William at the forge during the First World War, when her elder brothers were away serving their country.

A 1970s painting of the blacksmith's shop and cottage by Margaret Simpson, depicting life before the First World War.

Eric Gray recalled the AA sign attached to the outside of the smithy, yellow with black lettering and showing the distance to London. Today one is incorporated into a garden wall in Comfort Road. He also remembers:

Horseshoes festooned the old walls, hanging from hooks or lying about on the floor. The wooden bench was covered with gritty dust, boxes of nails, rasps and knives. The drum bellows were pumped with a long handle and the cinders turned into a white hot glow. No wonder this was a meeting-place for the older men to gossip, smoke their pipes and warm up at the same time. The metal horseshoes would be heated and then quickly taken to the anvil to flatten, bend and shape with rapid hammer blows, finally hardened with a hissing sound as they were placed in the trough of water outside. The horse would be in the wooden stable section and by taking its hoof between his knees, the blacksmith, clad in a leather apron, would fit the new shoe.

Ovens for the Cornish ranges were made and mended at the smithy, and David Rees was frequently to be seen walking through the village to deliver a newly repaired range oven. Dredges were repaired for the oyster men, and when horses were no longer used on the farms there was more time to be spent on the manufacture of decorative wrought ironwork. Fine examples of this are to be seen around the village to this day. Sadly, the smithy was demolished when the property was sold for development, but Lemon Cottage survives and is known simply as Blacksmith's Cottage. Another house was constructed on the site of the smithy and is called The Forge.

Road Improvement and Transport

From the late-eighteenth century and throughout the nineteenth there was a steady improvement in transport. Wheeled vehicles, drawn by horses or donkeys, were made for every purpose. A range of conveyances for personal use, not unlike present-day cars, were used by the more affluent and appropriate horses had to be kept for the various carriages. Within the parish,

the Overseers of the Poor were in charge of roadworks, financed by the rates. Dr Olivey, in his *Notes on the Parish of Mylor*, gives some extracts from the Overseer's accounts. From this we see that in the last three months of 1826, a sum of ten pounds was set aside for labour on the roads. For February of 1828, the cost of labour was £7.14s. In 1829 a pauper employed on the parish roads was paid one shilling and sixpence per day if he had a wife and six children. A single man was paid only nine pence per day.

The main roads improved and turnpikes linked all major towns. Lumbering and slow freight wagons, such as were run by Russell's out of Falmouth, were complemented by stagecoaches. These cut days from the time taken to travel from Cornwall to London, but were expensive and quite beyond the reach of most people.

Farm Vehicles

Farmers and others took advantage of improved roads to employ a variety of vehicles which were built locally. There was plenty of work for wheelwrights, carpenters and blacksmiths. The essential vehicle was the farm cart, of heavy construction, with a tipping butt. It was usually called a dung cart since taking dung from the farmyard to the field was its principal function. Bigger farms had a four-wheeled wagon, with a detachable framework fore and aft to carry sheaves of corn from field to mowhay. This required two horses. A lighter vehicle was a wain which had large-diameter wheels and a single axle. Detailed design varied from county to county, or even more locally. In Mylor the traditional colours were royal blue and Venetian red.

Steam Power

The first great innovation was the advent of steam power applied to transport, which ultimately affected everyone. No railway passed through our parish, but Penryn station was conveniently close. Steam road vehicles could be seen such as the threshing-machine, needed by all the larger farms, and the very occasional traction engine, delivering such heavy objects as granite gate-posts and quoins (stone blocks used to join walls). After 1894, when the County Council came into being, steamrollers came regularly to the village. They towed a tar boiler, the contents of which were sprayed on the road and then stone chippings were spread on the hot tar. A few turns over the surface by the roller kept most of the chippings in place, but rain and passing vehicles flung much into the ditch.

Bicycles

At about the same time, the bicycle became a practical form of personal transport. In its earlier form, the penny farthing had been expensive, hard to pedal and control; not much more than a plaything for rich young men. The safety bicycle, not dissimilar to those of today, became useful and, with mass production, more affordable. The poor road surfaces and primitive pneumatic tyres forced cyclists to become proficient in tyre repair and a handy, inexpensive kit was available. Bicycles were usually known as push-bikes, as our steep hills were always ascended on foot.

Motor Cars

Mrs Hearle with one of the family's vehicles, an Austin Heavy 12/4 of 1936 with a Hoyle fabric body, c.1936.

The twentieth century saw the arrival of the motor car. It transformed the way people lived more radically than any invention of previous centuries. Up to the First World War, only the rich could hope to own such a machine. Cars in the Mylor area were a rarity but one belonged to the Tremaynes of Carclew. It was a massive Daimler, such as that used by King George V, which they kept until about 1930. An early local example was Mr Chamberlin's Star 15-horsepower tourer.

To start the engine one needed to fully retard the ignition on the quadrant by the steering wheel. The starting handle was swung rapidly and then with luck the engine would start. The ignition was advanced when the engine settled to run sweetly, then the heavy clutch was depressed and a low gear selected. Then the hand brake was let off, simultaneously allowing the clutch to come back. If engaged too quickly the car would stall and the whole procedure would have to be repeated. Changing gear required double-declutching and precise timing, or horrible screaming would come from the gearbox. Cars often had brakes only on the rear wheels, so going down a steep hill, such as that which leads to Weir, had to be done in low gear. The road surfaces caused frequent tyre punctures and fitting the spare tyre was sweat-inducing work.

Motor Buses

In the last years of Queen Victoria, Mr Porter of Church Road had a horse-drawn bus which ran to Flushing, where the ferry would take passengers to Falmouth. The earliest motor bus appeared in the 1920s and took passengers to and from Mylor and

Flushing. It was a Model T Ford with two longitudinal rows of seats facing each other and was run by Johnnie Harcourt.

In 1927 came two new bus operators, Mr E. Hearle and Mr G. Johns. Mr Johns ran a French Laffley, 20-seater, the chassis of which had seen service as an ambulance during the war. Mr Hearle had a 20-seater Thorneycroft. Shortly after came CMT (Cornish Motor Transport), serving towns and villages all over West Cornwall. On some days of the week, three buses would leave Mylor for Falmouth at precisely the same time. The local buses ran via St Gluvias Church Hill, and the CMT via Carclew and Lane End. Competition was fierce and the return fare was set at nine pence for Falmouth. It stayed at this low level until 1948.

After running the Riviera bus for just over a year, the Hearle family suffered a tragedy. An exploding tyre struck Mr Hearle in the face, causing a broken piece of dental plate to lodge in his windpipe. It was necessary for him to be taken to St Bartholomew's Hospital in London where the piece was removed. In those pre-antibiotic times Mr Hearle succumbed to pneumonia and sadly died soon after returning to Mylor. His widow Mrs L. Hearle ran the service for a further 20 years and for 17 years the Riviera bus was driven by Phil Rogers.

There were changes in operators. Mr Johns was replaced by Mr W.J. George of West Pelere and the CMT became part of the much bigger Western National Omnibus Company, which survives as First at the time of writing. Timetables soon stabilised and remained basically unchanged for many years. The number of services varied from day to day – Saturday was always the busiest, including the 10.30p.m. from Falmouth, which waited for the last films to finish at each of the three Falmouth cinemas. On some days the services would go to Restronguet or Mylor Church at particular times. On Wednesdays, the Riviera bus went to Truro, starting from Flushing. Passengers were mainly farmers, sometimes accompanied by their wives.

In 1930 the first Labour government brought in a Traffic Act, which had far-reaching provisions. Buses had to obtain a certificate of fitness, similar to today's MOT certificate. Inspections were carried out by ministry engineers and were very stringent. Hundreds of vehicles were taken off the road; drivers and conductors were licensed and tested, with a Traffic Commissioner regulating services. This was resented at the time, but did introduce higher standards of safety.

When Noel Hearle returned from the Army, he took over the running of the bus business. By then this had been much expanded by taking over the tour business of Lewis Motors, whose pre-war fleet had been destroyed by enemy action during the war. As increased numbers of people were coming to Falmouth on holiday, this aspect of the business expanded and by 1960 the company ran a fleet of six

Four charabancs on Falmouth Moor, taken in the early morning of a municipal outing to Land's End in 1921. Silver Cars of Falmouth bought the four Dennis Army lorries and had the bodies built with the popular bench seats in the style of the charabanc. These had a door to each row of seats. This proved to be far too ambitious and two were soon sold, one of which was bought by Mr N.E. Hearle. He and his vehicles are on the left of the picture. For this outing the fleet was re-assembled. These vehicles were unsuitable for bus service and the Dennis was exchanged, first for a Fiat, then for the Thorneycroft with which Mr Hearle began the Mylor bus service.

Left: *Brochure advertising outings with Lewis Motors of Mylor.*

Below left: *Conductor Mrs Hearle and the 1946 Maudsley 33-seater.*

Below: *The first bus operated by the Hearle family of Mylor in 1927, a Thorneycroft 20-seater, the Riviera Bus.*

AEC luxury coaches. This was in addition to the service buses between Mylor, Falmouth, Penryn and summer services to Falmouth beach. There was a steady reduction in passenger demand as more and more people bought private cars. Mr Hearle realised that the bus business had peaked, so he moved into the retail motor trade. The Mylor service was sold to the Western National and at last a single operator served the people of Mylor. In recent years, the Truronian service has been introduced which gives Mylor the increased benefit of good, regular bus services – not always the case in rural areas.

Commercial Vehicles Between the Wars

An increasing number of commercial vehicles appeared in the 1920s and '30s. Oddly enough, no one in Mylor started a haulage business – perhaps this was because Falmouth ran a large fleet of ex-Army Dennis lorries. The grandest lorry which brought provisions for Frost's shop was run by Trounson's of Redruth. It was a massive Thorneycroft which had seen service in France, but with a civilian attire of scarlet and lime green. The most regular van was a black Model T Ford owned by Harry Beer, a baker of Flushing. Vans became more common, but Mr W.E. Rollason, butcher for Mylor and Flushing, used a traditional butcher's cart until he retired.

The Lemon Arms

Lucky the man who set forth up Lemon Hill and had his nostrils assailed by home-brewed beer on the left hand side and newly baked bread on the right.

The Lemon Arms in the centre of the village, c.1975.

So stated a past villager. According to the Records of the Manor of Restronguet, there has been an inn on the site of the Lemon Arms since at least 1765 when the landlord was Abram Bythewood. At this time it was known as the Griffin Inn and was used for meetings of the Manor Court when rents were paid and other business transacted on quarter days. In 1877, a villager recorded that:

... the passage boats at Restronguet being dangerous and inconvenient for passengers, require speedy repair. Also the sand quarry to be viewed in order to its being repaired by the Lord of the Manor.

After the meetings, the tenants were entertained to a glass of ale and a cut of roast beef.

In the early days, the inn stood further back from the road. It is likely that it had been enlarged by 1821, when it was known as the Red Lion. It was used by the Overseers of the Poor to hold meetings of the Vestry, a body that dealt with the business of the poor-house, which stood on the other side of the road. In 1829, the Overseers' account reads 'it was agreed that a dinner be ordered at the Red Lion', showing that the inn was used for entertaining in connection with official business.

Records show that by 1837 the inn had become the Lemon Arms and that early in the twentieth century it was still used for the collection of rents with tenants waiting outside to pay. In those days when beer was brewed on the premises, water was taken direct from the village pump by hose-pipe to vats in the brew-house. The story goes that on one shocking occasion Mr Rollason fell into the vat of boiling beer! Fortunately he was rescued in time, but his boots had to be cut off. What happened to the beer doesn't bear thinking about. When the extensive Carclew auction of 1920 took place, the Lemon Arms (rent £24) was offered – the only bid for a time was £300 and an intimation was made that it would be withdrawn. 'Beer is dear now', remarked one of the audience as a bid of £400 was put in. Further advances were made up to £750, but the reserve was not reached.

The Lemon Arms and the village pump, 1930s.

Perran Creek, c.1840. On the left is the tidal creek leading to Carclew Bridge and on the right is the canal leading to Perran Wharf, where various cargoes were unloaded, including limestone for the kiln beside the Norway Inn.

The Lemon Arms has always played an important role in the life of the village. It has served as a venue for meetings, both formal and informal, and many other gatherings. In the 1920s and '30s it was a tradition for wassailers to perform there every Boxing Day, and even in modern times the annual Harvest Festival Auction is held there and it is the centre for many more activities, as well as providing good hospitality.

The Foundry – A Noise-Filled Valley

This was Perranwharf in the 1840s when the foundry was at the height of its powers. Ellen Fox writes of the noise of the steam-driven hammer filling the valley with loud, regular thuds and bumps. So impossible did it become that it was later moved to Devoran and then to the viaduct near Ponsanooth where the buildings can still be seen at the time of writing. Perran Cove, now Perranwharf, is on the north-west side of Mylor and before the days of the foundry, coal, lime and timber arrived by sea while copper ore was shipped to other parts of Britain and abroad. The timber, mostly from Norway, was off-loaded at Restronguet, made into rafts and floated up to the timber ponds on a high tide. These ponds were large, one covering an area of over two acres.

Ellen wrote: 'On the opposite side of the lake-like river, floats of timber baulks for the mine house were pushed up its tide by stalwart men, big Jim Martin was the finest specimen.'

In 1769, the Quaker Fox family had leased the south side of Perran Creek from Lord Mount Edgecombe for their wharf, timber ponds and sawmill, and in 1791 they established their foundry. Although businessmen, they had no technical engineering experience so a partnership was formed with three experts: Thomas Wilson, a copper smelter; William Wood, an iron master at Neath Abbey foundry in South Wales; and Peter Price who had trained with

Abram Derby of Coalbrookdale.

Casting may not have begun until 1795 although buildings were in place. However, by 1797 a condenser and air pump were being cast. The main buildings comprised of the machine and fitting shed, moulding shop, smithy, pattern shop, brass foundry, sawmill, stores, drawing office and manager's office. The gasworks were installed by William Murdock from Redruth and produced gas for the foundry, its counting house and nearby cottages and houses.

There was in the counting house a dear old clerk of who can say how many years standing, out of whose desk used to come secret stores of sweetmeats, whose sweetness was added to by his fierce looks as he gave them in a secret surreptitious way.

The counting house was also used for business meetings and was the timber-fronted terrace on the wharf, since made into private homes.

The site produced the whole range of foundry, smithy and cool metalwork, including some of the largest cast-iron boilers and cylinders for steam engines ever made. The vast beam engines could drain passages hundreds of feet underground, haul ore to the surface and crush the viscera of tin and copper from it. At its peak the foundry employed between 400 and 600 men. Work was laborious and the average age span was 40 years and, for miners, much less.

In 1815 a huge beam was cast for Dolcoath mine – the deepest Cornish mine. It weighed 25 tons and was cast in two parts.

We went to Perran Foundry, met there Derwent Coleridge to see them cast 14 tons of iron for the beam of a steam engine. The excitement displayed by Richard Cloke, the foreman, was quite beautiful.

The Revd Derwent Coleridge was the son of Samuel Taylor Coleridge. In 1842, Barclay Fox records that the

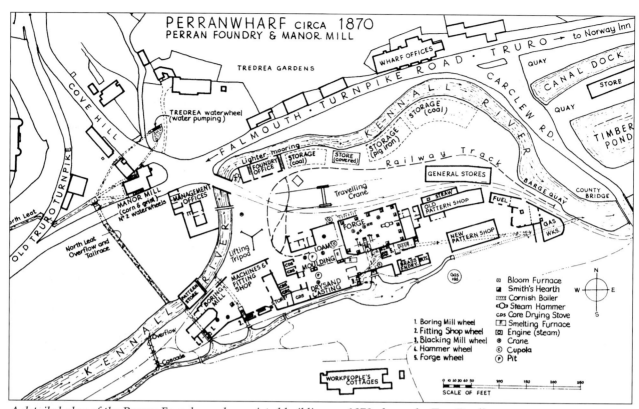

A detailed plan of the Perran Foundry and associated buildings, c.1870, drawn by Tom Bradley.

(BY KIND PERMISSION OF MRS T. BRADLEY)

largest piece of wrought iron ever made at the foundry was completed – an axle for the main machine at Tresavean, weight 46cwt. This machine was for lowering and raising the men in the mine shaft and was the result of a competition run by the Royal Cornwall Polytechnic Society. Engines were built and sent to Mexico in 1824, Holland in 1846, Australia and Spain in 1871–76, the Forest of Dean in 1869 and to South Wales in 1873.

The wharf too, was full of interest. Pairs of mules, led by a considerate horse, brought ore from the mines there to be embarked in lighters for foreign sale. Copper ore itself was a sparkling thing to inspect as it lay in great heaps on the wharf.

While under the control of the Fox family and partners, the foundry established a high reputation in the finish, accuracy and quality of its work. Men's lives were valued more than profits and there are records of many feasts and happy times. At the defeat of Bonaparte in 1814, the numerous workmen were given a public dinner and in the evening the women and children drank the best China tea at the Fox house. When the Foxes relinquished control of the foundry, each adult was presented with a bible and the Band of Hope children received a New Testament. These gifts are still treasured in many families today.

An amusing incident occurring at one celebration is well recorded. It used to be the practice to mount one or two guns on the foundry lighters and an old naval pensioner, Hannibal Roberts, fired the salutes. On one occasion, the old hero forgot to sponge out and when he re-loaded, the charge ignited and he was blown overboard into the river. However, he was fished out and a month's holiday restored him to normal. Hannibal was between 70 and 80 years of age at the time.

The works became known as the Williams Perran Foundry in 1858 when the Foxes sold their shares to the partners, Mr Michael Williams MP of Trevince and Mr William Williams of Tregullow. There was great rejoicing in 1866 when Mr W. Williams was created a baronet. All the employees were driven to Tregullow to be fêted and feasted. Beer was plentiful and free. Another great occasion was the passing of the Nine Hours Act. Formerly working from 6a.m.–6p.m. (5p.m. on Saturdays), the men successfully petitioned for a 53-hour week and they were entertained in the pattern loft to a great feast and sing-song with a band from Truro.

With the closing of the copper mines and the development of the railway and roads, business changed. Marine engines, water tanks and chimneys were made. Parts of the Lizard lighthouse and sections of the swing-bridge of Penryn were completed before trade dwindled. The foundry finally closed in March 1879, but in its time it had a huge influence on the engineering and industrial development of the nineteenth century.

At the time of writing, the future of the foundry looks bleak. Although English Heritage has identified the Grade II site and Cornwall's last surviving foundry as being at risk and urgently needing repairs, the huge costs involved have deterred various companies from developing and preserving the buildings. The latest

A group of workers from the Perran Foundry, taken before its closure in 1879.

(PICTURE KINDLY LENT BY MRS RUTH CHAMBERLAIN, WHOSE GRANDFATHER, JOHN HENRY WILLIAMS, KNOWN AS 'BRASSY JACK', IS SEATED ON THE LEFT.)

Above: *View of Mill Quay, as it looked in the mid-1900s. It is reported that during the coal strike in 1927, when the coal yard was run by Mr Tallack, all tenants had to sign a form to enable them to have coal which was limited to one cwt per household and was delivered by horse and wagon, owned by Mr J. Gilbert of Rose Hill Farm.*

Right: *Mr and Mrs Bryant with son Will, standing outside Mill House, early 1900s.*

idea is to convert the foundry into an hotel and shopping complex, but sadly this would be the end of the foundry as we know it. Meanwhile, the old buildings are steadily deteriorating and make a sorry sight.

Mylor Quay and the Mill

In 1417, the records of Restronguet Manor property include 'two water course mills, with rents of six shillings and eight pence per annum each,' but the first available lease is dated 1771. This refers to:

> ... two grist mills called Restronguet Mills with a small garden and two dwelling houses; a small stable, barn and mowhay, also a field called Cliff Close all near Mylor Bridge, with water courses and leats.

The first mill referred to was Restronguet Manor mill, which was fed by the leat running through the village. The leat was six to eight feet wide and 18 inches deep. The fall from end to end was probably only a couple of feet and the flow was low. The digging of the leat would have been carried out by unskilled labourers under manor staff guidance, a simple but expensive task. The 'cut' was about 2,000 feet long, involving at least 20,000 cubic feet of spoil, which was distributed alongside the leat. It required accurate setting out, levelling, digging out, waterproofing and reinstatement on completion.

The first recorded miller in 1771 was Martin Hoskin, and the last was listed as Thomas Moore, grocer and miller. By 1906 it seems that the mill was no longer working. The site of the mill-wheel can still be traced behind one of the houses facing the quay. The second mill referred to in the lease may have been a tide mill. Where the stepping-stones are today there was an embankment and a small building holding the mill machinery – this is clearly shown on the 1939 map. At normal tides the high water reached Mylor Bridge. The water would be collected between the bridge and the embankment and held there by closing the sluice-gates. When the tide had fallen sufficiently, the head of water would be released to turn the wheel inside the building. The leat was filled in some years after the Second World War, but water still appears at the side of the road near the quay after heavy rain and the basement of the butcher's shop is flooded occasionally.

Joseph Eddy ran a coal yard at Mill Quay. Many of the reminiscences involved collecting coal from the quay in a wheelbarrow and children would play on the coal barge which brought coal up the creek to Mylor Bridge.

The Brickworks

Frank Curnow remembers walking along Comfort Road:

> On then to the Comfort road, which was a ford over a river and to Brick Kiln or Brick Hill, where there was

MYLOR BRICK WORKS.

To Merchants, Iron Founders, Builders, and Others.

Sale of 100,000 Building Bricks, Workshops, Machinery, &c.

MR. ROBERTS

WILL SELL BY PUBLIC AUCTION,

On Monday, February the 17th,

At Two O'clock, at the above WORKS, near MYLOR-BRIDGE.

About 100,000

Building Bricks

50 DOZEN PAN TILES,
Large quantity of Broken Bricks.
100 WOOD LAUNDERS,
12 to 20 feet long, 14 in. by 11.
BRICK-BUILT DRYING SHED.
WOOD-BUILT WORKSHOP.
WATER WHEEL,
16 feet diameter, with shaft and bearings.
LARGE PUGGING MACHINE,
with Fly Wheel, &c.
2 CAST-IRON ROLLERS,
with Iron Frame and Gearing.
PATENT PRESSING MACHINE,
by CLAYTON.
IRON SHAFT, DITTO GEARING
FOR THREE TRAM WAGGONS.
ABOUT 200 FIR POLES.
Lot of Old Iron and Brick Moulds, a quantity of excellent Firewood, a Large Lot of Scaffolding Boards, Bearing of Barrows, Grindstone, &c.

The whole of the above may be viewed on Friday and Saturday preceding the Sale.

For further particulars apply to the AUCTIONEER, at his Offices, Arwenack-street, Falmouth.

Dated 23rd. January, 1873.

Notice of a forthcoming public auction of the assets of the Mylor Brickworks which appeared in the Penryn Advertiser *on 8 February 1873.*

a brickworks. It is stated that Mr Lemon of Carclew made considerable money out of the brickworks. There are hundreds of bricks buried at Brick Hill and the late Charles Gilbert told me that he was the last person to carry by horse and wagon, bricks that went down to Flushing for house-building along Trefusis Road. He also *said that he took two loads of 500 bricks with a single horse, or two loads of 850 bricks with two horses from Devoran as a day's work. Further up the road from Brick Kiln is a small wood. Among the trees are two small pits, now filled with water, from which clay was dug, but eventually the supply gave out.*

Mr Jimmy Andrews says:

Years ago there weren't any bricks, only for chimney pieces mind. With bricks you would get a straight chimney and they would bend with the wind. It has to give a bit with the wind in order to get a good draught and not smoke you out.

The Wood Yard

James Thomas writes about a wood yard operated by a family called Rendle along Comfort Road between 1941 and 1948:

They used a flat bed lorry with which they collected wood for local fires. They had the rights to clear the Mylor end of the Enys estate, behind Jones' farm and up to Broads Lane. As children we would often accompany them on these forays, and considered ourselves to be a great help. Chain saws did not exist and the trees were felled by means of axes and large two-handled crosscut saws. Once on the ground they would be sectioned with the aid of the saws and then one of the men would use an auger to drill two or three holes in the trunk and pack in black powder and detonators. Fuses were run and lit and we would all be shepherded back to a safe distance while the ensuing explosion split the wood up. It then became the job of us youngsters to load the pieces onto the lorry for transport back to the wood yard, where it could be rendered into logs with the aid of a large circular saw mounted on a bench in the yard and powered by an old paraffin engine housed in a tin shed. The resulting firewood was distributed around the village at a cost of one pound for a lorry load, or a shilling for a full bushel basket. I can still smell the fresh turpentine smell of the cut timber!

Flower Growing

Many smallholdings and farms used to grow flowers and in the early 1900s, this small industry employed several people. At that time the flowers were picked by the men and bunched by the women. They were packed in wooden boxes and then taken by horse and cart to the railway at Penryn for the London market.

In the 1920s and '30s, women were still helping with flowers on the smallholdings. Becky Bunny (née Rawlings) remembered working for Mrs Johns at Rose Hill Cottage, where she bunched daffodils, violets and gladioli. Some other small farms known to grow flowers were Albion (Mr Osterton), Plaisance (Mr and Mrs Evans), Cogos (Mr Denman) and Bellair. The

Vera and Hazel Gray in the 1930s, bunching daffodils at Greystones to be sent to Covent Garden, with Edwin Thomas looking on.

latter was a pig farm, but Mr Jones also grew flowers there. Many different flowers were grown including violets, tulips, daffodils and wallflowers, stocks, sweet peas and polyanthus.

On a larger scale, Henry Pike at Woodlands was well known for his flowers. He had a barge for collecting seaweed from the rocks, which was landed at Tregatreath and taken to Woodlands by horse and cart to be spread as fertiliser. Another source of manure was dung supplied by Greenbank stables and brought by barge to be sold at Mill Quay.

Henry Pike's son, Fred, developed his own flower business at the top of Passage Hill. He had several fields stretching from Passage Hill to Bells Hill and rising to the Clump. He also had greenhouses on Passage Hill for growing tomatoes and he built himself a house there called Greystones. Vera Moore remembers her work on the farm in the 1930s. She started when she left school at 14 and bunched flowers with other women while the men did the picking. In wintertime, the shed was very cold! They made attractive bunches of violets with their leaves around them but, if it had been a cold spell, the leaves turned brown and they used coltsfoot leaves instead. They also bunched anemones in winter and then, with the spring, the trade turned to daffodils followed by tulips. In the summer, she stayed on to sort bulbs, while Mr Pike sold tomatoes. The flowers were packed in cardboard boxes and taken to Penryn market for the train to London. It was Fred Pike's brother, Phil, who gave the land for the bowling club in Mylor.

Mr Rickard of Trelew Farm has given a description of the hard work involved in flower growing (see section on Trelew Farm, later). Anemones and violets were also grown by the Rowes at Tregatreath.

Daffodil growing and the cultivation of vegetables became an industry at Carclew Enterprises until 1985, providing regular work for about ten men and 15 women. In the early years, daffodils were picked in bunches of ten and were arranged attractively for sale in flower. Later, they were picked in bud to survive the journey and reach the markets in fresh condition. Bulb growing, carrots for factory use and sprouts were other enterprises from the Carclew and Carsawsen fields.

Another enterprise, which prospered for a while, was the growing of *Pittosporum* trees, for flower decoration. These can still be seen around Mylor, but the trade faded in the 1980s due to foreign competition.

Treseder's Nursery

The family firm of Treseder, Seedsmen, Nurserymen and Florists, was in existence at the time of the Battle of Waterloo, but it was in 1820 that James Treseder began developing the business at Trehavern on the outskirts of Truro. He married one of the Garland daughters of Illogan and that name was perpetuated as the second name of the eldest son of each succeeding generation. The family moved to Mylor, where a market garden, with greenhouses, was established on the landward side of the bridge, the parents and four children living in a small thatched cottage on the side of the creek, now no more.

In those days, when large families were commonplace, James sent three of his sons – John Garland, Thomas and Charles – to take their chance in the Australian gold fields. John and Thomas soon became disenchanted with that life and started nurseries near Sydney and later opened a flower and seed shop in the Sydney Arcade. John became an authority on landscape gardening, designing many of the parks and public gardens in New South Wales. The brothers also introduced into Britain many of the hardier plants they came across on their travels, including the tree fern. Their main clients were the big seed businesses of Europe and the United States. With his brother, John wrote the first book to be published in Australia on *Gardening in the Colonies*. John told an amazing story to the family back home at this time. He had been visited by a vagrant artist and offered him hospitality. A painting was produced from the wanderer's portfolio and its subject proved to be the family's creekside home in Mylor Bridge!

Following his father's death in 1897, John returned to Cornwall to take over the family business, acquiring a lease of the nurseries, Truro, from the Enys estate. There he was joined by his eldest Australian-born son, Ira Garland, and later by a second son, Jack. Between them they formed a talented team designing and landscaping parks and gardens far from their Truro base. Jack later founded his own nursery business in Brixton, London, from where he introduced such subtropical trees as the New Zealand Dracaena palm and the Chinese fan palm.

Ira's son, Neil Garland Treseder, was born in Truro in 1913 and was educated at Truro School and Exeter University. When his father retired in 1955, he took over the business, developing one of the largest collections of ornamental plants in the British Isles and considerable export trade. He was an authority on magnolias and camellias and other plants at home in Cornish gardens, such as the popular *Ceanothus* 'Trewithen Blue'. He introduced over 50 plants.

Neil retired in 1976, leaving his son, Andrew Garland (b.1941), in charge of the ever-growing family firm. He had gained wide experience at the Royal Horticultural Society's garden at Wisley, Surrey, and on a Dutch nursery at Boskoop. Andrew became a Truro City Councillor and the youngest ever mayor of that city (1981–82). He and his wife had returned to Mylor to live at Bellair. He is remembered for his cheerful, outgoing, charming disposition. Tragically, in 1983 and at the early age of 42, Andrew Garland died of cancer.

His father wrote 'I do not think it was quite by chance that Andrew went to live in Mylor.' No, indeed, for the important firm of Treseder had come full circle and no new generation remained to continue. Four years later, the Truro Nursery was sold for housing development.

The following is taken from a newspaper item, from 15 February 1850:

> MYLOR NURSERY, NEAR FALMOUTH
> *J. Treseder, thanking the Nobility and Gentry for their liberal patronage, begs to announce that he has just received direct from one of the first seed-growers, an assortment, comprising all the best varieties of kitchen-garden and flower seeds, which, together with the choicest sorts of Fruit Trees, Ornamental Shrubs, Forest trees and general nursery stock, may be had at moderate prices at the Nursery, or of J. Treseder, in Falmouth or Redruth markets. Intending Emigrants supplied with good selections of Seeds of all descriptions, in convenient parcels, and carefully packed for voyages.*

❖

Chapter 5

Harbour and Creek

Mylor Royal Naval Dockyard, HMS Ganges, *The* Queen Transport *Tragedy, Mylor Yacht Harbour,*
Mylor Yacht Club, The Fal Oyster Fishery, The Oysterman, A Coasting Ketch, Tregatreath Boatyard, Penarrow.

Mylor Creek looking west, c.1930.

(BY KIND PERMISSION OF THE NATIONAL MARITIME MUSEUM, GREENWICH)

Mylor Royal Naval Dockyard

A map of 1767 shows the only buildings at the entrance to Mylor Creek to be the church, the Vicarage and Lawithick. From 1793 to 1815 Britain was more or less continually at war with France, and at times with other countries as well. The Fal estuary and Falmouth Bay were in a good position to serve as a base for Royal Navy ships operating at the entrance to the English Channel, in the Western Approaches and for blockading French ports.

In 1805, the Admiralty Commissioners initiated the construction of a Royal Naval dockyard for victualling and watering HM ships. They bought 15 acres of land near the mouth of Mylor Creek from John, Lord Wodehouse. He owned the Killigrew estates by marriage to Sophia Berkeley, their heiress. Notices were placed in the local paper of the time, the *Sherborne Advertizer,* for tenders to build a house, shed and cooperage, a reservoir, a stone quay about 270 feet long and other buildings. Later advertisements were for fresh fruit and vegetables, through the agency of John Mitchell. These entries continued for many years. The stream in the valley was diverted to the carefully stone-built, clay-lined reservoir. Over the years further buildings were erected and coopering barrel staves of

inadequate naval quality were advertised for sale.

After Waterloo, when the wars ended, some facilities were made available to the packet service, which had been operating out of Falmouth since 1689 serving an increasing number of destinations. Packets were frequently attacked by pirates and French privateers. It was found that these ships could achieve faster and therefore safer times for delivery, as well as avoiding raiders, if their underwater hulls were coppered. This was done at Mylor, saving time by not having to be sent to Plymouth. When the former boat shed was being converted to a restaurant in 2003, the roof slates were found to have been attached together with coppering nails. In the 1841 census there were seven naval personnel living at Mylor Dockyard – but none at all in 1851.

At the time of the Crimean War the dockyard was reopened for the repair of ships. A safe anchorage was provided for shallow-draught ships in Mylor Pool. The year 1866 saw the arrival of HMS *Ganges* as a training ship for boy sailors.

In the great depression between the First and Second World Wars, some ships were laid up to the north of the dockyard closely packed together, and many more in the river above Turnaware, the maximum number at any one time being 86 in 1933.

These ships had skeleton crews and personnel rowed ashore to the dockyard for mail and also milk from Lawithick Farm. Water was obtained from the Admiralty reservoir at Kingsmoor and delivered by water boat, the *Cascade*. Mr John Hamilton had a coal yard at Mill Quay, Mylor, and kept a dump of coal at the dockyard. This was for supply to the laid-up ships for domestic use and for engine testing. Manoeuvring these big ships was done by Falmouth harbour tugs which included *Lynch, Northgate Scot, Victor, Durgan* and *Joyce*.

In December 1939, the *Stanwood's* cargo of coal was found to be on fire whilst she was lying in Falmouth docks. She was towed into the Carrick Roads on 10 December and sank off Trefusis on the edge of the main channel near the north bank buoy. The crane on the old quay at Mylor Dockyard was installed as part of an attempt to salvage her. She was still visible in 1947. Some of her cargo was dumped at Mylor and coal was still being dredged up by oyster fishermen in 2003. On 5 July 1940 the *Tascalusa* was bombed in Falmouth docks and caught fire. She was towed out of the way and beached on the Mylor bank. She was sold later for breaking up by operators working from Mylor Dockyard.

In 1940, after the German occupation of Northern France, coast defences at Mylor were manned by the Bedfordshire and Hertfordshire regiment. They were billeted in the Admiralty buildings at Mylor Dockyard. Later these duties were undertaken by the Home Guard. There is still a Second World War pillbox on the low cliff just beyond Restronguet Sailing Club's dinghy park.

Colonel Stewart Menzies, who had been head of the Special Intelligence Service in Paris from 1926 until the fall of France, set up the SIS in Falmouth. This was later removed to Mylor Dockyard as being more secluded, occupying the building at the end of the quay. They stayed there until after the loss of *L'Emigrant*. She had escaped to Cornwall on 6 December 1940 with the French agent leader, his wife and children. On a mission to Brittany she was intercepted by a German patrol – the three Breton crew were sent to Buchenwald. The unit then moved to Helford.

In 1942, American troops started arriving in the South West of England. Some were stationed in a Nissen-hutted camp at Lawithick Farm. A grid for the maintenance and repair of landing-craft was constructed to the west of the dockyard. These craft were moored offshore between two dolphins – one of these still remains outside the postwar quay, and is a Grade II listed building. The other was damaged (and later dismantled) in the construction of the slipway to the east of the new quay. The landing-craft were berthed on a cradle and winched up broadside on so they could be repaired and repainted. This work was done by American Sea-bees, a US Navy pioneer corps unit.

HMS *Ganges*

HMS *Ganges* was built from Indian teak in Bombay in 1821. She was the last wooden-wall sailing ship to be used as a flagship on a foreign station, her final assignment being to bolster British authority during the Frazer River Gold Rush crisis in 1859. She arrived back at Spithead in 1861.

In about the middle of the nineteenth century, when the Royal Navy turned to steam propulsion, the government was faced with the problem of what to do with the hundreds of old wooden sailing ships now redundant as fighting vessels. It was decided that five were to be distributed around estuaries and used as training establishments for boys. This also helped to reduce the pressure on local authorities looking for a way of avoiding responsibility for hundreds of orphan and pauper boys, costly to keep in workhouses throughout the land.

HMS *Ganges* arrived in 1866, towed by paddle tug *Gladiator*, to be anchored in the deep St Just Pool with her shore establishment based in the Royal Naval Dockyard at Mylor, which had been developed in the days of the Napoleonic Wars. In command of HMS *Ganges* was Captain Frederick Hildebrand Stevens with 180 boys transferred from the training ship *Wellesley* in Chatham, Kent. There was accommodation for 500 boys. Additional entrants between 15 and 17 years of age were asked to volunteer for a career in the Royal Navy with at least one year on board the training ship before joining the fleet. They were to be fit and be able to read and write, and training would include seamanship (i.e. sail, mast and yard drill as well as knots, splices and boat handling) and gunnery. General schooling was included.

But these high ideals did not get off to a very good start as far as HMS *Ganges* was concerned – the intake of boys was less than for the other training ships. Reports of harsh and brutal treatment occurring on the ship were brought to the notice of the Admiralty: a wardroom steward serving aboard the ship had written to the *Army and Navy Gazette* complaining that 'the abuse and tyranny to which we are subjected is unbearable.' He gave details of a beating that had been inflicted on two local boys with a birch that had been pickled in brine to make the punishment even more cruel, and he also threatened to write to the newspapers. The steward, distressed when his letter became public and depressed by his treatment on board and by his creditors, shot himself whilst on night leave.

The senior officer of training ships, Captain Tremlett, was ordered to proceed to Falmouth to hold an enquiry into the matter. He reported that a 'strong feeling exists on shore against Commander Stevens because of the birching of local boys, Edward Earle and George Finch.' The mother of the latter was a fish woman who begged Captain Tremlett to remove her son from *Ganges*. Mrs Finch then went down to Mylor boatyard armed with a bludgeon with the aim of chastising Commander Stevens. She was in a very excited

Above: *Painting of HMS* Ganges, *by kind permission of the artist M.W. Cockell.*

Right: *The* Ganges *memorial, a granite obelisk erected by the boys of HMS Ganges in 1872. On it are engraved the names of 53 boys between 15 and 17 who died whilst in training.*

Wanted, for the Royal Navy.
FINE BOYS, who can read and write,
Between the ages of 15 and 16 ½
years.3, 500 are
annually required. For all particulars
apply by letter
or otherwise to COMMANDING
OFFICER H.M.S.
"GANGES" at Falmouth.

Above: *A recruitment notice for boys for HMS* Ganges.

Right: *Wistful expressions on the faces of the boy sailors of the* Ganges *in 1890.*

state with drink. At that time, a new consignment of recruits arrived and were persuaded by her to return to their homes. Captain Tremlett's report found that Commander Stevens had given punishments not laid down in Training Regulations and had prevented the ship's company from taking due leave. Both he and the First Lieutenant were removed and a new Commander appointed.

As the clamour died down, the number of boys joining *Ganges* rose gradually and there were no less than 478 boys under training by the end of the year. The ship's official history records what life for the boys was like:

They rose each day at 5.30 am and scrubbed down the decks. Trousers were rolled up above the knees and feet were bare even on the coldest days. (Shoes and socks were worn only when going on shore in uniform and attending the sick bay.) Breakfast consisted of hot cocoa made without milk and little sugar. Hard ships' biscuits when dunked, frequently proved full of weevils, which then emerged.

Boys were taught to swim by being lowered over the side of the ship in a crate with floor boards set wide apart to let in the icy water. Add to this the barnacles covering the base, which cut their feet, and it followed that they either swam or sank. Ship's police carried big bamboo canes and the instructors knotted ropes called stonnickers. At 11.30 am each day, boys had to gather on deck to witness the punishment of their erring fellows, who were birched over a gun.

On Saturdays, they all had a bath using one of six baths. By the time they had finished, the water was filthy but they then had to set to and wash their clothes in it. Recreation amounted to drill with dumbbells or Indian clubs with the occasional football match or long route march on shore.

After the last meal of the day at 3.30 pm, the boys sat by candlelight playing draughts or ludo. Ill-fed, herded between decks without heating or adequate ventilation, small wonder it was said that deaths amounted to some 34% more than other training ships. It was a harsh introduction to service life but matched the rawness of existence of many in the late nineteenth Century. It turned boys into the men who were the back-bone of the greatest navy of the time.

On 28 August 1899, HMS *Ganges* was towed away to end her days at Shotley Gate, Ipswich, Suffolk, where she gave her name to a naval shore-training establishment.

In 1929, *Ganges* had her final move – to Plymouth, where she was broken up. In 1971, Revd Jack Burgoyne, chaplain to Captain J.M.C. Dunlop RN, was asked to deliver two items to Mylor Parish Church. One was a colour photograph of a painting of HMS *Ganges* in Falmouth Harbour which hung in the wardroom at Shotley and the other a plaque showing the *Ganges* crest. Captain Dunlop hoped that they would be considered suitable as permanent souvenirs of the old association. They now hang on the left of the choir vestry in the church.

The Queen Transport *Tragedy*

Because of Mylor's proximity to the sea, there are gravestones in the churchyard which tell of wrecks and drowning. None is more tragic than that with a ship carved upon it, inscribed: 'To the memory of many buried beneath, who perished in the wreck of the *Queen Transport* on Trefusis Point on January 14th, 1814.'

The ship was bound from Lisbon and Cadiz to Portsmouth carrying home casualties of the Peninsular War. It being January and the weather stormy, she took shelter in the Carrick Roads, where she remained at single anchor for four days. The gale became increasingly violent until, between four and five o'clock the next morning, after dragging her anchor, she parted her cable and went on shore at Trefusis Point. She became a complete wreck 20 minutes after she struck. There were more than 330 persons on board, of whom many were invalids. Some had escaped the dangers of Lord Wellington's campaign and now were returning joyfully home accompanied by their wives and children. These dependants numbered more than 120.

The *West Briton* newspaper reported that the horror and confusion which ensued was indescribable. Those who reached the deck were either swept off by the waves or maimed by the fragments of rigging and spars that flew in all directions. Numerous passengers, trying to struggle up on deck, were drowned or crushed to death by floating planks and timbers as the vessel's bottom was speedily beaten to pieces. Gigantic waves soon made an end to the ship.

The alarm brought every able-bodied man in the neighbourhood down to the shore, whilst womenfolk prepared to receive and accommodate the survivors who were washed ashore. Break of day revealed a tragic spectacle. A total of 213 people perished. The newspaper concluded:

The hearts of those who witnessed the shocking scene were particularly moved by the sight of the corpse of a lovely female, wife of one of the officers, washed on shore with that of her infant which, even in death, she clasped to her bosom.

Mylor Yacht Harbour

Between the wars the Admiralty had sold the dockyard and land to the Trefusis estate. Soon after the Second World War, Captain R.T. Dixon RE arrived to live at Mylor Dockyard, bringing with him his yacht skipper, George Corke, and George's wife, Gladys. When Captain Dixon died, he bequeathed his estate, including Admiralty Cottage and his interest in the dockyard, to George. The sheltered anchorage had already proved attractive to yachtsmen, although there was little else in the way of facilities ashore apart from the dockyard buildings and the stone quay.

On 25 March 1953, Henry Trefusis sold Kingsmoor

The boys of HMS Ganges, *the Royal Navy training ship moored in St Just Pool and serviced by facilities at Mylor Dockyard, 1866–99.*

Above: *The naval hospital, part of the* Ganges *establishment at Mylor Dockyard, as it was in the early-twentieth century. This building has since been converted into holiday accommodation.*

Below: *Painting of HMS* Ganges, *a copy of which is in St Mylor Church.*

The memorial to the women and children who perished in the wreck of the Queen Transport, *14 January 1814.*
(Drawing by Jean Clapham)

Mylor Dockyard shortly after the Second World War, showing the two 'dolphins' used for mooring naval craft.

This view of Mylor Dockyard, crane and pier was taken in c.1960.

and Mylor Dockyard, quay and reservoir to George Corke for £6,000, with the stipulation that the six existing recipients should continue to be supplied with free water from the reservoir. Also the road and drains had to be kept in good order. The buildings included the guard house, Admiralty Cottage, the boat-house on the lane to Churchtown Farm, part of old Admiralty House where the Ganges restaurant is at the time of writing, Kingsmoor Cottage at the end, a wash-house and a lean-to shed. Gradually, the basis of a yacht harbour began to be developed, with investment from some wealthy yacht owners.

In 1962, Mylor Yacht Harbour was set up with three directors and George Corke as managing director. The marsh was drained and the valley developed for winter storage of boats. A chandlery was established in the old boat-house by Derek Rowe. A public lavatory and telephone kiosk were built to serve the increasing number of visitors and other businesses associated with yachting. Restronguet Sailing Club left Weir and built a new clubhouse on Trefusis land beyond the private houses east of the harbour. This was later extended to the east with a large dinghy park and a second slipway to the beach.

When George Corke retired in 1970, Derek took over as managing director and was responsible for the development of Mylor as an internationally known sailing centre up to 1997. It became clear that to provide for the rising demand for marina development, major financial investment would be needed. So, in 1997, the whole harbour was sold to Roger

Graffy and since then it has been transformed into a marina with every facility. Exeter Archaeology was employed to make a site survey before work was begun, making two reports in 1998. Cornwall Archaeological Unit kept a watching brief throughout. The area had to be thoroughly cleared and dredged. This was a long job as the spoil barges could only be towed out to sea in wind force 4 or less. Sometimes, to suit the tides, dredging went on noisily all night.

A full range of services has been set up with new buildings in the valley. Included are a shop and café, wine bar, windsurfing school, a yacht hoist and basin for hauling out. The 41st Sunbeam yacht, *Milly*, was launched and raced to celebrate the millennium. There are opportunities for yacht and boat hire and winter lay-up in the valley and on the filled-in inshore end of the new quay. The Second World War scrubbing grid is preserved in situ underneath. There is a shower block, a launderette and a chemical disposal point with non-potable water. There is dinghy and mast storage and some businesses rent premises on the site. There is also a water-taxi service during the season.

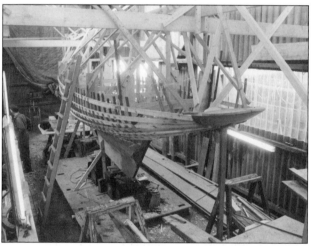

The Sunbeam is a keel boat designed by Alfred Westmacott in 1922. Here we see the Sunbeam Milly *under construction at Mylor Yacht Harbour in 1999. She was the first one to be built for 16 years and the first ever to be built in the port of Falmouth.*

Looking to the future, Roger Graffy writes:

Sheltered in the centre of the Fal Estuary, one of the largest natural harbours in the world, Mylor Yacht Harbour has been attracting visitors for many years. It has become a yachting and sailing centre of excellence and the home port for the last oyster fishing fleets still working under sail in the world. Man's relationship with the sea is a very special one. Cornwall's position and coastline makes her relationship extra special. These two things come together at Mylor.

By understanding the history and the unique location we can ensure the future is secure for this very special place. Over the last five years the harbour and its historical buildings have been sympathetically restored

Mylor Yacht Harbour as it looked in 2003, a thriving marina.

creating a regeneration project that has not only secured the future of the old jobs but also created 45 new ones. This is not just based on the beautiful location but also the skilled trades employed at the harbour. For the new millennium the first Sunbeam was built for 20 years. It is a fine example of a gentleman's racing yacht and a testament to the skills of the Mylor men who built her. Keeping alive these traditional skills and passing them on to a new generation is a cornerstone of the work at Mylor.

The future of Mylor Harbour is exciting; the constant work of maintaining and enhancing this unique Cornish harbour will continue and the traditional skills will be maintained, making Mylor Yacht Harbour a good place to keep a boat in Cornwall.

Mylor Yacht Club

Mylor Yacht Club was established in 1963 in what was once the guard room of the smallest ever British Royal Naval Dockyard which dated back to 1760. The now-extended and modernised clubhouse stands on the end of the harbour quay from where there is direct access to a number of pontoon berths enclosed by a new and substantial wave-break pontoon which also houses a fuel berth and space for alongside visitors'

The headquarters of Mylor Yacht Club on the end of the pier, once a naval guard house. It is seen here in 2004.

berthing. The club was founded in 1963 by George Corke and the then directors of Mylor Yacht Harbour primarily to give them a place to meet, where they could enjoy a drink or two after sailing. At that time membership was strictly by invitation so apart from being fairly exclusive it was also very friendly. But the exclusivity was not too restrictive and the membership soon began to expand.

The original building consisted of what is at the time of writing the centre section of the clubhouse, although at that time it was somewhat narrower than today's building. In the winter of 1967 a concrete barge, which was being used as a mooring pontoon, broke adrift in a gale and smashed into the north side of the quay, demolishing a large section of the structure of the quay itself and sending most of the clubhouse into the sea. As the bar area was on the north side, all of this plus its contents disappeared into the waves. Over the days, weeks and months following this event much of the bar stock was recovered from the shores and beaches of Mylor Creek, much to the pleasure of the local beachcombers.

The quay was rebuilt using concrete and at the same time the new clubhouse was made wider and given a new roof. A small lean-to was added, where the toilets are in 2004, to house a WC for the ladies. This was reportedly a most insanitary affair and not a place to linger. Having said that, sailing was mainly a male preserve at that time and those stalwart ladies who did take part were prepared to put up with some level of discomfort.

In 1973, the present entrance vestibule and much improved toilets were added, together with what is now used as the berthing-masters' office. The first ever Christmas Carol party, now very much a fixture in the MYC calendar, was held in 1977, as was the first New Year's Eve party. That year also saw the introduction of bread and cheese for Sunday lunches with profits going towards the purchase of the Club Bell, still in use today to herald closing times and call the members to order. In 1978, the first Silver Oyster Race was held. This race was, and still is, held on 5 November, the only holiday the dredgermen have during their working season. The date was set to commemorate a famous victory in court over foreshore rights.

The year 1985 saw improvements to the clubhouse with the addition of the 'D' section at the outer end of the quay, as well as a major internal refit. Two years later the club gained recognition as an RYA teaching establishment with the introduction of both theoretical and practical courses for yachtsmen and women wishing to gain various levels of RYA qualifications. The yacht club regularly hosts Feeder Races – two of the most successful of these events were held in 1992 and 1996 specifically for some of the many classic and traditional craft bound for events being held in Brest. Others have been held for those bound for Cork Week and various other local and distant destinations.

The Fal Oyster Fishery

There has been an oyster fishery, for *Ostrea edulis*, in the Fal estuary for a very long time. It is worked by traditional methods under sail and oar. At the time of writing the fishery is regulated by the Maritime Department of Carrick District Council, successor to Truro Corporation, which issues annual licences, currently costing £135 per dredge; in 1975 the licence fee was £18. To make a living, a boat has to go out on every practicable day. In the sense that anybody can buy a licence, it is a free fishery. The season runs from 1 October to 31 March and hours are limited to 0900 to 1500, Monday to Friday and 0900 to 1300 on Saturdays, with no dredging on Sundays. Only oysters larger than the statutory ring of $2\frac{5}{8}$ inches can be taken off the grounds.

A Mylor oysterman working aboard his boat Katrina *which was built in 1913 by Peter Ferris of Looe.*

Some of the boats were built especially for dredging, others have been adapted. Ease of handling and a man's familiarity with his boat, with the depth of water over the banks and with shore features, are of vital importance for success. Some fibreglass boats have been built, requiring vastly less maintenance. Sails nowadays are made of artificial fibres and halyards and warps are synthetic. This removes the necessity of drying sails, while both sails and ropes are stronger and longer lasting. It is not economic for Carrick to employ a full-time bailiff, nor should one be necessary. The regulations have been made to ensure the continuation of the fishery. Breaches of the rules are frequent with unfortunate long-term effects on the stocks.

In 1982, Bonamia oyster disease struck the fishery. This was probably caused by the re-laying of infected stock from elsewhere. Water quality is also important and is regularly tested by the Port of Falmouth Health Authority for sewage and harmful mineral residues such as zinc and cadmium waste, washed down from the mining areas. At very low spring tides some ground is exposed from which oysters may be gathered by hand.

The fishermen do not dredge on 5 November – a custom to mark the confirmation of their right to free lay-beds on the foreshores in the creeks. Beds are marked by withies driven into the ground so that the tops show at high-water spring tides. Lately, races have been organised for over and under 25ft sail boats carrying all their dredging gear. Two model silver oysters are the prizes. These were made by Guy Sanders, a former oyster bailiff who was a sculptor. The only other closure is on Christmas Day.

Fishing is done by towing a dredge along the

This photo shows an oyster dredge. The diagonal strings are purely for photographic purposes to show expansion of the kit.

bottom. In a punt (rowing-boat) the oysterman rows away from an anchor, drops his dredge then winches himself back to the anchor, usually towing a single dredge. This he empties into the cultch board at the stem of the punt. A 25ft-plus boat can tow up to four dredges and is usually worked by two men and the smaller sail boats normally tow two dredges with a one-man crew. Oysters are bought by merchants who come round to the various landing places. The oysters are put in tanks of sterilised water for cleaning, prior to dispatch countrywide for uncooked human consumption. The oldest merchant firm is the Duchy Oyster Farm at Port Navas on the Helford. This has been managed for several generations by the Hodges family.

Although only a few oystermen live in Mylor, a majority use moorings off the dockyard. In an easterly blow many used to take shelter in the creek, picking up any available mooring vacated by a summer yachtsman, regardless of the size and windage of the

actual owner's boat. Other fishermen come out from Restronguet, Pill, Coombe and St Just.

The Oysterman

Frank Cock was a grand old man of the river who, in his nineties, loved to sit in his cottage above Restronguet Creek with his binoculars watching the fleet of Falmouth working boats dredge for oysters in Carrick Roads, and longed to be out there with them. He started dredging in 1920 when he was 15. His father had a boat called *Ida*, which he had converted to an oyster dredger, and father and son sailed together along the estuaries of the Fal, drifting with wind and tide. Frank said that his father taught him all he needed to know and that it was a healthy way of life from which they made a reasonable living.

However, the oyster trade was not a steady one, fluctuating as it did with the seasons, and Frank was encouraged by his father to learn a trade. He served his time as an apprentice shipwright at Cox & Co. in

Left: *The original* Six Brothers, *pictured here, was laid up in the Helford River during the Second World War and later bought by George Vinnicombe who, with his brother Frank, towed her back to Mylor. She was built in 1920 on Restronguet Creek by William Ferris. Tragically, she was wrecked on Greatwood Quay during a gale in November 1968.*

Oysterman Frank Cock on board his working boat Morning Star. *She was built about 1840 for a fisherman in Portloe.*
(REPRODUCED BY KIND PERMISSION OF ANDREW CAMPBELL)

Falmouth and enjoyed his time there, but by 1929 the firm had few orders and he turned to house carpentry. As war approached, the docks became busy once again and Frank returned as a charge hand with a team of 12 men. It was a dangerous period for men working in the docks and Frank often saw German planes drop their bombs. He lost friends and colleagues in raids and a brother-in-law was killed by a daylight bomb on Mylor village.

By 1946, Frank was married with a young son named John and that summer he skippered a boat taking tourists to Polperro and Looe. However, he was soon to return to oyster dredging which he said 'gets into your veins'. During the war the oyster-beds had been resting and hauls were good. For the next 30 years Frank and his partner, Harry Barnes, sailed their own working boat, *Morning Star*. In his heyday, Frank could catch 500 oysters a day but, surprisingly, he only once sampled an oyster and found it too salty for his taste. Many sackfuls were sold to the French who loved them, but Frank's best customer was Peter French of the Essex fishery and they traded together for more than 20 years.

It was a sad day in 1980 when *Morning Star* sank at her moorings and Frank decided it was time to retire from dredging. He still competed in sailing regattas and working-boat races in the summer. In his eighties he was frequently seen rowing his dinghy from Restronguet to Mylor Yacht Harbour, where he joined the crew on board the working boat for the race, then rowing home afterwards. He sometimes helped out on the rescue boat and spent time chatting to his friends in Mylor Yacht Club or the Pandora Inn.

When winter arrived, he was to be found sitting in his cottage perched high above Restronguet Creek, woodturning or knotting, and remembering his time on the water. He was a great character and will be remembered fondly by many for years to come.

A Coasting Ketch

The *Hobah*, a coasting ketch, was built at Trelew on the south side of Mylor Creek in 1879. Thomas Gray, a master shipwright, usually building in Falmouth, hired several labourers in Flushing and had a saw-pit dug out at the back of the beach 50ft from the present road. The men travelled to work by way of a footpath across Trelew Farm from Devil's Roost. Further down, keel blocks were laid across the beach. Edward Drew and his son, William, of Mylor, cut out all the timbers of the ketch. She was to Thomas Gray's own design and for his own use; when she was launched, she proved to be fast and of good carrying capacity. Her ketch rig made for easy handling. On her first voyage, the *Hobah* was rammed by a steamer and sank. She was re-floated, repaired and then traded for 68 years, often carrying Cornish granite as her cargo.

There is a story about the *Hobah* which is related in *The Merchant Schooners Vol. II* by Basil Greenhill and will appeal to all sea-going people:

In 1908, Captain Charles Lamey bought half the shares in her and became her master. His son, William, later took over from him. The latter had begun his career early, having sailed round the land in his father's ketch before he was five years old. He said of his father, 'Often, towards the end of his life, after we had brought the Hobah *into Appledore Quay, he would go down there after the day's work was over and sit watching her. I would say to him, 'What are you doing, father? Tis late now and you had best be coming home,' and he would say to me 'I'm just looking at the* Hobah, *son, I'm just looking at the* Hobah.' *At that time, I thought it was strange that anyone should feel that way about a ship, but I found myself doing the same thing before the end of my time with her.*

The *Hobah* was laid up at her home port of Appledore in 1946, when a mooring cable parted and she was washed so high up on the beach by spring tides that her old timbers were not worth salvaging. The use of sailing vessels, of which the *Hobah* was typical in the coastal trade, did not finally cease until the 1960s.

Tregatreath Boatyard

In 1963, Tregatreath Farm became Tregatreath Boatyard. The land, which was part of the Trefusis estate, was offered by Henry Trefusis to Terry Heard after he had stopped building and repairing boats from his home and foreshore at River View, Church Road. Terry had moved to Mylor Bridge from Bude, north Cornwall, in 1948 and his family took over the carpentry and undertaking business from Mr Tresise, which, at the time of writing, is the Village Butchers. In 1949, he married local girl, Thelma Evans, and for a short time worked at Mylor Dockyard for George Corke, before branching out on his own.

After the move to Tregatreath, the business took off building wooden oyster punts and motor boats for leisure, many of which are still being used in the area today. Terry, with his brother Colin and twins John and Brian van den Huvel as the workforce, established Gaffers and Luggers in 1965. The first GRP (glass-reinforced plastic) oyster punt was produced in 1968 and, despite numerous critics of GRP, Terry continued to build and expand the range of boats. He always stuck to the traditional type lines, but adapted them so that the owners spent more time either working them or enjoying them, rather than time in a boatyard having them repaired.

The first Heard 28 was *St Meloris* (wooden), from which the mould was taken to produce the GRP version of the 28ft craft. The original wooden *St Meloris* was sailed to Antigua by local sailor John Jackson, who sold her there. Three owners later she is still cruising those waters. Sales of larger boats declined and Terry introduced the Tosher 18 in 1975. These proved to be very popular but ceased to be built in 1988, when Terry's son, Martin, who now is

Above: *The coasting ketch* Hobah *built at Trelew alongside Mylor Creek in 1878. This photo is believed to have been taken at Appledore, North Devon, in the 1920s.*

Above left: *Drawing of the* Hobah.

Left: *Terry Heard, boat builder, who established the boatyard at Tregatreath in 1962.*

Marie Claude, *a 46-foot St Malo pilot cutter, built from an 1898 design at Tregatreath in 1996. On board is Martin Heard and his team of boat builders,* left to right: *Kevin Webber, John Moore, Phil Kernow, Tristan Jones, Henry Nathan, Martin Heard and Willie Claxton.*

in charge of the yard, introduced the Tosher 20 into the range. In 1980 the Heard 23 was introduced and is very popular for single-handed oyster dredging and pleasure. The most recent introduction to the fleet is the 35ft *Falmouth Quay Punt* which is ideal for cross-channel cruising. In addition, a small cuddy has been added to the popular 16ft *Clovelly Picarooner*, which is perfect for exploring the creeks and estuaries.

The yard lays up 130 boats over the winter and is kept busy with repairs and maintenance. The demand for new builds has declined slightly, but Gaffers and Luggers are in the midst of their biggest project to date, with a 65ft gaff ketch *Lady Grey* for a customer from the Solent. This follows hot on the heels of two 46ft Pilot Cutters. Sadly, Terry died in 1985 and was unable to share in Martin's recent successes. The business has continued to thrive and expand with a workforce of four. At the time of writing Martin has his son, Sam, learning the ropes.

Penarrow

Beyond the harbour and sailing club is Penarrow Point, marked by a stone pillar showing the boundary between Truro and Falmouth harbour jurisdictions. Another pillar at Messack Point marks the boundary on the other side of Carrick Roads.

Formerly, Truro's claims extended over the whole river and Falmouth Harbour as far as Black Rock, with the exception of Penryn which belonged to the monks of Glasney Collegiate Church. Truro had to relinquish its ancient rights over Falmouth Harbour in 1709 owing to the rising importance of that town as a leading packet station. (It was established as such in 1688 and operated until 1847.)

Later, Falmouth claimed more of the river and accused the Truro people of moving the pillars by night. In 1958, the case was taken to the House of Lords and Truro won the day, so every six years, a ceremony of beating the bounds is held.

Left: Helen Mary, *a traditional 28-foot oyster boat built at Tregatreath in 1975, undergoing trials in Carrick Roads with Ron Laity at the helm.*

Below: *Beating the Truro–Falmouth water bounds at Penarrow Point, Mylor, in 1878. The Mayor, Thomas Chirgwin, is flanked by his mace-bearers.*

Chapter 6

Farming

The Farms of Mylor, Mylor Farmland, Enclosure, Soil Improvement, Increasing Acreage of Pasture, The Coming of Machinery, The Tremayne Sale of Farms, Dairy Farming, Crops, Sheep and Pigs, Employment, Conclusion, Dowstall Farm, Crownick Farm, Landerio Farm, Elsie Rowe's Memories of Landerio Farm, Carvinack Farm, Trelew Farm, Little Tregew Farm, Harvesting Memories, Life at the Farm, Some Field Names, A News Item.

Elliott Nicholls with two horses ready for ploughing at Crownick Farm. This photograph was probably taken between the wars.

The Farms of Mylor

The farms of Mylor are divided by Mylor Creek. Those to the north side stretching up behind the village, over Mylor Downs and down to the main Truro to Falmouth road, were part of the Carclew estate, owned by the Lemons, then the Tremaynes. In 1920, Lieutenant Colonel Tremayne sold his estate and the farms were put up for auction, many farmers then being able to buy and to own their land for the first time. To the south of the creek is the Trefusis estate, the Trefusis family having owned the land since the thirteenth century. The farms have been sold gradually to their tenants, or new occupiers, during the twentieth century, with Trefusis Barton remaining with the family.

Many of the Mylor farms have old Celtic names denoting their antiquity. They were often sited with a sea view, in order to spy on sea-borne pirates. The farms changed little during feudal times, mostly serving their landowners. They had strict conditions on their leases as to how to work their fields, the rotation of crops and also as to their payment of tithes in labour and kind. The leases were usually for three named lives, a yearly rent being paid and a fine on the death of one of the named tenants. Looking at early maps, we find in Gascoyne's map of 1699, that Dowstall, Landerio and Carclew are shown as farmsteads. Dowstall was described as a gentleman's residence, because it was written in capital letters (as was Ennis). By 1748, in Martyn's map, more farms

are shown – Canara, Crownick, Halwyn, Carsawsen and Restronguet.

By 1842, at the time of the tithe map, which settled the apportionment of tithes in money rather than in kind, there were six landowners in Mylor. The two major landowners were Sir Charles Lemon, covering Carclew and Restronguet, with 2,049 acres, and Lord Clinton of Trefusis, owning Trefusis and Flushing, being 933 acres. There were three smaller landowners – the Church with its glebe lands of 21 acres, the Admiralty owning Mylor Dockyard, 14 acres, and Lord Wodehouse owning the manor of Mylor, 137 acres. This small manor around Trelew and Tregew was said by Olivey, writing in 1907, 'to have been exchanged a few years ago by Francis G. Enys for land on the west side of Mylor.' In total the cultivated area in the parish was 3,030 acres in 1842, with 479 acres of woodland.

The land around Mylor is exceptionally good arable land for the growth of crops of all kinds: oats, wheat, barley and turnips and all kinds of vegetables. The farms are small mixed family farms, mostly of 50 to 100 acres. Through the years, the balance of crops grown and livestock kept changes in response to national policies and new inventions.

Mylor Farmland

Mylor is fortunate in having high-quality land, which is generally very suitable for farming and horticulture. In fact, it is superior to that in any of its neighbouring parishes, according to the national Agricultural Land Classification. In this system, by which all land is classed within grades from one down to five, most of Mylor's land is grade two. Where the land rises to 240 feet above sea level, at Mylor Clump, the height affects the land classification, which becomes grade three in some areas.

The system classes land according to the limitations it may impose on cultivation, crop yields or harvesting. Thus it takes into account the climate, the land's topography and the soil condition, particularly its content of stones and its wetness or dryness. The character of the Mylor soil is described as fine and loamy; it is a permeable, finely structured loam with slate or stony layers. However, land around Crownick and Restronguet, near to the sea, is of a different type, having soil with a high mineral content, and this is excellent for cereal growth. The soil is described as spar land and its produce is much sought after by grain merchants.

The favourable climate, as in West Cornwall generally, allows cultivation of potatoes, brassicas and flowers. Being near the sea, the warm winters and early springs can give a long growing season of up to ten months. However, livestock are grazed for somewhat less so as to avoid the damage that can occur from cattle treading, and thereby compacting, the soil structure in wet winter weather.

The average rainfall is close to 1,000 millimetres (40 inches). The permeable soil allows the water to drain rapidly, so that excess winter rain is quickly lost. Salt-laden winds can be severe at times and, in some seasons, cereal crops can suffer from drought.

The soils are naturally acid and require regular liming. However, past applications of sea sand and lime have greatly improved the quality of the topsoil, raising the pH to around 7. The land is regularly treated with ground limestone at two tons to the acre. Contractors also spread sea sand from Gwithian on the north coast. Fertiliser needs vary with the crop to be grown, potatoes especially being heavy users of potash. All crops require high phosphate fertilisation, at one time provided by basic slag but now no longer available from the steelworks.

For hay and silage, two hundredweight per acre of compound fertiliser is needed on average. With the present financial restrictions and the rising cost of fertiliser, the quantity used may reduce in future. The quality of the land in Mylor has been so much improved by good management through the generations as to stand in good stead for the future.

Enclosure

There were commons in Mylor for the common pasturing of the tenants' animals. These are shown on the Trefusis maps of 1764 and 1767, as open downs from Tregew to Mylor Bridge, and on the north side, as Restronguet and Goonree Downs. During the eighteenth and nineteenth centuries, the commons were gradually enclosed. The Carclew estates are said to have cleared moorland at the time of the war against Napoleon in the early 1800s. The price of wheat had risen dramatically because the war prevented corn being imported. Enclosure allowed extra arable cultivation in new fields. It improved the health of cattle too, because the stone hedges gave better protection and made possible the growth of roots and clover for their fodder.

An account of the enclosure of Mylor Downs is given in a letter written by John Pascoe Treneer. He remembers as a boy working with his father for the Carclew estate and assisting his father in ploughing up Mylor Downs with horse teams, a stretch of 56 acres. This was

probably in about 1870 and resulted in Mylor Downs becoming four large fields of about 50 acres together, now farmed by the Nicholls family at Solanum.

As a result of enclosure the area of land under cultivation increased to 3,590 acres in the parish, as given in Kelly's directories both in 1923 and 1939. The chief crops remained constant, being oats, wheat, barley and turnips. The most recent enclosure is the creation of Devichoys Farm, resulting from woodland cleared during the Second World War.

Soil Improvement

There was a new interest in improving the soil in the nineteenth century, farmers using limestone, guano and sand. It had long been known that limestone would alleviate the soil acidity. In the nineteenth century there were two limekilns built on Mylor Creek, to burn lime for spreading on the fields; one at Trelew and one on the north side near Mylor Quay. The limestone was heated to drive off carbon dioxide and leave quicklime. The kiln was fed with limestone and coal in order to produce this quicklime, which was more easily absorbed on the fields. The limestone was brought by boat from Plymouth and up the creek by barge. The coal came from South Wales to Portreath and then by rail to Devoran, from where it was collected by horse and cart.

During the nineteenth century a trade developed in guano, which was rich in fish protein. It was imported from Peru in South America, and was sold to and collected by farmers. Europeans discovered this natural fertiliser, made from bird droppings, in around 1800. Fish-eating birds – cormorants, grey pelicans and boobies – nested on the rocky shores of islands off the Peruvian coast. It was estimated that a million birds nesting on one island could create 11,000 tons of guano in one year! Farmers were able to obtain guano locally from the Williams at Perran Wharf and Restronguet Passage. It was costly, however, and by the end of the century artificial fertilisers ended the trade.

Farmers also used their own cattle muck for manure, where their cattle were housed. Sand was brought by the cartload to spread on the fields, the north-coast sand being preferred and still being used in 2004. The collection of sand to spread on the fields was a medieval right and earlier, local sand was much prized. W. Borlase, who says it was renowned as the best fertiliser, gives an account of the Collaline sands of St Mawes in the eighteenth century. It was dredged with canvas bags below the tide level and taken up river by barge. He states that a barge load of sand in 1750 cost ten shillings and dressed an acre of land.

The right to collect sand for the fields came into question in 1833. It seems that the lords of Ennis and Vyvyan had been restricting access for the collection of sand for some time but, when the Dean of Exeter ordered fences to be erected in order to collect a toll for sand, there was an outcry. Four to five hundred

'Miler' map. Gascoyne's Survey of Cornwall, 1699.

This limekiln at Trelew was one of two built along Mylor Creek. The other is on the north side near Mill Quay. The limestone was brought by boat from Plymouth and up the creek by barge. Coal was collected from Devoran by horse and cart.

farmers and their labourers from Truro and surrounds marched in angry protest to tear down the fences. At the Assizes in 1834, it was stated that 'farmers had been using Towan sand for manure from times beyond the memory of man.'

Increasing Acreage of Pasture

In 1840, much of the land in Mylor was used for growing corn and other crops. However, during the second half of the century dairy farming increased.

After the war against Napoleon, home-produced corn was encouraged by the protection of the Corn Laws, restricting the import of foreign corn. Arable production increased, and farmers had good prices for their corn. However, this kept the price of bread high and there was much protest from the working population in the cities. When, in 1846, the Corn Laws were finally repealed, there were fears that foreign corn would swamp the market. Twenty years later, when grain had begun to flood in from the new American grain fields, the price of corn was falling steadily, and in the 1870s there was a serious national farming slump. This continued for 20 years or more and the price of corn did not recover until the onset of the First World War in 1914.

As a result, from the 1880s Cornwall became more of a dairy county, with arable fields changing to pasture land for cattle and most farms having a few dairy cows. Marketing of dairy products was helped by the use of railway transport. In addition, after a serious outbreak of cattle plague in 1865–66, many town dairies were wiped out and milk started to be brought long distances to the cities by rail from country farms.

This trend seems to have affected Mylor, in that in the parish the number of cattle kept increased from 734 in 1868, to 969 in 1906, an increase of 235 cattle. The number of acres in pasture also increased over the 30 years before 1900. There was a new emphasis on milk, butter and cream production. Mixed farming continued alongside, with varied arable crops being grown. Most farms also kept pigs, sheep and poultry.

As well as the bigger farms, there were many smallholdings where fruit and vegetables were grown for sale. Market gardening and flower growing prospered well up to the 1950s.

The Coming of Machinery

During the second half of the Victorian age onwards, machinery gradually appeared on the farms. It was used increasingly through the 1900s, greatly reducing the need for labour.

Iron ploughs replaced the old wooden Cornish ploughs, which had easily been turned on steep hillsides and in small Cornish fields. Drills came into use instead of hand sowing, where seed had previously been lost and wasted. With the use of drills, turnip

production increased. The reaper-binder saved cutting and tying the corn sheaves by hand. Eric Gray describes it in about 1939:

I remember at the age of 15 spending the whole summer holidays working at Halwyn Farm, which gave me some insight into the hard graft involved. We had horse-driven reaper-binders with flailing arms and a neat device that tied the sheaves with oil-smelling binder-twine before throwing them on the field. The sheaves were then stacked to form an upright stook and left to dry. Carting would then begin with the sheaves being pitch-forked onto a wagon and taken to the farmyard to await the threshing-machine.

A reaper-binder at Landerio Farm in the 1930s.

The travelling steam threshing-machine saved the work of the flail. Elsie Rowe, in her *Memories of Landerio Farm*, describes the great day of the arrival of the threshing-machine with all its noise and dirt. Other memories of threshing come from Eric Gray and Rose Rogers. It was a long and exhausting day for the farmers, their wives and neighbours, but it was also a time of companionship in sharing the work with their neighbours.

These inventions, as well as reducing the need for labourers, also improved the quality and yield of the grain at sowing, reaping and threshing. At the same time, local mills became abandoned and farmers began to buy machinery to grind their own corn for feeding their animals. Imported grain became available from Penryn or Devoran and later in the twentieth century concentrates took over, produced by local mills specialising in animal feed stuffs.

All these changes came in gradually and perhaps were adopted more slowly by the smaller farmers. Each invention added to the gradual revolution in reducing

Gordon and Elsie Rowe serving 'croust' in the basket at threshing time during the 1950s. This meant a very well-earned break with heavy cake, saffron buns and plenty of tea.

Gordon Rowe in 1951 on the grey Ferguson tractor, loading loose hay onto the rick with his father-in-law Charles Rowe.

manpower needs, and changed the way of work on family farms. Major tasks such as threshing and haymaking became times when families helped each other, shared resources and much fun and laughter came too! A much greater revolution was brewing, however, with the coming of tractors from 1950 onwards.

The Second World War brought an emphasis on food production. Local agricultural committees were set up to encourage the growing of extra crops, and continued for some years after the war, giving the farms quotas for how much they should produce. Ploughing of all these extra acres was done at first by horses. Crownick had three or four heavy horses for ploughing, tillage and carting.

After the war, tractors gradually appeared. Eric Nicholls reports his first was a standard Fordson TVO with iron wheels. It was hard to start and difficult to get round the ends of fields, being apt to slide. Then came the Harry Ferguson, which was more sophisticated; it had rubber wheels and special instruments to make working easier, as well as a hydraulic lift. In the 1950s, the Ford diesel tractors arrived. Horses were largely superseded, with a couple kept for carting. As tractors developed, so did the implements they could attach to help with haymaking, muck spreading, tillage and all farm work.

The Tremayne Sale of Farms

During the First World War there was great demand for home-produced food. The price of wheat finally rose to 80 shillings (£4) a quarter (28lbs) for the first time for a quarter of a century. Farming had a brief revival as the price held up until the slump of the 1920s.

In 1920, the Tremayne family decided to sell their farms, lands and cottages in Mylor and St Gluvias, and held an auction over two days. Not all the property was sold at the auction, but some sold later by negotiation. Ten Mylor farms were for sale ranging in size from Dowstall (104 acres), to Bellair (39 acres) and the smallest, Albion, of 12 acres. Restronguet became the biggest holding at 343 acres, being an amalgamation of seven leases. Some of the previous farm tenants bought their holdings and others, such as Restronguet, changed hands. The Rogers family at Tregunwith Farm and the Nicholls family at Crownick, who both had been tenants since the 1800s, were able to purchase their farms. Notably, many of the farms purchased are still in the occupation of the same families and their descendants in 2004.

Besides the farms, smallholdings were for sale, there being 17 of these ranging in size from one to 28 acres. The smallholdings were mainly around Comfort Road and between Bells Hill and Passage Hill, where there were many small fields. Land at the present Cogos Park development was included. Presumably, negotiation took place in the following years. During the first half of the 1900s, these market gardeners grew much produce, which they sold locally and at Penryn. Mylor people have happy memories of visiting the growers to fetch vegetables and fruit in season. Rose Rogers gives us a lovely memory of Mr Williams, in Passage Hill, selling raspberries by the pint in a cabbage leaf!

The memories of Mylor people of the 1920s and '30s tell us much of the village life then, in which local produce and local work played such a big part. The farms were then, as today, places of hard work, fulfilment and companionship, above all governed by the seasons and the weather.

Dairy Farming

At the same time as farm implements developed, the dairy industry was changing rapidly. Before the war most farms had a few cows and milking was by hand, done by a team of three or four people, usually the family. At Crownick, 25 Shorthorn dairy cows were tied in sheds over winter and milked there. Horse and cart took the milk churns to the crossroads, where Nestles collected it for the Penryn creamery.

In the 1940s, machine milking began with the milk stored in ten-gallon churns. It was a big improvement when the Milk Marketing Board drove up the lane and collected the churns off the milk stand. The milking system changed again in the 1960s when the cow house was adapted into a milking parlour. The cows stood in stalls, eight at a time, and four electric milking units were used together at one time. The cows gathered in the collecting yard and jumped onto a three-foot platform, allowing the operator to stand below. The number of cows increased at Crownick to 30 or 40, but the breed remained Shorthorn.

A dramatic change occurred in the 1970s with the coming of the bulk milk tanker throughout the county. The cows lay in cubicles and the milk parlour enlarged to take seven each side, with a pit for milking. Milk was refrigerated in tanks. Holstein-Friesian cows replaced the Shorthorns because of their much greater milk production. Holsteins produced up to eight gallons per day compared with only four gallons per day from the Shorthorns. One man could now milk on average 100 cows and, consequently, herds grew larger. The quality of milk was strictly inspected and was tested for bacterial counts to a high standard. As a result of the need for bigger herds, the number of farms producing milk dived. At one time there were over 20 farms in the parish producing milk – soon there were only seven or eight. The capital input in dairy housing and equipment pushed many farms out of dairying. A few continued a local milk round but were discouraged by regulations and milk quotas and only the large herds could survive.

In the late 1990s, milk tankers were attending at farms only on alternate days, which required a greater capacity of milk storage and, therefore, higher costs to the farmer. In 2003 there were only three farms in Mylor parish producing milk, probably from over 300 cows.

Crops

Before the war, it was normal for farms to grow some corn to help feed their animals. They grew dredge corn (a mix of oats and barley), hay and a special long-stemmed wheat for thatching the ricks. All the corn was cut with a binder and big stacks built in the field and thatched. In the winter these stacks were threshed to provide grain and straw for animal feed. The arrival of the threshing contractor was a big event, originally steam powered and then diesel powered. About a dozen casual workers were employed for the day making it a busy day for the farmer's wife, providing meals or croust (a snack) for those involved. Later of course it all ended with the advent of the giant combine harvester and straw baler.

The reaper-binder at Crownick Farm with farm worker Dick Richards. Eric Nicholls is in front of him along with some visiting cousins in the late 1930s.

Some potatoes were grown, as well as mangolds for the cattle. The mangolds needed to be hoed and singled out and later harvested into stacks by the hedge, covered with straw or hedge trimmings. In winter, they were collected by Maun basket and chopped in half to feed the cows.

After the war, more pasture was needed to graze the increased number of cows, but some dredge corn continued to be grown for cattle fodder and bedding. Other crops grown for the cattle were rape and kale and fodder turnips. In dry summers the turnips are especially useful for grazing in August and September. A big change came in the 1970s, with the making of silage. This much relieved the effort of making hay in variable weather. At first the grass was cut and collected by buck rake, and run over in heaps by the tractor. Later silage clamps were built and filled by forage harvesters and a team of tractors and trailers. The clamps were then consolidated and covered with plastic sheets to provide high-quality winter feed. In recent years machines have been developed which pack the grass into round or square bales, individually wrapped in plastic.

Group of people in the harvest field at Crownick Farm seen here between the wars.

Sheep and Pigs

With the emphasis on dairy cattle, sheep and pigs have largely gone out of favour in Mylor. At Crownick, Eric's father, Rodney Nicholls, gave up having sheep after dogs, kept by the troops stationed on his land, savaged several of them. He became discouraged by this and never replaced them. At the time of writing, there is in Mylor possibly only one farm keeping sheep. Yet in the nineteenth century they were a usual part of local farms. In 1868 there were over 2,000 sheep in the parish, but 100 years later, in 1968, only 500. Pigs too had been kept. At Crownick they were fattened and then transported to Penryn station, en route to Bowyers in Wiltshire. It was usual for most farms to keep a pig or two for their own use.

Employment

Naturally, with so much mechanisation, numbers of people working on the land have plummeted and in the twenty-first century there is very little local employment in farming. Even the bigger farms are managed by their families with, at best, one or two helpers. Casual workers and pickers come in from outside, and contractors are on the increase for specialist jobs. General work has become much less physical than in the past. For example, half a hundredweight (25 kilograms) is now enough to lift, rather than the former one hundredweight sacks. Fertiliser and feeds now come in bulk 20-ton loads for lifting by tractor power. Silage made on the farm is also transported and lifted by tractor. So manual work has been largely superseded.

Conclusion

These are a few of the many changes that have affected farming in the twentieth century. The rise of European subsidies encouraged over-production and this was followed by quotas and restrictions. The disaster of BSE in 1996, followed by foot-and-mouth disease in 2001, has resulted in the loss of some of the market for British produce. The current crisis has reduced cattle numbers and forced many small farmers out of business. So, what of the future? Contractors are renting land, bulb growing is big business and vegetable growing is on the increase in the area. The farming community has to develop new ideas for the use of the land in the twenty-first century.

An account of some local family farms follows, showing their development and changes through the last century.

Dowstall Farm

Dowstall is an old Celtic name, meaning 'root of river', and there is no doubt that the land there has been farmed for a long time. Dowstall is shown on a map of 1699. It is good fertile soil and well situated, with the

Dowstall farmhouse in the 1950s, said to have been built from blocks of stone quarried from its own fields.

farmhouse in the middle of its fields. The farm belonged to the Carclew estate until 1920, when it was sold by the Tremayne family, together with the other farms on their extensive estate, and much other local property.

In 1920 Dowstall comprised 104 acres. At the time of the tithe map in 1839 it had been 114 acres, but this included Angarrick of 24 acres. Excluding Trefusis and Restronguet, Dowstall has remained one of the largest farms.

During the nineteenth century the Rundle family, who contributed much to the local community, tenanted Dowstall. Robert Rundle was 50 when he took the tenancy from Sir Charles Lemon in 1832 for £140 per year. Robert Rundle was married to Grace Carvosso, daughter of a famous Methodist preacher. It is likely that the Rundles were farming in Mylor before moving to Dowstall because, in 1818, Robert Rundle (yeoman) and William Pierce took a joint lease on the ground where the Methodist chapel had been built. He was, however, an Anglican himself and his name is found in the accounts of Mylor church pews in 1830.

Robert Rundle was succeeded by his son Charles in 1852, and Charles by his son William in 1886, so that for three generations and nearly 90 years this family steadfastly farmed their family farm, often employing two men and two boys. William became Chairman of Mylor Parish Council in 1894, 1900 and 1902. By the time of the Tremayne sale in 1920 he was 63 and perhaps happy to retire from such an active farming life.

At the Tremayne sale at Truro in 1920, Dowstall Farm and cottages were bought by Richard Dale of Penryn. The Dales still farm Dowstall in 2004, although there have been many changes. The first tractor came in about 1948 and mechanisation made a huge difference to their farming. Mrs Mary Dale, the owner at the time of writing, thinks that during the 1920–50 period the farm continued as a mixed stock and arable farm – pigs and cattle were kept in small numbers, but not sheep. Because of family friendships, Canara, their neighbouring farm across Comfort Road, has been worked in association with Dowstall since the 1950s, and the two farms remain together.

In the 1980s the Dales had a change of direction. With the government's emphasis on intensive farming, John and Mary set about expanding their dairy herd, so as to specialise in milk production. They built a new shed with milking parlour and cubicles for 60. This was a big change from having 15–20 cows and a few pigs. The sudden introduction of milk quotas in 1983, with attendant problems, followed by BSE in 1996, forced another change and, in 1997, they stopped milking and developed a South Devon pedigree cow and calf-suckler herd.

Crops on the farm have been diverse. Fifty years ago the crops were mainly grown in order to feed their own cattle. Dredge corn was popular – a mixture of oats, wheat and barley, as well as flat-ball cabbages, turnips and their own hay for the winter. At Canara and Dowstall they also grew all types of vegetables – broccoli, cabbage, potatoes and runner beans. Flowers were grown too, with the help of plastic tunnels at Canara from the 1960s, especially anemones and violets. All this produce was picked, bunched, packed and rushed to Penryn station to catch the train to London and Sheffield. Part-time casual women workers helped to harvest the flowers and vegetables.

Crownick Farm

One of the oldest farms on the Carclew estate is Crownick, its Celtic name meaning 'farm at the crossroads'.

Five generations of the Nicholls family have farmed this land, descending from John Stevens, who was at the farm in 1841 and whose daughter married W.H. Nicholls. They took over the farm in 1902 with their son Rodney, then aged seven. Rodney (known as Elliott), father of Eric, farmed Crownick until 1952, when he retired with Ellen his wife to Solanum. The family had purchased this smallholding at Mylor Downs, which had at one time been a game lodge. He lived there until his death in 1988. Eric Nicholls and his wife Jean have owned and farmed Crownick since 1952 and their son Stephen farms it in 2004.

In 1839, Crownick was part of the Carclew estate and divided into three tenements. In 1883 the old farmhouse was replaced and the old house was used as a barn. The new house is thought to have been built of local stone. Oil-lamps and paraffin lanterns were used, as electricity did not arrive at the farm until 1944. In 1920 the farm, together with others of the Carclew estate, was put up for auction in Truro. At this time the Nicholls family bought Crownick Farm.

Elliott Nicholls recalls:

It was a mixed farm growing hay, potatoes, mangolds and turnips for their own use, and buying in some corn for stock feed. They had about 18 Shorthorn milking cows and their own bullocks to fatten and heifers to rear for replacements. They also had 40 ewes, 100 pigs and 100 fowl. The milk was sold to Nestles and collected at Stickenbridge. The bullocks were walked to Truro market when ready for sale. The pigs were walked to Penryn and after 1896 were transported by train. They had four or five heavy horses for farm arable work. After the First World War they bought their own horse-drawn reaper-binder in order to cut and harvest hay and corn.

During the Second World War, troops were billeted at Crownick, taking over about 20 acres of farmland on both sides of the road. The army camp for British troops was built at the Clump, and searchlights set up near to the farm. Across the road towards Restronguet, an anti-aircraft site was set up, with heavy guns and machine guns. The noise of the guns was fearsome to the horses. One of them even broke a leg one night by panicking in the stable. It was a hard time for the family who had extra quotas of crops to produce with little help, as well as their normal arable work, twice daily milking and care of their animals.

Landerio Farm

Landerio, meaning enclosure of oaks, has remained in the same family since Charles Rowe took out a lease from the Trefusis estate in the 1920s. The old thatched farmhouse was falling down, so Henry Trefusis had a new one built. The old farmhouse is still in part use for farm buildings, but is now tin-roofed. A lease for 1929 shows Landerio Farm having 53 acres, with a rent of £115 for 21 years.

Charles Rowe had previously farmed at Little Tregew at Flushing and had a milk round in Mylor and Flushing. He continued with this at Landerio and had a herd of milking cows, calves and young heifers (between 36–40 cattle) and one bull. He was the first farmer in the area to have Friesian cattle and the herd became accredited against TB. Working horses played a big part on the farm until the arrival of their first grey Ferguson tractor in the 1950s. This date also saw the arrival of electricity. Until then, milking had been done by hand and a milking machine operated by a generator. Lighting was by gas Tilley lamps and candles and cooking was done on the Cornish range or a Primus stove. Water from the well in the yard was pumped into an elevated tank and gravitated into the house.

Mrs Katie Rowe had a dairy in the house, making butter and cream, which she gave up in the 1950s when government regulations became so harsh that it was difficult to comply. The main crops grown were corn and hay for the cattle and extra potatoes during the war. There were seven children in the family and when Charles Rowe died in 1958 his son, Edmund Rowe, took over and later, Trent Meyers, who was brought up on the farm and worked with his uncles after leaving school, was in charge. He and his wife Jackie became sole occupants in 1982 when the acreage was 70 acres. In 2004 they no longer farm the Penscove fields and houses in Penmorvah and Saltbox Close were built on one of their fields.

Top left: *'Shocks' of corn in Green Close Field, Crownick Farm, in the 1930s. In the distance is Restronguet Point with very few houses at that time.*

Top right: *Reaper-binder drawn by a team of three horses at Crownick Farm, very early in the 1900s with a view of Restronguet Creek in the background.*

Far left: *Elliott Nicholls of Crownick Farm, prior to the Second World War.*

Left: *Elliott Nicholls later in life, after the war.*

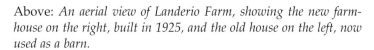

Above: *An aerial view of Landerio Farm, showing the new farmhouse on the right, built in 1925, and the old house on the left, now used as a barn.*

Right: *Haymaking at Landerio Farm – 'Captain' the horse with Joe Bowden and Mr Roberts on the trailer in the 1940s.*

Charles Rowe using a scythe to cut corn round the field edges before the reaper-binder cut the centre of the field, 1940s.

Charles Rowe and his son Elliott cutting corn with the reaper-binding machine, early 1950s.

Landerio is now a good compact unit and the house has been modernised.

Up until 1982 the farm was largely dairy with a mixed-breed milking herd. Trent and Jackie decided to expand the number of dairy cows and to build up a new herd of Friesians. Dairy quotas and other regulations made such difficulties that in 1994 they decided to give up milking and sold their dairy cattle and young stock.

Landerio is very good quality arable land. Trent has been growing corn, barley, wheat and cauliflowers commercially, and cabbage, calabrese, sprouts, cauliflowers and courgettes for local sale. A new development over the past few years has been the production and sale of haylage. The advantage of haylage is that two or three crops of grass can be harvested each season, since the grass is cut young. It is very popular with horse owners. Prices for farm produce continue to fall, especially the price of wheat, in 2000 being half of what it was in 1982 (£62 a ton compared with £120 a ton).

In 1984, Jackie opened a farm shop to sell produce directly to the public. This proved popular locally in spite of the competition from a new Asda supermarket. She also provides bed-and-breakfast accommodation at the farmhouse and stabling for a few horses. In 2002, Jackie decided to expand their livery business and to close the farm shop. Trent has diversified into garden contract work, running a hedging and tree-lopping business and a garden-waste removal service.

Such variety of enterprise has been essential during the current farming crisis.

Elsie Rowe's Memories of Landerio Farm

Elsie was born at Landerio in 1927 and has many memories of helping on the farm as a child. Jobs to be done were varied and included collecting eggs, picking up stones from the fields and delivering milk to nearby homes on her way to school in Mylor. She attended cookery classes in Penryn when she was about 12 years old and, on her way home, she would drive Mr Lawrys' bullocks back from near Bissom to Penscove Farm.

There was always plenty of help needed in the dairy. Elsie remembers turning the butter churn by hand and the rose-imprinted butter splats that her mother used. Milk for the cream was scalded in a large pan on top of the copper and then allowed to cool. If the weather was very hot when the cream was separated, her father would put it in the cool of the well. There was no pocket money in those days for these tasks but, for a special treat on Sundays, there was cream and sugar spread on a cracker. Delicious! Life on the farm was not all work; a lot of fun was had, especially the games of rounders which were played in the front field.

When Elsie left school at 14, she became a milk-maid. She still has the milking-stool she used when helping with the milking. These were very busy times, as several members of the family had become involved in war activities, which meant extra work for those at home. They had a young evacuee from Plymouth staying with them, who shared a bedroom with Elsie and her sisters.

When her father gave up going on the milk round with the horse and cart, Elsie took over the round with her stepbrother. She always wore a white coat and drove the van. They delivered milk, cream and eggs to Mylor and Flushing. Some of the milk was in bottles and some was in cans, from which it was poured into the customers' own jugs. One-third-pint bottles were taken to the schools in Mylor, Flushing and Penryn for the children to drink at break-time. Elsie remembers filling these by hand and putting the cardboard caps on, which had little push-out tabs to put the straw through.

The milk round was a lot of hard work. After milking, the milk was left to cool. The bottles, which had Landerio stamped on them, were sterilised in a big steamer in the yard before being filled once again. Elsie also helped her mother with the dairy work and housework. One of the weekly jobs was to clean the brass trims on the Cornish range with Brasso and to blacklead with Zebo. The cooking was done on the range but, to save time, the early-morning cup of tea was made on a Primus stove.

Above: *The Landerio Farm horses Captain and Colonel with brothers Eddie and Elliott Rowe cutting corn in the 1940s.*

Below: *Captain and Mr Roberts of Trevissome Cottage cutting hay in the 1940s.*

The Rowe family enjoying a cup of tea brought out to the tractor and trailer by Elsie Rowe (in the print dress), 1950s.

Haymaking, harvesting and threshing were very busy times both in the fields and in the house. Mrs Rowe would provide croust mid-morning for the many helpers. There would be heavy cake, yeast or saffron buns and herby beer. This was made from Masons Extract. Balloons were placed on top of the earthenware jars, so that when the yeast fermented it did not crack them. At midday, a roast lunch was served in the farmhouse and later, at teatime, tea and sandwiches were brought outside.

Before the coming of the threshing-machine, Mr Rowe had an old binder and two horses, called Captain and Colonel, which Elsie used to lead to and from the rick, whilst it was being built. Threshing lasted two days and then everyone moved on to the next farm to help. Despite all the hard work at threshing time, one man found time to play a joke on Elsie. She was going to a dance at Mylor and had worn her old shoes up the muddy track, changed into her smart ones and put the old ones in the hedge ready for later. When she returned, she could not find them. They had been hidden!

Elsie has so many wonderful memories of her family and farming. It is good to know that the tradition is being carried on through her sister, Christine Mitchell and her family at Trevissome and nephew, Trent Meyers and his family at Landerio.

Carvinack Farm

Carvinack (meaning fort or camp) is on the Enys estate but is in the parish of Mylor. In the 1950s it was a farm of 30 acres with mixed cattle, pigs and poultry, but no sheep. At that time it was tenanted by Herbert Tregenza. In the cottage next door lived the Johns family, and as a child Heather Johns loved to help with everything on the farm. Some of her memories of life on the farm follow.

The Tregenza family had been in the village through the nineteenth and twentieth centuries. In 1923, John Tregenza was at Carvinack and Thomas Tregenza at Tregoweth nearby. An earlier John was sextant at Mylor Church in 1907. Much earlier, in 1816, Thomas Tregenza, a farmer, leased a plot of land in New Row where he built two cottages, which remained in the family until 1877.

At Carvinack Farm in the 1950s, tractor power was beginning to take over from horses. The first tractor was a Fordson TVO. All the corn grown was for use of their own stock. Flowers, especially anemones and violets, were picked by local helpers and taken to Penryn station for the Covent Garden market. Milk was the main product and was collected in churns by the Milk Marketing lorry. There was no electricity or running water.

Carvinack Cottage, where the Johns family lived, was a substantial three-bedroomed Victorian house, with coloured glass in the front door. The front doorstep was polished with cardinal red. In the kitchen was a big Cornish range and every Sunday afternoon Mrs Johns gave it a blackleading and also polished all the brasses. Nearby, at Bagatelle, lived Heather's uncle and aunt, Ron and Brenda Johns, on their small farm. Their produce was famous, people coming especially to buy their goats milk and Kea plums. Near to them, on Rose Hill, Bertie Brewer sold special tasty tomatoes, while the Tregenzas sold honey from their own bees.

After the Johns left in 1959 and the Tregenzas gave way to the Bromleys, Carvinack Cottage was pulled down to make way for a new hay barn. Although it is sad to see the old give way to the new, it is good that so many happy memories remain. (With thanks to the memories of Heather Sanders, née Johns.)

Trelew Farm

Arthur Rickard and Barbara have lived at Trelew since 1958. They rented the farm from the Trefusis estate until 1973, when they gave up farming the fields, but have remained at the farmhouse, keeping seven acres.

Trelew is a very old house, perhaps 400 years old. The present house was built for one of Nelson's captains.

When HMS *Ganges* was anchored at Mylor in the late 1800s, Trelew Farm had outbuildings that were used as an abattoir for slaughtering animals for the ships. The meat was then ferried from Trelew Quay down the creek to the ships. Arthur had a picture of the *Ganges, Implaccable, Foudroyant* and *Cutty Sark* being anchored in the bay. The old boiler used to be in their outhouse and some of the ironmongery is now at the Maritime Museum.

After their marriage in 1956, Mr and Mrs Rickard lived for a few years at Penoweth and farmed there on a small farm of about 14 acres. They moved to Trelew and farmed about 50 acres there, where they had dairy cows producing milk, collected by the Milk Marketing Board. They also had pigs and were fattening beef cattle on the grass. When they gave up farming, the land went back to the Trefusis estate, and was later sold to the Perkins and farmed by the Dales until recently. Mrs Rickard has bred sheep dogs.

Penoweth farmhouse when Harry Nicholls lived there before the building of houses on Penoweth land, 1940s. The car is a Baby Austin owned by Mr Brewer.

The Rickards also grew vegetables and flowers in their fields. The flower business involved much hard work as they grew several rows of anemones, planting about 38,000 corms. They had three rows of daffodils, three rows of sweet peas (each colour kept separate (pink, mauve and white)) and three rows of cornflowers – these were two blue and one pink, being the best-selling colours. They grew calendulas, stocks and violets – the violets were a good crop to grow as they flowered all year round. They planted out the runners in the summer and divided the plants, then they were ready to flower again in the autumn. Much of the flower crop was sold to Lawrence at Falmouth. He used to deliver flowers four days a week in his Austin car to Truro, Newquay, Penryn and Camborne. He was the son of Lawrence, the Mylor policeman. Mr Rickard employed help to pick and bunch the flowers – hoeing was done by hand but there was a horse-drawn hoe for use between the rows of violets.

Little Tregew Farm

Arthur was born and brought up at Little Tregew Farm in Pillars Road. His father kept a dairy there and delivered milk locally. He took milk around in churns by horse and cart, selling it direct into the customers' own jugs, then later he used bottles. The farm was 29 acres and became 54 acres after the Second World War, acquiring some fields from Penoweth when it was sold for building.

During the war, Mr Rickard senr was ordered to plough in the daffodil bulbs. After the war the flower business never recovered – high labour and transport costs were reasons, as well as low prices, and later the imports from abroad. In 1975, he died aged 88 having been blind for 27 years. He had lived at Little Tregew for about 80 years. The farm at Little Tregew was given up in about 1977.

Arthur remembers that there used to be three cottages at the site of the present house and another house further up the road. The cottage he and his family lived in was thatched and his grandmother lived next door. In one of the cottages lived an Irishman who kept a sow under the table. He said the pig helped to pay the rent so it had a right to live in the house! In his youth, Arthur's father had worked at Tregatreath where he rented cows and milked them there. It was a small farm of about 18 acres.

Harvesting Memories

Eric Gray, working at Halwyn Farm in his holidays aged 15, remembers:

The thresher, with its steady rhythmic hum and shiny leather belt going round and round, was a delight to watch, the chaff flew around as the corn tumbled down into sacks. The days were long for men and horses at harvest time but refreshment (croust) was provided at intervals, together with enamel cups of tea. When time allowed, out would come the Robin Redbreast tobacco and pipes lit or maybe a puff on a Woodbine cigarette would suffice.

As children, we looked forward to harvest time and, armed with sticks and stones, would wait until the area of corn left to be cut was small, and the rabbits bolted for safety; this is when we struck with our seemingly deadly weapons, usually to no avail. On one occasion, however, a stone brought blood from the head of one of the boys, needless to say we were threatened never to continue this practice again.

Cows had to be milked twice a day and the horse and cart took the milk churns to a point on the main road, from where they would be collected. Taking the horse to the village smithy by myself was a daunting task as Prince seemed a very big animal.

Rose Rogers writes of her experience of threshing at Tregunwith Farm:

Stacking sheaves onto the trailer at Crownick in the late 1930s. In front is Elliott Nicholls, with left to right on the trailer: *young Parkyn, Eric (Elliott's son) aged about ten and Father Parkyn of Oriel Cottage.*

When the threshing-machine came to the farm the men had to have lodgings either in the farmhouse or in the village – breakfast, morning and afternoon croust and dinner; tea, dinner and croust for the extra men. The farmer also had to supply the coal for the engine. Water was fetched in wooden barrels from the river in the middle of the village, sacks being placed over the top of the barrels to prevent the water splashing over. My first experience of threshing was three weeks after I was married in September 1940. I had never taken much interest in cooking so was rather worried having to cope with extra people, but felt very proud when my mother-in-law told me I had done something she had never done all the time she had lived at Tregunwith – she always had help when they were threshing whereas I did it on my own.

Life at the Farm

Dorothy Congdon writes of her work on a farm in the early 1920s. She went as a young woman to work on a farm where the farmer's wife was an invalid and there were two young schoolboys:

All the water had to be fetched from the pump across the road, what hard work but what lovely water; this was one of my jobs. I was there three years: cooking, cleaning, washing, scalding milk, etc. I learnt how to clean the fat off the pigs' bellies, which was very often because the pigs fattened up quickly. The man to kill them came from Mylor. I remember the killing house, and the wash-house with a large copper of boiling water that I had fetched there, and the sharp knife. I had to be very careful with that knife because if a slit were made in the pot, there would be an awful mess, and very little lard. After the bellies were cleaned the skins were delicious, stuffed with a suet paste and roasted. They could be bought at the butchers and they were soon sold out, because most of the families enjoyed them.

The farmer, Mr Charles Rowe, would bring a rib of beef every Friday and that had to last most of the week. That went on every week all the years that I was there. It was roasted when it came, and then cooked over and over again in pies, etc. I always made up my mind that when I had a home of my own, a rib of beef would never be eaten, and I cannot remember buying one.

The cream in those days was delicious. The pans it was scalded in were made of iron, an enamel bowl of milk put into the iron pan. When the cream was ready there would be a lovely crust with very fine bubbles around the edge. That would be carried to the dairy, and then another bowl put into the pan. That was every afternoon's work.

Other jobs included scrubbing men's corduroy breaches with a brush and board, standing in a tin bath. When I look back now I can hardly believe I did such work. I also prepared and papered the sitting room, white paper for the ceiling and red for the walls. No extra wages. I had ten shillings a week and often my mother would be glad of it.

Some Field Names

On an interesting map of 1764, field names are given; some quaint and reflecting their nature and history. Several fields bear the old Cornish names, like 'gew' meaning meadow and 'gweal', a big open field (the best pasture on the farm), as in 'gwealgarras' near Little Park and St Mylor Church. 'Park' itself means 'a field' as in 'park miler', 'park julian', and 'park jeffrys'. 'Park-an-hale' means 'field by the estuary'.

'Crocknagodna' is a very steep slope behind Flushing. There is also one in Restronguet and it means 'break the neck' – very apt. Posscatha, now Polscatha, a cove at the end of Church Road, means 'the harbour of little boats'.

A News Item

On 6 March 1835 a local newspaper (the *West Briton*) reported the following:

> An Inquest was held at Mylor yesterday, on the body of Jane Goodfellow, aged 64 years, wife of a bargeman, living at Mylor Bridge. On Wednesday evening, at about five o'clock, she went into a field near her house to milk her cow, and was shortly after found there quite dead. She had fallen off her stool, the bucket with some milk in it, standing between her feet. Verdict 'died by a visitation of God.'

Chapter 7

Restronguet and the Pandora

Restronguet, Restronguet Barton Since 1922, Restronguet Weir, Mining, Life at Weir 1900–27,
Pixie Wells' Reminiscences, The Pandora Inn.

Restronguet

In the Middle Ages, Restronguet was an important manor-house with its own chapel and lands. Mylor Creek, Perran Creek, Restronguet Creek and Carrick Roads bounded this ancient manor, mentioned in the twelfth century. Carclew and its lands were separated off by a lease of the thirteenth century. After this, Restronguet Manor remained in the hands of the Bodrugan, then Trevanion, families. It fell into ruins in the 1600s and in 1785 was sold to the Trefusis family. After 20 years, the Trefusis estate sold it again to William Lemon who already owned Carclew. Thus the Barton of Carclew and the Manor of Restronguet were rejoined after 500 years.

By 1840, Restronguet farmlands were divided into six or seven tenements, leased from the Lemon family. Much the largest was Ley's Tenement, being 109 acres and occupied by John Mitchell, but only until 1845 when he sold up to go abroad. The farm buildings and cottages were grouped together on the Weir road close to the site of the old manor-house. Many agricultural labourers with large families lived there, so the area was known as Restronguet Village. Along the road to the farm, the cottagers were given gardens to grow vegetables and potatoes for themselves and for the family pig. Also, there were fruit bushes and trees in orchards. On the Restronguet lands were also two quarries and a limekiln and quay on the north bank of Mylor Creek near to the village.

The farms grew corn and kept a few cattle and some sheep. At Restronguet Farm are the remains of an old horse round. This was driven by four oxen or horses walking round and round to drive the wheel of a threshing-machine or corn grinder, and was used before the coming of the new threshing-machines.

In the late 1880s the farms were tenanted together by Michael Holman. He was a thrifty farmer and also employed two or three stone builders, who built many of the local farm buildings with stone from the Weir quarry. In the early 1900s, he built a substantial new farmhouse for himself alongside the old. This has been used as the farmhouse through the twentieth century, but now Oliver and Rosemary Dale occupy the old farmhouse and yard at Kibben Cottage, the big house having been sold.

When the Tremayne farms were sold in 1920 the whole farm, including all the tenements, was sold to Captain Trewhella, a captain in the First World War and a wealthy farmer.

Restronguet Barton Since 1922

Captain Edward Trewhella bought Restronguet Farm from the Tremaynes in October 1920. Captain Trewhella came from St Ives and had been a pupil of Michael Holman, the long-standing tenant. He outbid Mr Holman for the purchase of the farm, despite the many improvements Holman had made there. Trewhella was a gentleman farmer and farmed Restronguet until he died. His widow sold up in 1957, at which time seven farm workers were employed. His brother, Bernard Trewhella, stayed in one of the cottages until his death at age 102.

In 1957 Dudley Dale and family bought the farm, having farmed previously at Tremough, Penryn. Restronguet is a mixed arable and livestock farm, of 364 acres, run by the family with few outside workers. It remains in the family today, Dudley being succeeded by his son Oliver and his grandsons, Matthew and Paul.

In the 1960s, with government encouragement of food from our own resources, they concentrated on pigs and corn, with barley as the chief crop, selling it to the Cornwall Farmers in Penryn for cattle food. This was the time of barley beef. They then decided to expand their dairy herd and to increase their milk production. With a large dairy herd they used more of their land as pasture. At one time, they also kept a flock of sheep and lambs, despite difficulties with dogs chasing sheep. However in 1999 they decided to give up dairy cattle, following the fall in the price of milk, the closure of the Milk Marketing Board and the difficulties of quotas. They were not alone in being driven out of dairy farming by political events.

The Dales have since reverted to arable crops and keep no livestock of their own. The farm is very good arable land and they are able to grow wheat, barley, fodder rape, silage, potatoes and vegetables.

Matthew and Paul Dale are now working the farm as an arable unit themselves. They have environmental concerns and take an active part in the Farming and

Wildlife Advisory Group. Some of their land is in stewardship, giving increased access to the public, and following strict guidelines for extensive farming.

Restronguet Weir

Res (a valley), Tron (a nose or promontory), Gas or Guys (deep or wood) – hence: 'A valley with a deep or woody promontory'.

Little is known of the prehistoric period of Restronguet, although barrows and burial mounds are numerous in the area. It is for this reason that the prefix 'Crock' or 'Crug', as in 'Crocknagodna' and 'Cruglew' (Carclew) occurs in the Restronguet area, as crug or crock, like cromlech, means 'burial mound'. The barrow at Crocknagodna has disappeared with extensive ploughing and farming in the last few hundred years, but was probably on the top of the hill as that was the usual burial place. As far as is known, the barrows in the Restronguet area have not been opened or explored, but they are thought to be late-Bronze Age and were probably burial places of important people.

It is also thought that a Cornish cross, or a menhir converted to a cross, existed at Restronguet; one of the fields at Restronguet Barton is still called Parc-an-Grouse, 'or field of the cross'. Most of these crosses were of pagan origin, about 3–4,000BC, and thought to be connected with phallic worship. Various old maps and charts of the Fal estuary are of interest, particularly perhaps the one made by Baptista Boazio in 1597, the original of which is in the Ministry of Defence. This shows the village of Restronguet comprising a number of houses.

An ancient cattle road, the signs of which still exist, linked the site of the present Restronguet Barton to a rope ferry across Mylor Creek for the transportation of animals to Flushing and Penryn, as it was the shortest route to Penryn. Crossing the animals in salty water would also remove some of the pests from their skins. A traveller making his way to slake his thirst at the Pandora creekside inn, may well catch his breath as he crests the hill at Crownick Farm. Looking over a gate at the turn in the road, he will see before him a very fine view of the creek and the countryside. Across the water lies the parish of St Feock, and between the two parishes a ferry plied for hundreds of years carrying travellers. There were two destinations on the south shore: one to Weir Beach and the other to the Pandora Inn. Very occasionally the ferry came into Bass Rock.

One may speculate upon the variety of those who journeyed this way; such as church dignitaries, monks and pilgrims making for Glasney College at Penryn which was, before the Reformation, the most important collegiate church in the South West and famous throughout the Christian world. They included families of naval officers resident in Flushing during the Napoleonic Wars and those of the commanders of the Packet Services stationed at Falmouth.

Sadly, most of the original records of Restronguet have been lost or were destroyed in the great fire which demolished Carclew House in 1934. It is only by references to Restronguet in published works or histories that any general account of the district in early days can be made. Dr Olivey in *The Parish of Mylor* published much of the original work on the history of Mylor, including Restronguet, in 1907; sadly it is now out of print and copies are becoming rare. Later there were some *Notes on Mylor* by Major Baird, which are held in the Royal Institution of Cornwall.

Mining

Weir Beach marks the entrance to the most extensive and once most intensely industrialised creek on the estuary. Restronguet Creek was tidal as far as Bissoe, and in bygone days was a loading-stage for tin. The Carnon Valley was one of the richest valleys and tin streaming was an early method of tin production. Tin and small nuggets of gold were found, as well as antler picks, wooden spades, deer bones, horns, logs of bog oak and a bronze axehead.

Before 1800, the tin deposits were worked by embanking areas to protect the workings from flooding, navigation being restricted to narrow channels. Sir William Lemon made a grant in 1796 to search for tin, copper and other minerals throughout the adjacent Restronguet Downs. In the mid-eighteenth century a port was opened up for the deep mining development at Gwennap. Four miles away, Perran Wharf was built and for a while it bustled, unloading Norwegian timber, coal, and other supplies and replacing them with cargoes of copper and tin.

In the nineteenth century Devoran could cater for ships of 300 tons. In the 1820s the first underwater mine in the area was sunk from islands which were then in the centre of Restronguet Creek. By 1835, a second mine had been opened, then a final one in the early 1870s.

Norwegian ships brought timber for the Gwennap mines into Restronguet Pool, where they anchored. There the cargoes were discharged and the timber rafted up the creek at high water, or left in an old timber pond, just upstream from the Pandora, to season and wash out the sap. An extract from the *West Briton* of 7 June 1811 recorded:

A Norwegian at Restronguet Passage ran away from his master, Captain Bendh Salveson, of the ship Hope, *now lying at Restronguet Passage, near Truro, his apprentice, Johannes Tollisen, a Norwegian, about 14 years of age, 4 feet 9 inches in height, brown eyes, can speak little English, and wore, when he left on Wednesday morning last, a blue jacket and trousers. Whoever will bring the above lad to Captain Salveson, at the Queen's Head Inn, Truro, shall receive a guinea reward. And whoever harbours or employs the said boy after this notice will be prosecuted.*

The remains of the old 'horse round' at Restronguet Farm which was used to grind corn for the Carclew estate farms in the nineteenth century.

This photo shows a similar 'horse round' in working order.

Kibben Cottage was the original Restronguet Farmhouse and is now the Dale family farmhouse. It is pictured here in c.1960. It no longer has a thatched roof.

Restronguet Farmhouse was sold with three acres by auction in 2002.

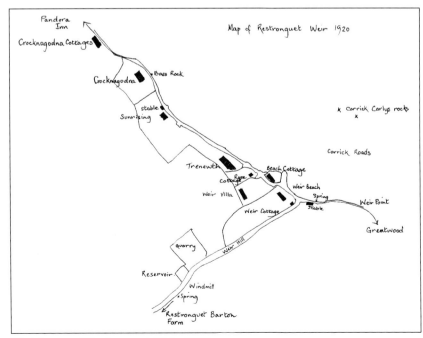

Sketch map of Restronguet Weir, 1920.

The slump in mining during the last quarter of the nineteenth century obviously took its toll, and the amount of commercial shipping gradually decreased. The barges, as the local trading sloops were called, sailed the waters of the Fal carrying coal, lime, sand, timber, local produce and stone from Porthoustock on the Lizard. They beached their flat bottoms on the mud and their cargo was manhandled ashore. Old men have mentioned boats trailing a heavy chain astern of a shallow sailing barge to stir up the silt, and a powerful tug, the *Pendennis*, was fitted with mud rakes to churn up the bottom of the creek on an ebb tide. Heavy silting caused larger vessels to anchor and the cargo was unloaded into barges, which were towed or poled to their destination. Two local steamers, the *Erimus* and the *Trefusis,* carried coal to Devoran. Sometimes it had to be unloaded at Restronguet.

Often, empty barges would dry out just off Weir Beach and sometimes they would lie on their sides and wait for the grain wagons to descend from Restronguet Barton Farm. The Chamberlin children would hear the cart-horses coming down the hill and they would rush out and enjoy washing the horses' hooves, and then the ecstasy of hanging onto the wagon as it trudged back up the hill to the farm.

The barge *Mary* used to anchor off Trenewth at Weir. Some of the crew would keep bicycles on board so they could cycle home if the vessel was stranded for the weekend. The local children used to dive off her.

Polwhele wrote in 1830 that 'mast money was a fixed payment of one shilling per mast as a due from every vessel passing the poles on the Carrick Carlys rocks.' The Rees family put the poles there and dues continued to their descendants. There was also a Rees family who ran the forge in Mylor just above the bridge. Amongst the general work of a blacksmith iron dredges were fashioned, and tailor-made for each oyster fisherman.

Restronguet is now a muddy if picturesque creek, due to the natural process of deposition accelerated by the mining of heavy metals such as arsenic, copper, zinc, iron, lead and cadmium. The only large vessels seen from Weir today are the ships being piloted up Carrick Roads to be laid up in the Fal at Tolverne.

Since 1950 further mining surveys of the creek have been made – a small mining company was operating up the Carnon Valley, and one of the largest and most up-to-date mines in 1970 was opened at Wheal Jane, the drainage from which also flows into the creek. Sadly Wheal Jane has since closed. In 1992, a pollution incident turned the creek reddish brown. It was not just Wheal Jane Mine itself that caused the trouble, for at least 50 abandoned mines are within the catchment area of the Carnon River, and the County Adit brings into it a flow of mine water from much further away.

The creek changed colour as millions of gallons of acidic water heavily contaminated with metals, including cadmium, poured in. Kim Stephens, who

Restronguet Point, c.1910.

owned Weir Beach, spent an hour turning over stones and seaweed to check for signs of life – there was none. He was on Restronguet Creek Society committee whose object is to safeguard the beauty and public amenity value of the creek by making representations to appropriate public authorities, industrial organisations and individuals, to ensure that the creek is not endangered. The society has now started 'Boatcheck'. Boat watchers alert owners to potential and actual casualties in the creek. In 1994, bodies of dead swans found in the Fal were subjected to autopsies, which revealed excessive levels of lead and zinc in the tissues and severe deterioration of specific glands.

In June 1997, the Port of Falmouth and Truro Health Officer, Andy Hopson, said there were algae in the Fal and he was worried that the toxins, which are produced by the algae, would get into the food-chain. Fishermen were advised to refrain from harvesting shellfish. On 20 November 1997, a non-toxic red dye was tipped into the Fal estuary by the Environment Agency. A survey was being carried out by Lyndhurst Oceanographics as part of ongoing work at the disused Wheal Jane Mine. Scientists were recording the movement of the dye within the water and its dispersion. Again, in July 1999, toxic algae were spotted.

Twice a year for the last four years Pamela Thompsett, a marine biologist, has checked the peacock-worm tubes at spring low tides on Weir Beach. Her last visit in 2002 showed plenty of tubes, thus proving the water was cleaner. In December 2002 and April 2003 two senior scientists from Plymouth University studied the tidal flow and water quality in the pool off the Pandora.

The existence of a fishing weir of unknown date at the entrance to Restronguet Creek is indicated by the names Restronguet Weir, Weir Meadows and Weir Point. Between October and the end of March, oyster boats can often be seen working off Weir. Since 1870, at least 210 oyster dredgers (working boats) have been involved in the industry, and 43 of the 111 boats for which the place of construction is known were built around the estuary. One has to admire this hardy breed, who are out in all weathers.

View down Restronguet Creek.
(BY KIND PERMISSION OF ANDREW CAMPBELL)

Punt used for oyster dredging, 1980s.

In the 1960s, Mary Prideaux, from one of the Greatwood cottages, spent several years fishing for oysters. She said:

Once they realised I pulled my weight and could do practically any job a man could do and didn't chicken out when the weather turned bad, the men were very helpful.

Many an amateur or professional artist has enjoyed painting the working boats scene. Shrimping was always great fun in the height of summer for the Stephens' children. The fruits of their labour were eaten for tea but there was one big problem – you had to peel your own shrimps! The shrimps started to disappear off Weir Point in the early 1980s. Another joy was to put out a net off Weir Point at about 9p.m. and then get up early at 5a.m. to discover what was caught. There were drawbacks, as you had to clean the

net afterwards and learn to gut the fish. Nancy Chamberlin taught her grandchildren a lot about sea life, searching for crabs, eels and lobsters and even using a seine-net with a group of friends.

Restronguet Sailing Club was founded in 1933 with the object of encouraging sailing and especially helping beginners. Prominent among the group of friends who founded the club were Major and Mrs Dorrien-Smith, the Chamberlins, Hilda Parker, Charles Stephens, the Vesseys and Mr Watson. Major Dorrien-Smith was elected the first Commodore and six boats comprised the entire fleet. The racing was organised on Saturdays as often as possible. The first regatta was in 1935 when a programme was arranged for seven classes and in the following year the regatta became part of Falmouth Fortnight. The club's activities ceased on the outbreak of war.

Weir Beach, Restronguet, 1959. Weir Cottage on the left was at one time the clubhouse for Restronguet Sailing Club. The cottage was later demolished and replaced with a new house.

In 1946, sailing was resumed from Weir Cottage, which belonged to the Chamberlins. The club grew rapidly, eventually making it necessary to move to the present premises at Mylor in 1962. We have had successful sailors who lived at Weir. Ben Ainslie was the World Youth Laser Champion in 1995. He won a silver medal in the 1996 Olympic Games and then went on to win gold in 2000 and 2004. In 2002, he won the World Finn Championship. Kim Stephens won the European Tornado title in 1975 and the European Dart Championship in 1982. Charles Stephens won the European Stampede Championship in 1984.

Life at Weir, 1900–27

Nancy Chamberlin (1905–89) lived at Weir all her life and draws a picture of her childhood in a tape-recorded conversation on 4 August 1988:

The Chamberlins, Smyths, Stephens and the Vesseys were all related and lived in nine of the houses down at Restronguet Weir. Our home, Trenewth, was originally a two-up and two-down cottage. Gradually extensions were made by my father (Henry Chamberlin) who added

Harry Smyth and his car at Weir, 1920s.

The Chamberlins on Weir Beach in 1902. Left to right: John, Aunt Dora, the children's nurse, Hugh.

two wings and a boat-house. The family stables and harness room were in Weir field. Later a garage was built for the car just opposite the stables at the bottom of the hill. The well was just behind Trenewth with the gas gallows. Don't forget that Trenewth was just one family house in my early days and father had all the land as far as Crocknagodna, where in fact my great-uncle and aunt Smyth lived. Behind the beach at Weir, we had the old cottage with greenhouses plus the vine and an orchard. The gardener lived there and with help from a boy provided the family with fruit and vegetables for the whole year. My father gave his sisters the land where Sunrising lies today.

We had a playroom upstairs at Trenewth, but we spent most of our time outside playing on the beach, or around the boat-house, and in the field behind. I knew every tree up in the Holman's field. The Pauls of Goonvrea (their father was our family solicitor), the children from Tullimar, and the Enys children would come and play, we would make tremendous camps down in the bushes and trees by the boat-house and hide-and-seek was always a great thrill. Bridget Tremayne and her brother from Carclew used to come over occasionally by pony and trap. They were a bit wild. One day Father found them riding Rosie, our pony, with no clothes on, another time he discovered them half walking, half swimming out to the poles at low tide. Mother used to play tennis at Carclew. She obviously was quite good for she won the Cornish Championships. We had an old tennis-court with a changing room, and a croquet lawn near the Restronguet Yacht Basin. The family often had picnics as far away as the Land's End or the Lizard. My parents went to lots of wonderful parties and dances at Carclew, particularly when the Navy came into the dockyard. Mother was a very keen member of the Women's Institute.

Regatta day was great excitement, all the flags were up. There was a special race for two men. One would row both of them from the Pandora to Weir Beach and the other on arrival at the beach had to run up Weir Hill and along the top road and down Restronguet Passage Hill. Meanwhile, the rower had to return and pick up his partner then row him out to the *Queen of the Fal*, which was often the Committee boat. The Chamberlin children had boats before they were ten, a praam, a

dinghy and the 16-foot motor boat that was used for outings. The family had a mooring just off the Prince of Wales Pier, so shopping in summer was quite easy for there were always little boys around who would look after the boat. They thought they were made if you gave them two pennies. Father would go to the Royal Cornwall Yacht Club and read his newspaper and gossip. When we got a car, he left it at Janes' Garage at the top of the High Street in Falmouth, just above the Old Curiosity Shop.

Father was very particular about going to church on Sundays. There were six of us children in all, four boys and two girls. We would all walk down to Wood Quay (Greatwood) in our Sunday best, and Father would row around, and then row us across Mylor Creek. I loathed dressing up and I was made to wear my straw hat with flowers. I would refuse to wear my laced-up boots. Sometimes, it was white sailor suits. The boys wore herringbone tweeds. We would enter through the side chapel door that creaked. It is now no longer in use. The Tremaynes always sat in the front pew, they came by carriage. The next pew was for the Trefusis family, and then came the Chamberlins. I used to bang my head on the angel, as there wasn't quite enough room for all of us.

Our early days we all had governesses, later the brothers boarded at Miss Crawford's Preparatory School in Falmouth and then Guy went on to Cheltenham and Sandhurst and Hugh to Repton and Cranwell, I can't remember what happened to the others. I was a weekly boarder at Truro High School. Father used to travel to Canada each year for a month or so to check on his building plots in one of the main streets in Vancouver. He took his old leather trunks on the train to London then off by ship to America. He used to send us postcards from the Rockies.

Weir Hill used to be stony with plenty of springs. There was an old man who sat on a bench by the cross. He had a sack around his waist and he would place stones between his knees and crack the stones with a tiny hammer. These stones were used on the roads around Restronguet Barton Farm. The roads, hedgerows and the ditches were always well maintained.

Descending Weir Hill there was a reservoir on the left-hand side that had a little moaning water-wheel pumping water up to the farm. The reservoir was *cleaned out every so often and one could find eels at least two feet long. The windmill was on the opposite side of the road and also pumped water to the farm. There are three wells, two on the hill and one on the beach, but sadly they have deteriorated over the years through lack of use. Mrs Knuckey, who was the housekeeper on the Holman's farm, used to bring the cream down to the first well to cool and thicken. The beach well, built up to prevent it being flooded with seawater, was used as late as the 1950s. Sewage came out from all the houses and went into the sea, but it never stopped us from bathing. Years ago, quarrying took place below the reservoir and in two places in Weir Orchard's garden.*

The saddest family occasions were the wartime telegrams arriving with the dreaded news. All my brothers were killed in action. Then Denys died out in the Gold Coast. (Denys Stephens was Nancy's first husband.) The Dorrien-Smiths at Greatwood lost two of their sons.

The size of Trenewth and the old cottage garden, plus one small son, just became too much for me to look after, so I sold Trenewth to Mr Norris, the 'Rum King'. He also bought Crocknagodna and Sunrising houses. In my youth all the other cottages were either owned by ex-Navy, or fishermen except Beach Cottage, which is probably the oldest. Count Leo Thun lived there with his housekeeper. He got extremely worried during the First World War because some people thought he was a spy.

Part of an old newspaper cutting records:

An inquiry was held yesterday by Mr E.L. Carlyon, county coroner, into the circumstances attending the death of Catherine Tallack, aged 55, single, housekeeper at Weir, Restronguet, the residence of Baron Leo Thun. The Baron had gone to Austria, and given the deceased notice to leave. That seemed to have depressed her. On Tuesday Mr Hugh Chamberlin sought for the deceased, whom he had not seen since Sunday, and found her hanging by a rope in the back kitchen quite dead.

A taped conversation with Phyllis Nichols (born in 1905) on 8 October 1987, records:

I came to help at Trenewth in 1921 and stayed for five years. There were five of us maids. My job was to rise at seven, and in wintertime I had to clean the grates and make the beds, use the carpet sweeper, mop, dust, and clean the floors. I was supposed to use the kneelers, but I never used them. No wonder my knees are so bad! Fanny Thomas used to come in and beat the carpets in the back field behind Trenewth. All the maids would be upstairs waving out of the windows when the oyster boats sailed out of the creek. Miss Fisher from Delta Cottage came in daily and cooked the breakfast and main meal. Old Bill Harris would bring in some lovely fish. You don't taste fish like it today.

Mr Richards who came from Penryn used a horse-drawn covered cart for our deliveries. On one occasion,

Mabel ordered a quarter pound of saffron for a cake and Mrs Chamberlin had to come down and sort it out. Mr Tripp, the baker, also came from Penryn, but unfortunately he would arrive just as we were going to bed. Rollason, the butcher, came from Mylor. Albert Blackler who worked on Mr Michael Henry Holman's farm (Restronguet Barton) brought the milk round in cans. Trenewth had a big old Cornish range; oh! I used to polish 'ee. When Annear's coal lorry came, the coal had to be brought through the back passage causing tremendous dirt and dust for the maids to clear up. I was never allowed to feather dust the lovely objects on the mantelpiece or in the great display cabinet in the drawing-room.

Mrs Chamberlin spoke French, and she enjoyed talking to the Breton onion men. They cycled out from Penryn with two long strings of onions thrown over their handlebars. Trenewth owned two parrots; one was Australian and the other African. There was an aviary at the back of Trenewth for many of the family's foreign birds. My aunt remembers a boy who collected grass seeds for the budgerigars. I can remember the geese that occasionally chased people.

Nancy continued:

I remember Mr Moore wearing his straw boater and big white apron. He had the general store next to Ash Villa. He was fond of his drink and unfortunately one day he fell head-first into the great flour bin. When Mr Moore retired, Mr Williams took over, later followed by his son, Escott. I do remember the high old-fashioned counters in the two Miss Frosts' shop. They ran a general grocery plus haberdashery. Rosie, our donkey, would refuse to leave the shop until she'd been given a treat. Then there was a carpenter's shop. He built the far wing at Trenewth. Of course the Rees family ran the blacksmiths.

Phyllis remembered: 'They had about 15 children.' Nancy commented:

I can remember the children crawling over the street with no shoes and trousers on. The leat nearby was a great attraction to the local children especially when it was tadpole season. Do you remember the postman, Sammy Harris? One day he made his usual stop at the Lemon Arms but stayed longer than usual. No one received their letters that day. A paper chase was later found in the fields on the way to Greatwood.

Becky Bunny was born in 1908. Her maiden name was Rawling. The following extract is taken from a tape she recorded in 1993:

When we were living in the middle cottage at Greatwood, my father carried a two-handled basket once a week to collect all the maids' white caps and frilly aprons and cook's big aprons from Trenewth for Mother to wash. She would use a gophering iron, heating it over a methylated stove and wiping it clean before she ironed. She did it for a good many years. Mrs Chamberlin would call on the poorer families in the village and often she would come to our cottage with a basket of cakes. We were brought up to respect the Chamberlins.

The fun we had at the Pandora when it was regatta day. Mother took all we little children along with a bun each or a cake in a box. There were three or four tiny stalls selling bouncy balls full of sawdust, sticks of sweets, and teasers. Old man Turtree had tubes of teasers that he filled up with water. We would squirt them at the boys, and then throw confetti so it would stick. You could play hoopla and then there was always the greasy pole off the end of Jack Ferris' quay. There was usually a local band on a barge.

The Blacklers used to do jobbing around the village. They would kill people's pigs. The belly skins used to be washed in the pond and then stuffed with mince beef, herbs and onion then placed in a great dish with potatoes around the dish. When it was nearly ready suet pastry was placed on top and the gravy would come up.

Frank Cock's taped conversation, 2 February 1994, is as follows:

I came here to Restronguet in 1919 and went to Truro School. I would row across each day and pick up my push-bike and cycle into Truro. I started oyster fishing in 1921, but my father wanted me to learn a trade so I served a five-year apprenticeship with Cox and Co. at the docks in Falmouth, but I later went back to oystering. When Morning Star *was bought from Harris there were big gaps between the planks, and all the decks were gone. It was ready for the scrap yard, but Harry Barnes and I bought it for £250. On one occasion it was blowing fresh and raining so Harry got under the tarpaulin. 'What time is it Harry?' I asked. 'Half past ten' came the reply. 'How's that you'd never looked at your watch?' 'Oh! I can see the old mail van down at Mylor Dockyard out through the seams here.' In those days we did five or six drifts a day, and we also had to bail out 60 buckets of water.*

In summer I took people out to Looe, Polperro, Fowey and Mevagissey in my boat Primex. *Harry's boat was called* Y Not. *I remember the porpoises snorting as they swam up the creek in rough easterly winds. We rarely see them now. You would see rowing-boats on their way to the gardens at Point so full of seaweed. My mother, who was a Vinnicombe, remembered seeing seven large sailing vessels moored in Restronguet Gut. Now if you climb the rocks under Trenewth to Crocknagodna you will find the remains of metal stakes that had big ring bolts – these were used for tying up the boats. On one occasion on a high spring tide, Andy Campbell, when he was at the Pandora, asked me to bring along my fishing rod and sit in the lower room and fish – the water came up to my knees. The hatch was open and I could see barrels of beer floating around. I have seen mackerel flapping and jumping around on the mud. I have no idea what drove them in, perhaps a seal.*

Pixie Wells' Reminiscences

I was born at Restronguet many years ago. When I was small, the inn only had a beer licence (a spirit licence was bought about 1934). The clientele then were local people: sailors, fishermen and farm workers. Sometimes they had a singsong outside after closing time. The fishermen dredged oysters from October to April (9a.m. to 3p.m.) and kept their boats in the pool – that is a deep-water area of the creek. When a gale got up from the south, all the boats would be moved to shelter under the east side of the creek. The oysters were taken to the Helford River to be washed because there were too many minerals in the Restronguet Creek and a lot of tin. The silt that comes downstream makes the sand red. This extends further each year and the creek dries up at low tide as far as the Pandora Inn. Up to 1939, the creek was dredged and enough tin washed out to be viable.

My brother and I had a variety of boats as children and we used to be told off by the fishermen if we did anything wrong! At least they kept an eye on us. Nowadays, no one bothers so no child is allowed on the water without a life-jacket. We also had bicycles, which we rode along the footpath to Weir – about eight of us in line. Luckily, not many people walked along there in those days.

Restronguet Hill is steep, 1 in 4½, and was rough stoned until 1947/8 when it was tarred. There is a spring in the old orchard of the bottom house on the right-hand side, which provided the water to all the houses as far as Weir Beach. Mains water was laid on in about 1965 and nearly all the houses have it now. Just upstream from the Pandora Inn is an old timber pond: a semi-circle of poles between which the pit props were put to season.

When Captain Tremayne, who at one time owned Restronguet Farm, was alive, he drove his pony and trap from Greatwood to Carclew along the footpath and woe betide anyone who blocked his path. Our house next to the Pandora was also a shop which had a balk of timber as a step. He regularly threw this over the wall onto the beach as it interfered with his trap wheel. This was before the great Carclew sale of 1920 when all the cottages and holdings were sold, many to sitting tenants.

The Pandora Inn

H.L. Douch wrote in his book *Old Cornish Inns* that without question, the Cornish inns most strategically placed were those by bridges and ferries. There were Ferry House, or Passage House inns on all the estuaries of the Fal. The Pandora stands on the Restronguet Creek in the parish of Mylor. From there, a ferry operated from the thirteenth century – the first, it is said, in the area.

When Edward the Confessor founded a Benedictine monastery on St Michael's Mount, it was so important that it became an object of pilgrimage. Another was in Penryn. Glasney College was founded in 1265 and was to become a great ecclesiastical centre of church life in

Aileen and Hugh Chamberlin with their daughter Nancy in their dark green 15hp Star, first registered 26 April 1909. It is seen here in 1911.

Rosie the donkey with Nancy Chamberlin and her nurse, 1907.

The start of the Pandora Race, 1980s.

(BY KIND PERMISSION OF ANDREW CAMPBELL)

The Pandora Inn, pictured here in the 1930s.

Cornwall. The estuaries of the Fal were a major difficulty for pilgrims and those travelling on horseback or on foot to these destinations. The Passage House service at Mylor was let out and operated by an innkeeper at a rent of 8s.4d. a year in 1468. Primitive refreshment and fresh horses would be available.

So monks would come in singing procession with others to Feock and cross the creek by rowing ferry, summoned by a bell. They would continue to Venton Vean on the banks of Mylor Creek with a further rowing ferry to Trelew, which was not far from Flushing, where a third ferry would carry them to Penny Farthing House on the site of the present Greenbank Hotel in Falmouth. Glasney College was in nearby Penryn; St Michael's Mount more distant. Another pilgrim route was to St James de Compostella in Spain. Falmouth skippers had the right to transport pilgrims to and from Corunna.

From parish records, we learn that the Restronguet crossing was from 1250 the postboy route and from 1468 a pack route existed via Passage Hill to and from Penryn. Tonkin, the historian, wrote in 1730, 'There is a passing boat kept here, it being the post road and much the nearest cut from Falmouth to Truro and the East... .'

Between 1789 and 1912 there were 12 deeds regarding the passage tenement and the inn. In 1791, the *Exeter Flying Post* reported:

In September, the passing boat was crossing with several passengers and three horses aboard. In midstream, one of the horses took fright, the boat upset and three persons, including Miss Pellow of Penryn, were drowned.

Two years earlier a fisherman named Thomas Harvey took a lease of:

... a cottage... called the Passage House adjoining the Beach at Restronguet Passage together with the stable

and pig's house at one end of the dwelling house... also of that ferry... together with two Boats, Ores, Ropes, Grapples and Materials thereto belonging and the liberty of passing and repassing to the opposite shore...

In 1920, several oystermen and the licensee were fined for keeping late hours and five years later, John Ferris, innkeeper, was fined for illegal Christmas Eve hours and the inn not being well kept. Until 1920, the Pandora was owned by the Tremayne estate, and was a beerhouse only until 1936. It was open six days a week. The building was one room deep until 1935, but many additions have been made over the years.

How did the ancient Passage House eventually become known as the Pandora? The long-accepted opinion was that a Captain Edwards was sent in 1790 to capture the mutineers from HMS *Bounty*. He was in command of the 24-gun frigate *Pandora*. On the return journey, the ship was wrecked on the Great Barrier Reef, Captain Edwards was court-martialled and dismissed from the service. He retired to Cornwall, bought the inn – at that time known as the Ship – and renamed it after his last command. However, this story is disputed by a former owner of the inn, Mr Andrew Campbell. He believes that Captain Edwards was court-martialled but acquitted, becoming an active Flag Officer when war broke out with France in 1793. On his death in 1815, he was ranked 48th most senior officer in the Royal Navy.

Mr Campbell further discovered that a Packet Brig *Pandora* was built in 1833 – one of the six last packet ships to operate. Furthermore, a wooden board which had been removed from over the front door of the inn was examined by Mr Campbell and bore a picture of a packet ship.

Today, this distinctively-thatched hostelry – one of Cornwall's best known – continues to flourish in the beautiful setting of Restronguet Creek.

A drawing of the Pandora as it was in 1900. It was drawn by Joan West in the 1980s.

A painting of the Pandora by M.J. Cockell to illustrate how it appeared during the twentieth century.

Chapter 8

Churches and Chapels

The Coming of St Mylor, St Mylor Parish Church, The Churchyard, A Previous Vicar,
All Saints Church, The Methodist Church, The Bible Christians.

The Coming of St Mylor

Christianity was brought in through the close relationship between Cornish Celt and Roman. Cornwall formed ties with the Celtic brethren in Wales, Ireland and Brittany. Among the travellers of the fifth and sixth centuries were missionaries coming to reinforce the faith – one from Brittany was St Milor. These saints were not canonised but missionaries who, with holy zeal, spread the word of God to pagans for whom fear and superstition were part of life.

Drawing of the north side of the church, by Jack Holt.

The saint would have attracted the populace by means of a bronze handbell. Canon Miles Brown, in his book *The Church in Cornwall,* gives us a picture of him 'clad in a white tunic with a rough coat of fur'. To us, his appearance would be grotesque by reason of the Celtic tonsure, the head shaved in front of a line from ear to ear, the hair hanging down behind. He would also have had a long beard. It is believed that St Mylor was martyred in 411.

Who was this saint who gave Mylor its name? Canon Doble, an authority on Cornish church history, wrote: 'The truth is that the Melor honoured at Mylor... was... a pan-Celtic Abbot-Bishop, who is also honoured at Trémeloir in Brittany.'

The area of the churchyard has been associated with burial from pagan times and nearby are fields known as 'cregoes', which is Cornish for 'barrows' or 'burial places'. Together they cover over 50 acres of Trefusis headland. We cannot be certain what happened here as there was no documentary evidence until the thirteenth century, but the site, place-name and dedication to a Celtic saint suggest a very early origin. Permission having been given by a local ruler for the founding of the community, land would be allocated with a portion for a cemetery. Our churchyard is large and reflects the importance of the site.

Mylor became a Christian settlement because the sea was Cornwall's highway. It has a sheltered harbour, accessible yet hidden from sea-borne marauders, and swamps made beaching easy. A supply of water would be needed for the saint, for a growing community and also for the baptising of the newly-converted. Mylor Churchtown has many springs.

St Mylor Parish Church

In this county of beautiful country churches there can be few to compare with St Mylor. The approach road descends between hedgerows colourful with wild flowers in their season, such as primroses, violets, bluebells, cranesbill, Queen Anne's Lace and, occasionally, the purple-spotted orchid. To the left of the lych-gate, the road plunges steeply to a breath-taking view of the busy harbour. But we walk through the gate and take the churchyard path which leads round to the right of the church, where the cross of St Mylor stands outside the south porch.

Cornish cross outside the south porch of St Mylor Church.

When the Normans came in 1066, they carried out far-reaching reforms. It was a time of rigorous rebuilding and, according to Henderson's *Cornish Church Guide*, St Mylor is one of 135 of the 220 Parish Churches in the county with some original Norman stonework. About one in three Celtic holy sites became new Christian centres.

In the early days three Celtic princes endowed the church with land. Included was the manor of Treliever, which was in turn presented to the Bishop of Exeter. The area comprised Mabe, Mawnan, Budock, Mylor and Gluvias. These special parishes were known as Bishop's Peculiars, in which his own official performed the functions carried out by the Archdeacon elsewhere. Therefore, questions of probate, divorce, slander, immorality, church rates and so on, were directed to Exeter rather than Bodmin, the Archdeacon's seat. Thus it was that many ancient papers, such as household inventories, so valuable to historians and students, were destroyed in the Blitz on Exeter in the Second World War.

In 1308, St Mylor Church was rededicated and made parochial. A priest, Sir Simon de Tralees, was instituted vicar, with a messuage, a dwelling-house with outbuildings and ten acres of land, all altarage (the fund to maintain the priest) and small tithes and tithes of hay, the fishing mortuaries and the garb tithes of Cregoes, which is the area adjacent to the vicar's land.

In the sixteenth century, a notable addition to the south porch was an elaborately carved outer arch of Caen stone which, together with the Trefusis Chapel window tracery, has been confirmed as coming from Glasney Collegiate Church in Penryn, dismantled during the dissolution of the monasteries.

Other rebuilding periods were: the thirteenth century (1260 to 1320); a fifteenth-century enlargement; the great restoration of 1870 and a complete re-roofing in 1900. In 1869, it was discovered that the walls were very dilapidated, especially the south one, which was held up by a massive granite monolith discovered to be the ancient churchyard cross with its head buried in the ground and used as a buttress. It was dug out and re-erected in the traditional position near the south porch. In the great restoration, several coats of whitewash were removed from the interior walls and damaged frescoes were revealed.

Near the Norman doorway on the north wall was pictured a right arm in black and grey, holding a white staff. Close to the Carclew arch was a woman in a red garment, her hair in a fitted cap with curls escaping. Also near the north door were several long-skirted figures on a yellow ground with lines of black and red, although the lowered roof line had removed their heads. There were several inscribed ribbon scrolls of church text overlaying more figures and a church tower in black on white. On the south wall was a similar scroll with the date 1638. At that time, Thomas Peter was the puritan vicar of Mylor. His gravestone is the oldest in the churchyard.

A squint was opened in the wall between the south chancel aisle and the sanctuary in the fifteenth century, with a flat stone base used as a credence, a small side-table used for Eucharistic elements before consecration. Underneath can be seen the ancient pillar piscine, a perforated stone basin for draining the water used for rinsing the chalice after Holy Communion. It is said that this was unearthed in removing the foundation of the Old Vicarage House.

Some portions of the fifteenth-century rood-screen, retaining the original colouring, were pieced together and replaced as nearly as possible in their former position. On the panels are the words, possibly in Cornish, *'Iarys Ionai Iesw Crest'*. This is probably 'Mary, John, Jesus Christ', referring to the original rood.

The three bells in the detached bell tower were recast in 1888. No. 1 is medieval and retains the legend *'In honore Santi Georgii'*; No. 2 is dated 1637 and bears the legend *'Ergo me preco se clamando conterimus audite venite'* (I and the town crier both wear ourselves out by clamouring harken and come); No. 3 has the date 1664. The small bell in the church tower is dated 1767.

On entering the porch, you see the holy water stoup and ancient parish stocks. For a first impression of the church interior, let us take a look at entries in the visitors' book from June 2003:

A visitor from Guernsey: 'So beautiful, so spiritual!'
From London: 'A place of peace and hope.'
From Shrewsbury: 'Walked in and gasped. Oh, it is so beautiful!'

Although the present church is mainly fifteenth century, substantial parts are of twelfth century Norman building. Hanging above the entrance is a representation of the Royal Arms of the Stuart sovereigns and a copy of a letter from King Charles I, thanking the Cornish people for their loyalty in defending his rights. Dated 10 September 1643, it was sent from his camp in Sudeley Castle.

The lower part of the north wall is Norman and a carefully preserved doorway has an ancient method of fastening consisting of a heavy wooden bar sliding into holes cut deeply into the walls.

The pulpit is a charming piece of wood carving from the time of Queen Elizabeth I and the diamond-shaped hatchment (i.e. deceased armorial bearings) is of the Tremayne family of Carclew. Another hangs on the south wall and is of the Trefusis family.

Both church and churchyard are dominated by the sea. A screen between the chancel and Trefusis Chapel was erected in memory of the 31 men, women and children lost at sea in the motor vessel *Darlwyne* on a pleasure cruise from Mylor on 31 July 1966. Further tragedies are recorded on tablets on the walls of the church. There is Edmund Yescombe, commander of the *King George* Lisbon Packet who lost his life bravely defending his ship against the enemy in 1803. Then

This illustration of 'Mylor Old Church – South Porch' reproduces a pencil drawing of unknown origin and shows the church before the 1870 restoration. The famed cross is shown head downwards, supporting the bulging south wall. The sturdy figure to the right is Mr Boucaut, a Guernsey man who occupied a cottage to the north side of the church.

Two of the seventeenth-century frescoes discovered during the great restoration of 1870.

Above: *The detached bell tower.*

Left: *Interior of St Mylor Church, east end, 2004.*

there is John Warren, RN, who was in command of the slaver HMS *Ranger,* which he was taking to St Helena in 1862 when he 'caught a fever from the negroes' and died. Another is James Burke, son of Sir Thomas Burke of Galway, Ireland, who came to Cornwall for the benefit of his health – but even the pure air of the Carrick Roads did him no good and he died in 1812, aged 18.

There can be few inscriptions more tragic than that outside the church on the gravestone of a local man, James Thomas, 33, killed by a customs officer who took him for a smuggler as he rowed home from St Mawes in December 1814. The distinguished Cornish writer, A.K. Hamilton Jenkin, avers that the dead man was no smuggler but the victim of an excise man's aggression. He was, in fact, returning from a fishing trip when fired on and fatally wounded.

Officious zeal in luckless hour laid wait
and wilful sent the murderous ball of fate,
James to his home (which late in health he left)
Wounded returns – of life is soon bereft.

The Churchyard

There is a story recorded in the annals of Trefusis which confirms the marshy ground on the seaward side of the church.

Drawing of the church tower, artist unknown. The picture probably dates from the twentieth century.

After a night of cockfighting and gaming, the family came down to Mylor Church by the drive which led over the Cregoes. The huge unwieldy coach with attendant footmen ranged behind suddenly came to a standstill then sank lower and lower in the soft mud till carriage, horses, and all but Trefusis, his family and footmen went out of sight, and there carriage and horses remain!

By the time the tithe map of Mylor was drawn (1840) some drainage work had been done by the Admiralty because, to the north-east of the church a storehouse stood, and two gardens, a wood and an orchard were established. The storehouse was later converted into a dwelling-house, occupied by a Mr Boucaut, whose son was born there and became Sir James Penn Boucaut, a judge of the Supreme Court of Southern Australia. An addition to the churchyard was made in 1845 by the gift of the Admiralty, called Naval Burying Ground for the burial of those who died at sea.

The Boucaut house was vacated in 1866. In that year, the Naval Training Ship HMS *Ganges* moved into St Just Pool with her shore establishment in Mylor Churchtown. Another extension to the churchyard was given by the Admiralty in 1866 and another in 1871.

There follows an account of the rediscovery of the Cornish cross during the restoration of the church in 1870 by Revd J.W. Murray, vicar at the time and reported in *Notes on the Parish of Mylor* by H.P. Olivey:

At the commencement of the restoration, a granite post which had long done duty as a flying buttress against the south wall of the church, had to be removed. On clearing away the earth in which it was deeply embedded, it was discovered to be a ponderous monolith, a granite cross of the 'round-headed' type, 17ft 6ins in length. On each face... is a Greek cross with central boss enclosed within a circular rim... the shaft is ornamented with concentric rings and marginal lines.

It has been suggested that the latter represent the pagan sun symbol and that here we have a 'Christianised stone'.

Leading into the churchyard from the west is the lych-gate, the superstructure of which is in memory of Lady Mary Trefusis and is a gift of the parishioners of Mylor and Flushing.

Lady Mary Lygon became a Woman of the Bedchamber to Queen Mary in 1895 and married Henry Walter Trefusis in 1905. At that time he was serving in the Scots Guards. She continued to undertake her duties for Queen Mary, spending part of her year in London. In Cornwall, Lady Mary became involved in many activities and, in particular, formed the Cornwall music competitions and in collaboration with Cecil Sharp she pioneered the revival of folk-dance competitions. There are many in Mylor who remember her work with village choirs. When she died in 1927, the lych-gate at St Mylor was made into a memorial to her.

Lady Mary Trefusis, who was a lifelong friend of Queen Mary, consort to George V, and a great benefactor to the parish.

The superstructure of the lych-gate was a gift of the parishioners of Mylor and Flushing in memory of Lady Mary Trefusis. It is seen here in 2004.

On either side of the large lych-stone are seats and on the ground a Cornish stepping-stone stile or cattle-grid of granite bars.

In the *Ganges* burial plot is an obelisk erected by the boys of the ship in 1872. The names of 51 dead boys are recorded there with an average age of 16; a sad reminder of the harshness of life under naval training in Victorian times.

It is said that there are few gravestones surviving from before the end of the seventeenth century. In St Mylor churchyard we have a flat slab one of 1654. This marks the remains of a puritan vicar. Below his crest is inscribed 'Thomas Peter, preacher of Mylor above 20 years, died the 57 year of his age in the year 1654.' In his will he wrote 'my body, to be interred over against my study windoe near the brow of the hill near the pathway to the diall.' This ancient sundial, of which only the original pillar remains,

now stands in a different place with a new top and dial plate as a memorial to Howard Spring, the novelist who lived at nearby Hooper's Hill.

The variety of gravestones in the churchyard is very wide, representing every age since Parson Peter. Yet there is little pretension, for the Mylor of the past was largely a parish of farmers and fishermen pleased to use the locally available granite and slate and there was no dearth of stonemasons in the area. Whilst the local stone could be readily worked, it was durable enough to withstand the ferocious storms of winter which brought so many – like the *Queen Transport,* which sank in 1814 with the loss of over 200 lives – to lie here forever.

Among other graves is that of Joseph Crapp, shipwright, who died in 1770 at the age of 45 as a result of an accident and whose inscription reads:

Alafs Friend Joseph His End war Allmost Sudden
As thou the mandate came Exprefs from heaven
his foot it Slip And he did fall
help help he cries & that was all

After the Second World War, Mylor gradually grew in importance as a yachting centre and is now a very busy place. Among those who take a short cut through the churchyard to a day's sailing, there are some who find time to sit awhile to catch a view of sea and sail and to appreciate the peace of this much loved, holy place.

The churchyard well, dressed with flowers by Junior Church members for Rogation Sunday, 2002.

Above: *The vicar in 2004, Charles James, and his wife Dorothy, pictured outside the south porch.*

The interior of All Saints Church beautifully decorated for a festival.

Above: *Three views of All Saints Church, Mylor Bridge, showing the exterior and the gates which were dedicated by the vicar, Revd Conrad Sargisson MA, in December 1983.*

A Previous Vicar

As well as being the longest-serving vicar of Mylor in the twentieth century, Frank Martin was the best known and had become something of a national figure, as he wrote for the *Daily Sketch*. The incumbent at the time of writing, Charles James, remembers, as a boy, seeing the name Frank Martin in the newspaper. Frank Martin also wrote for the local paper, the *West Briton,* and is particularly remembered for his long-running 'Persuasions' column, and the humorous anecdotes of life in the imaginary St Ingy. He was a great figure in the village – folk remember him taking the children for religious teaching, out of Mylor School and marching them up to All Saints Church. It was said that he, the village policeman, Bill Kent, and the head teacher, George Pyper, used to run the affairs of the village. They would meet at the Pandora Inn. The young lads of the village were afraid to do anything wrong as they were bound to find out about it.

Of the future of the church, the vicar, Charles James, says:

Now a new age may be opening in the history of St Mylor Church. The long chain of incumbents, the rectors and vicars, each with his own personality and talents, may possibly be coming to an end. When I go, Mylor could become part of a group ministry of all Anglican churches in and around Penryn. Things change. Forms of administration and outreach change, but the gospel of Christ remains the same and so does the commission to make disciples of all nations.

All Saints Church

All Saints Church, Bells Hill, was built between 1869 and 1892. There was a need for a church in the growing village as the Parish Church was two miles away from the village centre and most parishioners had no means of transport. Lieutenant Colonel Tremayne leased the land for a new church with the proviso that, if it were no longer used, the land should be returned to the family. Mrs Tremayne laid the foundation-stone.

Both Methodists and Anglicans helped in the building of the church and local farmers brought stone in their carts. The total cost was £600 and villagers contributed by paying a halfpenny a tile towards the roof. When it was completed in 1892, it could seat 200 people and there was great celebration. The vicar at that time was Revd Charles Taunton.

In the winter of 1927 there were exceptionally severe storms and All Saints, like many other buildings in the village, was badly damaged. A new roof and ceiling were needed at a cost of £250. Revd Gilbert Young, vicar of St Mylor from 1924 to 1936, felt the need for new vestries at All Saints, since only a curtained part of the sanctuary was available. He gathered an enthusiastic band of local helpers and work began with Mr

Harris, a builder from Probus. The cost was to be £340, but only £50 was in the church accounts. Voluntary subscriptions and fund-raising followed and Colonel Trefusis gave his support by allowing a grand fête to be held on his property in August. Thus, in late 1927 the foundation-stone to the new vestry was laid at a special evensong. The vicar officiated and the two eldest sidemen, Charles Rowe aged 80 years and Charles Burley aged 78, laid the foundation-stone. Colonel Trefusis and Mr Tresise led the procession from the church door to the building site.

Also, in September 1927, Lady Mary Trefusis died. At her funeral, the Revd Young gave a moving address, describing how she had longed to see the enlargement of the mission church and of all the help and encouragement she had given to the work there.

Under the care of Revd Young further improvements were made, including the raising of the choir floor and the reconditioning of the heating system. A legacy left by Mrs Burley was to provide electric lighting when electricity came to the village. In 1936, an oak standard and candlesticks were given in memory of Canon Young by his family. Other gifts came from William and Winifred Chance, who were active in the church from 1920 to 1981. Mrs Chance became the first verger of All Saints in 1941 and was also the parish clerk. The electric lighting was eventually installed in 1958 and overhead electric heating replaced the old boiler.

Communion was celebrated at All Saints every Sunday morning and frequently on a weekday. Evensong was held each Sunday. However, during the 1930s, attendance at evensong declined, due it was said to the coming of the motor buses, which enabled villagers to take days away, and to wireless sets, which provided entertainment at home. A family communion service for the whole parish was started on Christmas Day and Easter Sunday. Advent Sunday was also celebrated at All Saints and a service of carols at Christmas.

Numerous other activities in the church included the Junior Guild, which became the choir club in 1958. Nowadays the St Mylor Junior Singers and the Mylor Youth Band meet in the church and there are monthly meetings of the All Saints Fellowship to discuss a wide range of interesting topics. The millennium has seen the coming together of Anglicans and Methodists with joint evening services held alternately in All Saints and the chapel. These advance the longstanding hopes for Christian unity, in the creation of 'Churches together in Mylor'.

The Methodist Church

In 1992 Mylor Methodist Church published a *Bicentenary Brochure* which not only included celebratory messages and a list of events, but also an historical account and members' recollections, to which reference is made in this article.

Although the first Wesleyan Society was formed in 1792, nothing is known of the first building which was replaced in 1836. During that period William Carvosso, a pioneer of Methodism, who had come to live with his daughter, Grace, at Dowstall Farm, despaired of the 'indifference, coldness and deadness of the people at Mylor Bridge,' but was soon to be cheered by their change of heart! Galleries were added to this new building in 1860 and the present pulpit installed in 1879. In 1873 a Sunday school was built adjoining the rear of the chapel. These two rooms were used as vestries when a larger separate school-room was erected in 1887. Now they are used as a kitchen and the minister's vestry, with a toilet suitable for disabled persons recently installed.

The 1964 Harvest Festival showing the decorated pulpit which was installed in 1879.

In 1909 major alterations were made to the chapel, in that the walls were raised to accommodate a new pipe-organ installed the following year. This necessitated re-roofing and the unusual tin ceiling was raised by 4 feet and 6 inches. At about this time the ornate façade with pediment and pilasters would have been incorporated with the front wall. In 1928 the following payments were recorded in the accounts: 'Organist: three guineas, Chapel fund: £1 and worn out ministers: ten shillings'!

Rose Rogers (1910–2003), who lived as a child on Rose Hill, made this observation:

Preachers used their arms a lot more and voices were a lot louder. On each side of the pulpit there were ornamental brass stands to hold the lamps – these often shook! The preachers arrived by push-bike, horse and trap or motorbike, and some walked. If they were to take two services they

went to different homes for dinner and tea. When Sister Florence came to our house she had to lie down on the bed after dinner. Another, the Revd Charles Bone, had to lie on the settee.

Becky Bunny recalled that she and her three brothers and two sisters were christened at the chapel and attended the three Sunday services: 'Best Sunday clothes and shoes were worn but had to be taken off on reaching home. This meant that one seemed to spend all the day dressing and undressing.'

Vera Moore, a lifelong member and dedicated worker, was a pupil, along with Margaret Richards and Barbara Rogers, in Rose Rogers' class, and remembers:

We had Sunday school from 10.30 to 11a.m. and then went into the service. At 2.30p.m. we came back to Sunday school for an hour and then the evening service at 6.00p.m. Each week we learnt more of the catechism which was recited in the afternoon. We earned one mark for saying it correctly, one for attendance and one for being early. For the annual tea treat we marched up to a field, following the band, and then had games and saffron buns [a tradition which still remains an important event in the calendar]. We had good congregations but, more especially, for the Anniversary and Harvest Festival, when the chapel was packed and extra forms were put upstairs. On the Harvest Friday evening we started to decorate and all the teenagers would be there to help, having a good time together, ending up in pairs on the stairs.

Ivy Collins (1898–1993) recalled the renting of seats which, unaffected by inflation, averaged at five shillings per annum for 50 years! Midweek gatherings took place regularly; prayer meetings, bible classes, choir and concert practices.

Rose Rogers remembered:

Winter sewing meetings for the Easter Bazaar, the stalls being decorated with daffodils, primroses and evergreens. Easter Sunday was an occasion for new clothes, especially in the ladies' hat department! I can remember Mr Holman and Mr Saul-Brown with cut-away coats, striped trousers and high hats. The bowler hat was usual for Sunday wear, then the trilby and boater for summer. Most young men carried walking sticks, some their gloves and some wore spats.

At Christmas when singing Merrit's carols we were accompanied by T. Moore on the euphonium, R. Evans and E. Moore on cornets and R. Hawke on the flute. I think that all the

METHODIST CHAPEL MYLOR

A 2003 drawing of the Methodist chapel by Daphne Train.

HYMNS TO BE SUNG
AT THE
WESLEYAN SUNDAY SCHOOL TEA TREAT, MYLOR BRIDGE,
JULY 28th, 1869.

1st.   PRAISE OF JESUS.

1. To thee, O blessed Saviour,
   Our grateful songs we raise ;
   Oh, tune our hearts and voices
   Thy holy name to praise.
   'Tis by thy sov'reign mercy
   We're here allowed to meet,
   To join with friends and teachers
   Thy blessing to entreat.

2. Oh, may thy precious gospel
   Be publish'd all abroad,
   Till the benighted heathen
   Shall know and serve the Lord,
   Till o'er the wide creation
   The rays of truth shall shine,
   And nations now in darkness
   Arise to light divine.

2nd.   THE KING OF KINGS.

1. Low the infant Saviour lies,
   He appears in lowly guise ;
   Yet by faith we read the words—
   King of Kings and Lord of lords.

2. See ! he stands at Pilate's bar
   Most despised of all by far
   Still to him belong the words—
   King of Kings and Lord of lords

3. He who wears the crown of thorns,
   He whom man reviles and scorns,
   Yet demands as his the words—
   King of kings and Lord of lords.

4. On the cross 'tis still the same ;
   Never can he yield his claim
   To those ever glorious words—
   King of kings and Lord of lords.

3rd.   REST IN CHRIST.

1. Awake my soul, in joyful lays
   To sing thy great Redeemer's praise,
   He justly claims a song from me ;
   His loving-kindness, O how free !

2. He saw me ruined by the fall,
   Yet loved me notwithstanding all
   He saved me from my lost estate
   His loving-kindness, O how great.

3. Often I feel my sinful heart
   Prone from my Saviour to depart ;
   But though I have him oft forgot
   His loving-kindness changes not.

4. Soon shall I pass the gloomy vale
   Soon all my mortal powers must fail.
   O may my last expiring breath
   His loving-kindness sing in death.

4th.   THE GATHERING.

1. We gather, we gather, dear Jesus to bring
   The breathings of love, 'mid the blossoms of spring ;
   Our Maker ! Redeemer ! we gratefully raise
   Our hearts and our voices in hymning thy praise.
   Chorus—
   Hallelujah ! Hallelujah ! Hosannah in the highest.
   Hallelujah ! Hallelujah ! Hosannah to the Lord.

2. When stooping to earth from the brightness of heaven
   Thy blood for our ransom so freely was given !
   Thou deignest to listen while children adored,
   With joyful hosannas the blest of the Lord.
   Hallelujah, etc.

3. Those arms which embraced little children of old
   Still love to encircle the lambs of the fold ;
   That grace which invited the wandering home
   Hath never forbidden the youngest to come.
   Hallelujah, etc.

4. Hosannah ! hosannah ! Great Teacher we raise
   Our hearts and our voices in hymning thy praise.
   For precept and promise so graciously given
   For blessings of earth and the glories of heaven
   Hallelujah, etc.

5th.   HE WIPES THE TEAR.

1. When sore afflictions crush the soul,
   And riven is every earthly tie,
   The heart must cling to God alone—
   He wipes the tear from every eye.
   Thro' wakeful nights, when rack'd with pain,
   On bed of languishing you lie,
   Remember still that God is near ;
   He wipes the tears from every eye.

2. A few short years and all is o'er,
   Your sorrows—pain—will soon pass by :
   Then lean in faith on God's dear Son ;
   He wipes the tear from every eye.
   Oh, never be your soul cast down,
   Nor let your soul desponding sigh ;
   Assured that God, whose name is love,
   Will wipe the tear from every eye.

Gill & Son, Machine Printers, Penryn.

Hymn sheet for the Wesleyan Sunday school tea treat, Mylor Bridge, 1869.

Teachers at the tea treat in 1925.

members of the Rees, Rawling, Ralph and Bunny families were connected with the choir. Choir outings were looked forward to and sometimes as many as three coaches would leave the village, the back seats being booked well in advance. We enjoyed Mr Myatt playing the organ. His signature tune was 'Joybells' – a name he was known by! In those days the organ 'blower' was a very important person.

Vera Moore remembers that sometimes he would fall asleep and that the young people would giggle as the organ came to a stop.

Four years after the installation of mains electricity in 1934, the chapel was decorated at the cost of £100 and re-opened by Mrs Ralph who was 100 years old. During the war years gift days replaced many annual events but the Sunday services and mid-week prayer and fellowship meetings continued to give comfort in difficult times.

While the Revd Colin Sheffield was minister a safe was purchased so that a marriage register could be kept on the premises. Rose Rogers recalled:

Previous to this, the Registrar had to come from Truro and on one occasion he forgot his appointment at Mylor and went to a football match. The bride had to wait outside the chapel while someone went to fetch him from Truro! I remember telling Bob, when he went to enter the banns for our marriage, to impress on the Registrar the date and time. I warned him, 'If that man isn't there, I shall go home.' I'm glad to say he was there!

In 1958 the Annual June Fête was introduced. There are fond memories of the fancy-hat competition and a visit by the 'Pearly King' from London's East End. This event was replaced by the August mini-market in 1978.

Ada Stead (1914–2000) remembered:

One important date in March each year was the Sankey evening, greatly enjoyed by everyone. The chapel would be full of people and well supported by other chapels in the circuit. Aileen Cole, organist for over 50 years, would play the organ with all its power and the singing would be tremendous. Each chapel group would sing a Sankey hymn of their own choice with everyone joining in the chorus. We would order about 150 pasties for the supper afterwards, with cakes for those people who could not eat pasties. On one memorable occasion the appetising smell of pasties prompted Mrs Cole to call down to the Chairman, 'Mr Burnett, the pasties have come!' He replied, 'All right my dear!' and a somewhat lengthy service was drawn to a conclusion.

In January 1959 a Caravan Mission was held, which resulted in 13 young people attending classes for membership. In that year the chapel was refurbished by a team of volunteers and the present Communion table was given in memory of Henry Pike. Two Communion chairs were given in memory of Percy Lobb and Mr and Mrs Frank Porter, and the cross by Miss A. Prime.

In 1964 the Revd A. Pudner introduced the Christmas Eve service and also family services. At this time there were 26 children in the primary department of the Sunday school using the vestry during Sunday services. More accommodation was to be provided by the new primary room, a building linking the rear of the chapel to the large schoolroom and which was completed in 1966.

James Hawke remembers the annual tea treats of the mid-1960s:

About five or six coaches lined up outside the chapel to go to Carbis Bay and we would each get a saffron bun, a lemonade drink and a shilling. I remember on the beach, rows of beach tents which would be let out. Everyone dreaded the walk up the hill at the end of the day as the bus drivers refused to drive down to the bottom of the hill because it was so steep!

In 1988 the vestibule was enlarged and major re-decoration of the premises was made possible by the Manpower Services Commission who provided the supervised labour of NACRO. This mammoth operation was overseen by Dudley Dale, Church & Property steward and Len Simpson, Senior Steward, both of whom have given long and dedicated service to the chapel.

It was Dudley and his equally dedicated wife, Kathleen, who entertained Overseas Missions events at Restronguet Barton, an annual Garden Fête being held there for almost 20 years. Tregunwith Farm was also the venue for 'It's a Knockout' with organised competitions and games and in 1978 underprivileged children were entertained there.

Minnie May recalls that when the schoolroom was built her great-grandfather on her mother's side, Mr T. Moore, laid a stone plaque in the wall of the Sunday school. Rose Rogers, who was baptised in the Sunday schoolroom because of building works, had these memories from the early part of the twentieth century:

During the week, the Sunday schoolroom was used for the Bright Hour, the Band of Hope, various classes, concert practices, guild meetings and sewing meetings held on winter afternoons. The Bright Hour was started by Mrs Boon and the minister was the speaker at every meeting. Home-made yeast buns were eaten instead of today's biscuits. Water for cups of tea had to be pumped and carried from the village. It was then boiled in a copper in the wash-house, heated by a fire that needed constant attention. The musical plays produced included 'The Madcap Months' and 'The Doll's Wedding'. Mrs Boon and Miss Davies were the producers, helped by Mrs Rawling. The Mylor Feast was held on the Sunday nearest 25 October each year. Following the special Sunday services there was a tea and concert on Monday evening in the Sunday school. During the

First World War the soldiers billeted at Trefusis were fed and entertained in the Sunday school during their off-duty evenings. The Harvest Suppers were introduced in 1959 and as many as 130 people attended this event. Miss Sara and Miss Davies were day-school as well as Sunday school teachers. Mrs Boon, Miss Penhaul, Mrs Smith, Mr George and the sisters Mrs Wilmot, Rhoda and Ruby Frost taught at this time in the Sunday school. Alice Pike, who had a class of little boys, kept them until they were young men! The Sunday school was full of children!

Jean Calvert remembers that Willie Collins, Henry Pike, Herbie Rogers, Tommy Collett and Stowell Andrew were Sunday school superintendents. These were to be followed by Kathleen Dale, Keith Eells, Vera Moore and Joyce Mason.

Margaret Rogers remembers that, after the Caravan Mission in 1959, the Young People's Fellowship consisted of about 17 teenagers who met at the home of Audrey Prime. There was preparation for taking part in Sunday services, music-making for putting on concerts in the circuit and camping at Portreath in August.

A youth club was introduced in 1961 by Stowell

The teachers at the 1960 tea treat at Carbis Bay. Left to right, back row: *Audrey Prime, Herbert Rogers, Trixie Lane, Stowell Andrew, Ann Keast;* front: *Vera Moore, Chris Trevarthen, Valerie Rogers.*

Below: *Raising money for the organ fund, 1990.* Left to right, back row: *Margaret Simpson, Vyvyan Ping, Joyce Mason, Len Simpson, Vera Moore, Kevin Moore;* middle: *Graeme Wild, Linda Mooney, Susie Wild, Victoria Gilbert, Emma Grundy;* front: *Sarah Ping, Hayley Mooney, Tamsyn Rees, Helen Avis.* (By kind permission of *Packet Newspapers*)

Andrew. Subsequent leaders were Dudley Dale and Eskett Williams. Nan Williams recalled:

Eskett was glad to be keeping the young people off the streets and giving them interesting things to do. Bill Collins bought an old chassis from his garage in Falmouth for them to find out how the engine worked.

Junior Meeting Point was started in 1976 and met on Sunday evenings under the leadership of Robert Rogers. Margaret recalls a varied programme and an especially enjoyable coach trip to Trewint, John Wesley's meeting house.

For many years Mylor CP School has used the schoolroom for Class 1, one teacher describing it as the best reception classroom in Cornwall. However, in 2000, due to deterioration and storm damage, a new roof was required. As in 1990, when an appeal was made for the organ renovation, the generosity of Mylor villagers in support of chapel fund-raising events has been greatly appreciated. Another of these fund-raising efforts was the production of a Women's Fellowship cookery book which included the memories of the schoolroom used in this chapter. An exciting new era began in 2003 with total refurbishment of the schoolroom for use by Mylor Pre-School as well as church members.

Worship continues with services led by ministers, local preachers and chapel members. There are mid-week meetings in the form of Women's Fellowship, Friday Fellowship and Bible Studies. The children are

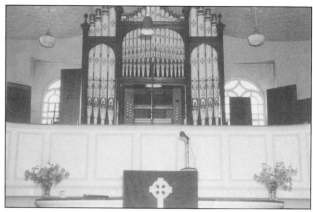

The Methodist chapel organ, built and installed by Hele & Co. of Plymouth in 1910. It was redecorated on 2 December 1990.

taught on Sundays and are an integral part of the chapel life. Helped by a small team of leaders they conduct five services every year and enjoy the special events organised for them.

In the years of the early twenty-first century, 'Churches Together in Mylor and Flushing' have held open-air services, Lent Studies, an Alpha Course and 'Songs of Praise'. So we look forward in hope, for the names mentioned in this record are but very few of the continuous stream of people who have served their Lord by worship, work and witness in Mylor and beyond.

The Bible Christians

The Bible Christians were an offshoot of Methodism. They were founded in 1815 by William O'Bryan and sometimes they were known as Bryanites. Their worship was simple but lively, enthusiastic and evangelical.

The Bible Christian Chapel in Passage Hill was built in 1882. In 1907, following the union of the Bible Christians, United Methodist Free Churches and the Methodist New Connexion, the membership took a downward plunge and the Mylor chapel was closed. It has since been converted into a private house.

The Methodist Sunday School tea treat of 2001 was joined by former members and friends as they enjoyed tea treat buns on Porthminster Beach, St Ives. The children were, left to right, back row: Charlotte Coles, Meriel Smith, Joanna Merrifield, Megan Jenkin; middle: Timothy Merrifield, Abigail Rowe, Gabrielle Rowe, Rhona Smith, Lucy Shermon, Kyle Johns; front: Joshua Rowe, Bethany Jenkin, Joanna Coles, Elizabeth Woodley, Rebecca Rowe, Rachael McKie. Others were Ruth Bray, James Hill, Philip Merrifield, Daniel Shermon, Christopher and Joe Timmins, Daniel Luke and Adam Johns.

The Bible Christian Chapel in Passage Hill was built in 1882. Closed in 1907, it is a private house at the time of writing.

Chapter 9

Famous People

John Leland, Robert Rundle, William and Thomas Lobb, Caroline Fox, Matthew Arnold, William Husband,
Sir James Penn Boucaut, Beatrix Potter, Charles Henderson, D.H. Lawrence and Katherine Mansfield,
Sir Peter Scott, Howard Spring, Princess Marthe Bibesco.

There have been a number of famous people, past and present, who have either visited or lived in the village. We have chosen to write about a few of those who are no longer with us.

John Leland

In 1533, John Leland was commissioned by King Henry VIII to investigate antiquities throughout his kingdom. He travelled widely, making many notes, and this is what he wrote about Mylor:

Betwixt the point of land of Trefusis and the point of Restronguet Wood is Milor Creek and there is St Milor's Church and beyond the Church is a good rode for shippes. Milor Creke goeth up a mile. Good wood in Restronguet.

'Good wood' meant oak for the King's ships. It is possible that the many fine oaks in Mylor are relics of Leland's 'good wood'.

Robert Rundle, Missionary

Robert Terrill Rundle (1811–96), one of five children born in Mylor to Robert Rundle (1778–1851) and Grace Carvosso (1781–1838), lived in Dowstall Farm, Bells Hill.

In 1839, Robert was accepted for the Methodist ministry and took a post as missionary and chaplain for the Hudson Bay Company in Canada, for the princely sum of £6.15s. per quarter plus £1.10s. for washing and stationery. In March 1840 he left with two other young missionaries, William Mason and George Barnley, for Fort Edmonton in Alberta.

During the eight years Robert was to stay there he felt that his best work was to be done away from the fort and for the Indians in their camps. He learnt the Cree language and had great success amongst the many tribes there. His influence on the Blackfoot tribe, although good at first, became diminished when his interpreter in Blackfoot, James Bird, refused to act for him and a replacement could not easily be found. This worried Robert greatly as he very much wanted to protect them from heathenism and the influence of the Roman Catholics.

Robert often dreamt of Mylor and of his mother, Grace, after whom he named an encampment Isle de Grace. His brother William had died suddenly at the age of 18 years and Robert was badly affected by this, so during his time in the Northern Territories he baptised 27 people with the name of William. He returned to England in 1848 as a result of ill health, intending to go back later. However, due to many changes in Canada, the decline in the Hudson Bay Company and scandal, it was decided to close the mission and Robert did not return.

In 1859, John Palliser, whilst on a surveying expedition in the Rocky Mountains, saw the great effect that Robert's work had on the Indians and renamed Terrace Mountain as Mount Rundle in his honour. There is also a Rundle Memorial United Church at Banff, Alberta, and a Rundle Mission at Pigeon Lake, which Robert had set up shortly before he left in 1848.

Mount Rundle in Canada, named after Robert Rundle, the missionary born in Mylor.

The Cornish Plant Hunters – William and Thomas Lobb

The childhood days of the four young Lobbs were spent near Wadebridge. But when Sir Charles Lemon offered their father the position of gamekeeper at Carclew, the family moved into a house on the side of the hill at Perran Wharf. The eldest son, William, born in 1809, was employed in the gardens and stove houses of Carclew. Later, he was joined by Thomas, the youngest son, born in 1817, and both boys were encouraged by their employer to study plant cultivation and botany.

In 1832, Sir Charles sent Thomas to work in the distinguished Veitch Nursery in Devon. William joined him there but left at the age of 28 to work at Scorrier House and Bochym. However, it was the latter, the 'energetic practical gardener with an ardent desire for travel and adventure', who was asked by James Veitch to go to South America in search of new seeds and plants. From Rio de Janeiro, he sent home several fine new orchids, passion flowers and *Begonia coccinea*. Next, he crossed primeval rain forest and pampas to Chile, where he discovered forests of *Araucaria araucana* (Monkey Puzzle) full of seed. These were enthusiastically greeted by an affluent Victorian society.

The Monkey-Puzzle tree, in front of St Mylor Church. The tree was grown from seeds collected by William Lobb on his travels in Chile.

William travelled four times to America, returning with new specimens such as the orange *berberis*, *escallonia*, *embothrium* and *crinodendron*; in fact, 100 plants suitable for Cornish gardens. In 1864 he was seized by paralysis of the limbs and died in San Francisco.

Meanwhile, Thomas had set out at the age of 26 in the opposite direction, to Singapore. He returned with thrilling prizes including many orchids and insect-eating pitcher plants. Next he sailed south to Java and found many more orchids; to Burma finding rhododendrons and in Nepal the giant lily, *Lilium gigantium*, a majestic plant growing ten feet high. In 1860, whilst in the Philippines, he lost a leg as a result of exposure. Sadly, his travelling days were over at just 43 years of age. Following this, he bought a secluded cottage off Bissoe Lane, in Devoran, and lived there alone for 34 years, tending his garden.

It is unlikely that either of the Lobb brothers had travelled further from home than Exeter when they set off on their long and hazardous journeys. We do not know the terrors or discomforts they suffered, but what is certain is that they rendered distinguished service to British horticulture.

Caroline Fox
(Taken from The Journals of Caroline Fox (1835–71))

Caroline Fox (1819–71) was a member of a distinguished Quaker family residing in Falmouth in the nineteenth century. The Fox family owned the leading shipping firm there and many important travellers of the day were entertained in their several family homes. Writers, poets, scientists, politicians and other highly placed personalities of the day were recorded in Caroline's journals as visiting her and Sir Charles Lemon at Carclew in Mylor.

Etching of Caroline Fox by Herkomer after a drawing by Samuel Laurence.

One was John Couch Adams, a Cornishman born on a small farm on Bodmin Moor, who discovered the planet Neptune in 1847. Another was Alfred, Lord Tennyson (1809–92), Poet Laureate of the time. Of him, Caroline writes, 'He wears a beard and moustache which one begrudges as hiding so much of that firm powerful but finely chiselled mouth.' Another poet visitor was Samuel Taylor Coleridge (1772–1834), who wrote 'The Rime of the Ancient Mariner'. Then there was Thomas Carlyle (1795–1881), the English historian and essayist, whose collected works filled 30 volumes. His deep study of German literature and philosophy brought new ideas into this country.

Davies Gilbert (1767–1839) was a Cornishman who lived at Trelissick. He wrote *A Parochial History of Cornwall* and the song 'And Shall Trelawney Die' and became President of the Royal Society.

And what of Caroline Fox herself? She was a lady of great charm. She managed to combine with her Quaker seriousness and idealism a delightful sense of humour, which is apparent in her journals.

Matthew Arnold

Matthew Arnold (1822–88), poet, critic and educationalist, was the son of Thomas Arnold, headmaster of Rugby School, immortalised in *Tom Brown's Schooldays* by T. Hughes.

Mr Harry Moore wrote in his reminiscences that his father had attended Sir Charles Lemon's school in Mylor Bridge and that on one occasion Matthew Arnold visited that school in his capacity as HM Inspector. 'He called upon my father to stand up and read to him,' related Mr Moore, continuing:

After a time, he asked my father to hand him the book and told him to go on reading, which he did, having memorised the whole book. There was only one book which was handed on to the children in turn, the leaves being kept clean by a mica covering.

Matthew Arnold's poems include 'The Scholar Gypsy', which tells the story of a brilliant Oxford scholar who forsook the intellectual life of university to wander freely, savouring the countryside and companionship of more wholesome, contented people belonging to a world which existed:

... before the strange disease of modern life, with its sick hurry, its divided aims, its heads o'ertaxed, its palsied hearts was rife... ['The Scholar Gypsy' had been seen]... *leaning backwards in a pensive dream, And fostering in thy lap a heap of flowers, Pluck'd in shy fields and distant whychwood bowers, And thine eyes resting on the moonlit stream...*

Is it fanciful to conclude that Matthew Arnold, famous HMI and great poet, envied those pupils of our village school?

William Husband

William Husband was the engineer in charge of the draining of Haarlem Lake, which gave 47,000 acres of rich agricultural land to Holland. This remarkable man enrolled in a Dutch village school and in six months spoke and wrote fluently in the Dutch language.

William Husband was born in Mylor in 1823 and was educated by a local curate before attending Bellevue Academy in Penryn. His father wanted him to be a sailor but young William ran off to Hayle and an apprenticeship with Harvey and Co., engineers and iron founders. Soon, he was involved in constructing the huge water engine, which would be used in his Dutch reclamation work for which he was admitted to the prestigious Dutch Institute of Engineers. In 1849 he suffered ague and was forced to resign his Dutch assignment. Returning home, he rejoined Harvey & Co., eventually becoming managing partner.

He designed baler safety plugs, and hydraulic and mining machinery including pumping engines and digging equipment. Being keen to promote Cornish engineering, he instituted science classes at Hayle. He died in 1887 and is buried at St Erth.

Sir James Penn Boucaut of Mylor and Adelaide

Whenever one has the opportunity to dip into that rare and valuable book *Notes on the Parish of Mylor* by Hugh P. Olivey (1907), one is intrigued by the plate 'Mylor Old Church – South Porch'. It is a reproduction of a pencil drawing of unquoted origin and shows St Mylor Parish Church before the 1870 rebuild.

The famed 17½-foot churchyard cross is shown head downwards supporting the bulging south wall, where it remained until boys from the training ship HMS *Ganges,* moored nearby, helped to dig it out to be re-erected where it now stands in the traditional place outside the south porch.

Yet more fascinating is the comfortable little figure standing by the chancel. Olivey tells us that this is a Mr Boucaut, who occupied a cottage on the north side of the church, which was not a part of the church burial ground until 1866. This house had previously been a storehouse and is shown as such on the 1840 tithe map. Olivey further writes: 'A son of this gentleman, who was born here became Judge of the Supreme Court of South Australia and an ex-Premier.'

What circumstances had carried a child born in Mylor churchyard in 1831 to a position of such great distinction in South Australia? Was there a story to be unearthed, like Mylor Cross?

Not many years ago, a modern heating system was to be put into the church and workmen began dismantling an old chimney. As the chimney-pot was removed, the whole structure crumbled, part falling through the church roof into the small vestry. A brass memorial plaque was discovered in the rubble which had been removed from the transept. It said simply:

To the Glory of God and for the comfort of those who worship here the Chimney in this Transept was erected in 1892 by James Penn Boucaut, Judge of the Supreme Court of South Australia, who was born on ground now part of Mylor Churchyard.

A book was published by Eric Gunton, a resident of South Australia, concerning cities, towns and villages in England with names which correspond with Australian places. As a result, a party of people from Adelaide visited Cornwall and was entertained by Mylor Women's Institute, which for some time had been in correspondence with its equivalent in Mylor, Australia. Thus it was revealed that Sir James Boucaut had actually named the latter, remarking when riding through Gum Flats, some 15 miles from Adelaide, that it reminded him of his birthplace. Here there was a hostelry, a staging-post for travellers, and the name of the township growing around it was changed to Mylor.

Mr Gunton was asked in a letter whether he could contribute more details to the personality emerging and the following information was received:

James Boucaut was a Guernsey man, the son of Capt. Ray Boucaut RE CS and Winifred, daughter of James Penn of Mylor. He was educated in Saltash before leaving with his father for South Australia when aged fifteen. He chose to study Law and was called to the Bar in 1855. His career in Parliament lasted 27 years. Although those were disturbed and stormy days in Australia, he took the opportunity to prove that he was skilled in management and strenuous in debate. His initiative resulted in great progress in the areas of education, public works and the railway system. His first Premiership of Southern Australia was after only four and a half years in Parliament. He became a QC in 1875. The second Premiership was in 1877, but the political strife was such that he returned to the judicial bench, where he sustained the high reputation gained as a politician.

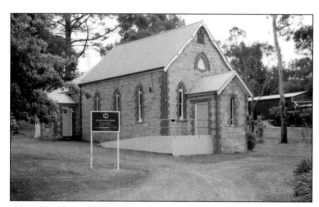

The church in Mylor, South Australia, 2000.

The school in Mylor, South Australia, 2000.

His knighthood was conferred in 1898 and was universally regarded as well deserved. 'He infused a new spirit into the public life of the province, lifted its politics to a higher level and inaugurated a new era in the conduct of affairs.' He retired in 1905. During his earlier colonial life, he had spent much time in the countryside and he never lost his interest in rural pursuits. He owned an estate where he bred Arab horses and wrote a book *The Arab: the Horse of the Future*. Also, he was a keen horse-racing man and enthusiastic yachtsman.

Sir James became a firm friend of John Langdon Bonython, the grandson of Thomas Bonython who had emigrated to Australia when the affairs of his family, once owners of Carclew House in Cornwall, were at a low ebb. John was editor of *The Advertiser* in Adelaide. He was knighted for his services to the Commonwealth in 1898, named his house in Adelaide, Carclew, and a summer residence bore the name Carwinow after a Cornishman he admired. Around this house he planted azaleas, rhododendrons and many bulbs acquired from the gardens of Carclew, Trelowarren, Lanarth, and Penrose in Cornwall. Both Sir James and Sir John felt a keen affection for Cornwall and were founder members of the Cornish Association in South Australia, which they helped to found in 1890.

In 1864, Sir James Boucaut had married Janet, daughter of Mr Alexander McCulloch, and they had five sons and a daughter. He died in 1916 at the age of 85 at Glenelg, a suburb of Adelaide, which is, like the place of his birth, by the sea.

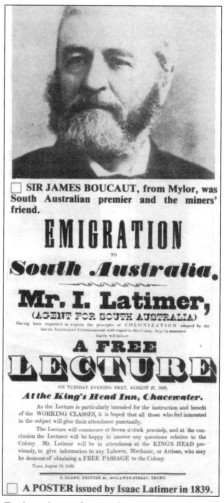

Emigration advert showing Sir James Boucaut, described as 'The miners' friend'.

Beatrix Potter

In the late-nineteenth century, Beatrix Potter, author of many children's books including *The Tale of Peter Rabbit* and *The Tale of Mrs Tiggy-Winkle,* visited Mylor with her father. She wrote a detailed account of the occasion, which was recorded over several weeks in *The Leader* newspaper in about June 1893.

She accompanied her father, who was photographing at Mylor harbour:

... where there is a naval yard and the training ship HMS Ganges, *which is moored high up in the Carrick Roads. The boys, mostly between 15 and 17, were sent to the ship when first recruited to learn the rudiments of drill and discipline. They were noisy and high spirited but always in the charge of an officer on shore, where their healthiness and clean merry faces make them a pleasure to look at.*

They looked the picture of health but the writer was surprised to hear that there had been one or two epidemics of diphtheria on board ship: 'Perhaps it was too full (500 on board) or the infection had come in with a new boy, or perhaps epidemics can spread even in the pure air of Mylor...'

Beatrix Potter noticed a number of blue jackets about the harbour (possibly Coastguards), apart from the white-clad *Ganges* people:

All are extremely orderly and have an objection to getting their feet wet when crossing to the ship in the rear of a certain lumbering wooden box, which the Corporation call a water cart!

Evidently, the conditions in which the *Ganges* boys lived had greatly improved over the 30-plus years in St Mylor Pool.

Charles Henderson

Charles Henderson was born into the landed gentry near Truro in 1900. From childhood he had a great love of all things Cornish and when he went up to Christ Church, Oxford, as a scholar in English, he became a close friend of A.L. Rowse, who later dedicated his book *Tudor Cornwall* (1941) 'To the memory of my friend Charles Henderson, First of Cornish Scholars.'

He is remembered not only as a writer of many books but also as an antiquarian. An authority without rival on every aspect of Cornish life, landscape, place-names, churches, families, his 'essays' included: 'Cornish Wrecks', 'Lighthouses', 'Bells', 'Crosses', 'Tucking Mills', 'Culver Houses', 'Woodlands' and 'The Origin of Cornish Towns'. But he is best known for the wonderful collection of Cornish material bequeathed to the Royal Institution of Cornwall.

His marriage in 1933 was radiantly happy but short-lived. A few weeks later on honeymoon in Rome he died. There he was laid to rest in the Protestant Cemetery. His death was an irreparable loss to Cornish scholarship. Concerning Mylor, he wrote:

Few parishes in Cornwall are more delightfully situated than Mylor and it is not surprising that the number of residents increases every year. Mylor must have been one of the first country parishes in Cornwall to attract the 'retired' class of resident, and the charming old-fashioned houses along the road from Mylor Church to Flushing were the 'neat marine villas' of newcomers a hundred years ago. I have been recently examining an interesting map of the parish made in 1764, when Mylor was still an unsophisticated place. Most of the field names are so picturesque that it is a pity that the builders of new bungalows do not revive them. One modern atrocity in particular with a high sounding title occupies a field, which in 1764 bore the more suitable name of The Little Pig's Close. What a delicious name for a house!

D.H. Lawrence and Katherine Mansfield

Sketch of D.H. Lawrence by Peter Clark, 2004.

In March 1916 the writer, D.H Lawrence, and his wife, Frieda, rented a cottage overlooking the cliffs near Zennor in West Cornwall. Next door was a larger residence converted from three cottages and Lawrence suggested to their friends, Katherine Mansfield and her companion, the critic John Middleton Murray, that they should come to Cornwall. He hoped they could set up an anti-war community of intellectuals.

Katherine and Murray arrived in April but, despite

the idyllic setting, which Lawrence loved, Katherine became unhappy with the situation, blaming the bleak landscape and the effect of the damp on her health. She also became disenchanted with the continuing noisy bickering of the Lawrences. The relationship between the four friends was far from stable. In May, Katherine and Murray began to look for another cottage on the south Cornish coast to take advantage of the milder climate. They eventually decided on Sunnyside Cottage (now named Quibo) along Church Road in Mylor at £18 a year. However, it seems the move did little to lift Katherine's despondent mood, despite the locals remembering that Sunnyside was treated to some very bright curtains during her stay there.

Sketch of Katherine Mansfield by Peter Clark, 2004.

Lawrence and his wife visited Katherine and Murray at Mylor in August when the four seemed to be in harmony for a while. Lawrence was at this time writing his book *Women in Love* and it is commonly believed that the characters were drawn in part from the four friends; Katherine and Frieda as Gudrun and Ursula, and Lawrence and Murray as Birkin and Gerald Crich respectively, although Murray denied he was in anyway like Crich and Katherine did not like the book at all.

In Murray's memory, Mylor was a pleasant and peaceful place with syringa and magnolias in the front garden and behind the cottage a kitchen garden that ran down to the water's edge. They had a maid called Mary, who brought them raspberries on a rhubarb leaf and gave them a kitten. There was a lot of sunshine that summer but Katherine was restless and not in the mood for writing. Murray recalls his memories of the cottage were of being alone in it.

Later that year, Murray became a translator at the War Office in London and Katherine moved there as well. Katherine married Murray in May 1918 and, although she later returned to East Cornwall to recuperate from an illness, it is not known whether she ever returned to Mylor.

Sir Peter Scott

In 1934, the Scott family had taken Greatwood House for part of the summer. It was full of dinghy sailors, their crews and girlfriends, as the big event of the season was the Prince of Wales' Cup being held in Falmouth for the International 14 class of dinghy.

Peter Scott, later famous as a naturalist and artist, had entered his boat *Eastlight* and hoped to win one of the six replicas of the cup. It was a long gruelling race. At one time *Eastlight* was becalmed in the lee of a large anchored merchant ship and could only manage sixteenth place. Peter was very disappointed. However, there were some compensations after the race, as the tension was over and everyone could enjoy themselves at Greatwood.

Peter did eventually win the coveted cup in 1937, sailing another boat named *Thunder* when the race was held at Lowestoft. In 1938 the competition returned to Falmouth and Peter, together with John Winter, sailed the boat *Thunder and Lightning*, trying out a trapeze for the first time. This amazed the other competitors, who included Robert Hichens, and *Thunder and Lightning* eventually won the race, four minutes ahead of the next boat. The use of the trapeze caused a lot of controversy and it was subsequently banned. It was another 17 years before it was allowed again for racing; this time for the Flying Fifteens.

Howard Spring

Howard Spring came to live in Mylor Churchtown with his wife Marion in 1939. He fell in love at first sight with a house called Hoopers Hill. The setting was perfect and, with land sloping down to the creek, it was the ideal place to moor his boat *Mildred*. Marion had known Mylor as a child and remembered Cornish cream teas taken at Lawithick. In her book, *Howard*, she describes the joy on first seeing the property. Soon their sons and friends joined them for a lovely holiday, the last before the start of the Second World War.

The Springs were allowed to sail in *Mildred* during the war, as long as they stayed within the confines of

Carrick Roads, and they caught fish for themselves and their cats. Howard joined the Home Guard and became a liaison officer for the Worcesters who were stationed nearby. The year 1941 was a memorable one for Howard – he was asked by the Minister of Information to join the battleship *Prince of Wales* in the company of H.V. Morton, author of many travel books. They were to travel with Sir Winston Churchill on board for a meeting with President Roosevelt in Newfoundland. This was naturally an awesome experience recounted in his book *In the Meantime* and Howard treasured a photograph of the battleship, signed for him by Sir Winston.

All through the war Howard continued to write. *Fame is the Spur* was published in 1940 and dedicated to his son David, followed by *In the Meantime* in 1942, inscribed to his younger son Michael. In 1944, he dedicated *Hard Facts* to both sons who were then serving in the RNVR. The Americans built a camp next to Hoopers Hill and they became very friendly with the Springs, especially when they found out that they had two sons in the Navy.

Both sons returned from the war safe and sound and the home at Mylor suddenly seemed too small. It was hoped to extend the house but permission was not granted, as immediately after the war all materials were needed to build council-houses. So in 1947, Howard and Marion moved to Falmouth. However, their son David continued to live at Hoopers Hill with his wife Runa after their marriage in 1949. Howard Spring died in 1965 and his ashes lie in St Mylor churchyard, within a few yards of the sound of water in the creek.

The historian A.L. Rowse wrote the following after Howard's death:

> In the end one thinks of the welcoming charm he and his wife radiated around them, the atmosphere of affection and sympathy they created, the kindly hospitality in that magic garden within sight and sound of the sea.

Many towns and villages have featured in novels and Mylor is no exception. In the book *All the Day Long* by Howard Spring, St Mylor Church becomes St Tudno, and Carclew House is Tregannock. He wrote:

> In many country parishes the church is in one place and the village in another... There were three ways of getting to the village. You could row yourself up the creek in the dinghy, and that was just about a mile. The village clustered round the head of the creek. Or you could go along the narrow road that followed the run of the creek, but you couldn't do this if you were driving any sort of vehicle, for the walls of fields closed in near the Vicarage so severely that no vehicle could get through. So the third way was by the wide road that made a half-circle sweep to the village, and that added miles...
>
> My favourite way of making the journey was in the dinghy, and that was the way we went on that May morning...

Marion and Howard Spring at the christening of their granddaughter at St Mylor Church in April 1955. In the centre is their daughter-in-law Runa, holding baby Susan, with Runa's mother, Rose Williams, beside her.

Sundial in Mylor churchyard, memorial to the author Howard Spring who lived at Hoopers Hill.

The tide had turned, and soon the upper half of the creek would be a mud-flat. But now it was all beauty, and how beautiful our creek was! On the side opposite the Vicarage, pasture land rolled steeply down to the water, and where land and water met small oaks grew thickly, and you could see the high tide mark drawn upon the leaves stretching away in front of you as clean as a ruled line... We just made it. Another half-hour and we should have been stranded... We had still about two miles to go, but before leaving the village we peeped in to the smithy opposite the Polperro Arms, and already a few old men, their pipes smoking placidly, were sitting near the forge. It was a regular club and parliament combined. Some of them snoozed and gossiped there through all of every day, going home only for their meals...

We had a fair way yet to go, for Tregannock was, on the other side, as far from the village as the Vicarage was on ours...

The gates of Tregannock opened upon a field big enough to house a village, with a road running through it. Beyond an iron fence, upon a slight rise of ground, the house stood with a lawn in front of it. Tregannock was no Blenheim or Montacute or Longleat, but it was an imposing house with a granite balustrade in front of it and a sweep of balustraded steps rising up to the entrance. Standing there at the head of the steps, you looked upon a great stretch of level agricultural land, but not far behind the house the land fell away in a vast escarpment, wooded, so that you looked out over that falling sea of oaks to a prospect of enchantment, blue and tender on a summer's day. The gardens were not gardens in the sense that the word conveys to most people: not a municipal park or the garden of a seedsman's catalogue. Like most great Cornish gardens, it was mainly woodland, but woodland composed of rare and splendid trees that had been brought to prosper in that favoured climate, under grown with blazing bushes that had known the steamy silence of forests climbing the foothills of the lonely Himalayas. It is all desolate now; and I often think how, from down there below the escarpment of oaks, where the road runs to Truro, night travellers must have looked up in wonder to see the great house flaming to death upon the hill.

Marion wrote that Carclew haunted Howard until he resurrected it in *All the Day Long*. Once, when visiting the gardens, they saw an old pond which they thought would be the perfect size for their own garden. Eventually they managed to purchase it from the estate and with much difficulty it was transported to Hoopers Hill on a builder's lorry, together with a granite sundial, which caught Howard's fancy.

Princess Marthe Bibesco

Princess Marthe Bibesco (1888–1973) was a Romanian beauty and intellectual, well-known in Europe during the first part of the twentieth century. She was a descendant of Emilie de Pellapra, a mistress of Napoleon, and many of her treasures and pictures came from that time. The daughter of Lahovary, a president of the Romanian state, she lived as a successful writer in Paris for many years. She won the prestigious 'Prix de L'Academie' at a time when she was a contemporary and friend of Marcel Proust and Jean Cocteau. Crowned heads and politicians were among her many admirers.

The German crown prince would meet her train in Berlin and their drive through the city would be heralded by the postillion playing the first three notes of Wagner's 'Siegfried' on a silver horn, denoting the approach of a member of the royal family. The British prime minister, Ramsay Macdonald, was captivated by her, as was General de Gaulle. She married Prince George Bibesco in 1886, grandson of a reigning Romanian prince and a diplomat who was his country's ambassador to Persia.

With the coming of the new Communist regime, the former royal family was stripped of the castles, estates and wealth. They were held under house arrest, until the family managed to escape in 1945. Marthe and her daughter Princess Valentine chose to spend their exile in Cornwall and were later joined by Prince George. Before buying the house called Tullimaar in Perranarworthal in 1957, Marthe and her daughter lived at a house called Plaisance on the Carclew road in Mylor. Their story ends sadly with a decline in their fortune forcing them to struggle to make a living from a small market garden. Marthe died in 1973 at the age of 85.

Sketch of Princess Bibesco by Peter Clark, 2004.

Chapter 10

Schools

Mylor Schools, The First Schools, Sunday Schools and the First Real School, Inspections and the Battersea Plan,
The Sir Charles Lemon School, Memories of the Old School, The Fire of 1921, The New School, Wartime,
More Recent Times, Awards, Mylor Pre-School.

Mylor Schools

In 2004 Mylor Bridge village school is a thriving busy place. Within its lively atmosphere and colourful environment there is a constant struggle to find space for the expanding numbers of children. The lovely old granite building was a prize-winning design in the 1920s and it has constantly been adapted to fulfil modern requirements.

Much of its success relates to the tradition of a village caring about education. This has been fostered over 200 years by many dedicated people. The most influential of these must surely be that compassionate benefactor, Sir Charles Lemon of the Carclew estate. His appreciation of intellectual life is shown by the estate's role in Victorian times as a cultural centre with many famous visitors from the literary world. It follows that he would have been concerned for the improvement in the standard of education for his estate workers.

The First Schools

Within educational development in the early-nineteenth century, there was growing national concern for the poor and, in particular, anxiety over the misuse of endowments intended for education. As a result, a select committee was appointed in 1817 with a questionnaire sent to every parish to research existing arrangements. It was reported by St Mylor's curate that there were seven day-schools educating 240 children. Most of these were dame-schools, run by individuals in their own homes. Two of these were seminaries for young ladies, or 'females of the higher class'. A curate ran a similar school for boys at the Vicarage. In 1822, he advertised in the *West Briton:*

The Rev William Whitehead receives into his family a limited number of Young Gentlemen to be educated in Greek, Latin, English and other branches of useful literature. Terms, thirty guineas per annum...

Old School House and clock tower in the 1970s.

Aerial view showing New Row School (circled) *and the present school, 2000.*

One wonders where he boarded them as the Old Vicarage consisted of a parlour, a hall 12 feet square, a kitchen, a dairy, two cellars, a barn and a stable. Sadly the curate died in 1823, just a year after opening his school.

Sunday Schools and the First Real School

Three Sunday schools taught reading so that children could read the Bible. The Baptists were the most successful with about 200 children, many of whom probably lived in Flushing. In 1824, Sir Charles Lemon inherited the Carclew estate from his father Sir William Lemon, who had bought the estate with wealth acquired from his mining and smelting works. Sir William had been MP for Penryn and Sir Charles would have been familiar with the needs of the poor in the area. There were many large families and with failures in farming and mining, deprivation frequently ensued. Sir Charles was a caring man whose generosity and compassion made it possible for the first real school to be built.

Sir Charles already supported two of the day-schools in the parish and he merged these into a new school which he established in Trenance Row, now New Row, with a house next door for the headmaster, John Mitchell. At this stage, Sir Charles maintained the school and paid the teachers' salaries (£60 per annum for the headmaster). The school was mainly for the estate workers but some would have come from a mobile community, travelling around the country to find work. Others were children from Mylor Harbour dockyard and later some connected with HMS *Ganges*, which arrived in 1866.

At the same time, Sir Charles built a workhouse for the very poor. This was the building we know as the Old School House at the time of writing. In 1834 the workhouse was enlarged, using stone from a quarry by the creek, but in 1840 the inmates were moved to the Union in Falmouth, an institution that cared for the basic needs of the poor.

Inspections and the Battersea Plan

At the invitation of Sir Charles Lemon in 1846, the school was inspected by Mr Joseph Fletcher, an inspector of British and other non-Anglican schools. A favourable report was given, which began with the words, '... the Mylor Bridge School is one of peculiar vigour.' Sir Charles was keen to be as efficient as possible and made sure that the latest teaching methods were used. His aim was to educate village children of both sexes and all ages in the same school. This involved teaching the boys and girls together in the mornings under the instruction of a master with a few monitors, following a method known as the 'Battersea plan'. Meanwhile the infants were in a separate room being taught by the mistress. During the second half of the day, the boys only were under the master's instruction, while the girls were learning to sew under the guidance of the mistress of the infants.

After 1846, provision was made by government aid for appointing pupil teachers who were better qualified than the monitors. Although the school had received no grant for building, as it had been donated by Sir Charles, some grants were made available towards salaries and materials. The children had to pay a penny a week, which must have been hard to find for some of the larger families.

The school flourished and on 17 February 1850 Sir Charles paid £70 to the churchwardens and overseers of the poor, transferring his school from Trenance Row to the enlarged workhouse building. He also gave the clock and clock tower, based on the Italianate design of one at Enys, where a small school for the estate workers' children had also existed for some time. The clock was made by Thwaites and Reed, Clerkenwell, London and is dated 1845.

The Sir Charles Lemon School

The school was now 'a public elementary school under some control or patronage.' Private schools still existed in the area though; in addition to a number of dame-schools, a private Church of England mixed school had also been in existence. This was owned by F.G. Enys of the Enys estate, but it was usually known as Mrs Enys's School and was situated in Broads Lane.

Joseph Mitchell was the headmaster of Mylor School in 1851, with some members of his family appointed as teachers. A son and two daughters of the Lemon family also became teachers at the school. In the 1861 census, we find that Philip Ashton, aged 24, from Abergwili, Carmarthenshire, had become a teacher at the school, but it was not until 1881 that he took Joseph Mitchell's place, when the latter retired.

In 1868, Sir Charles Lemon died at the age of 83 having devoted much of his life to the development of Mylor School, which had been named after him. He had carried on single-handed for many years and finally gave the buildings to the parish by deed under

A school photo from c.1902 by the Church Hall. Pictured are, front: (fourth from left) Percy Gray with Ivy Collins behind him, (seventh from left) Frank Gray with Irene Gray behind him; second row from the back: (far right) Robert Rogers.

Above: *Sir Charles Lemon, c.1860.*

Right: *Notice of a vestry meeting.*

PARISH OF
MYLOR.

The Parishioners are hereby requested to take Notice that a ~~Vestry~~ Meeting will be held in the Vestry Room at Mylor Bridge, on Thursday the 12th day of July at 7 o'clock in the evening for the purpose of deciding upon the future position of the National School of the Parish.

C.W.S. Taunton, Vicar

Matt. H. Doble }
J.P. Lawrance } Churchwardens.

} Trustees of Mylor National School.

} Overseers.

Dated this 6th day of July 1894

trustees as a Church of England school for ever. As he had no surviving children of his own, one can understand how he wanted to help the children of the parish.

Having no heir, the school passed to his nephew, Lieutenant Colonel Arthur Tremayne, who took control until 1894. Lieutenant Colonel Tremayne was a strong military man, famous for being one of the 600 cavalry at Balaclava. Some changes in the Education Department made it more desirable for the school to be handed over to a committee of management, but it continued to be carried on under the terms of the trust deed granted by Sir Charles.

The year 1870 was the beginning of a new era. Elementary schools were established and in 1874 Mylor became a board school. Two years later the government ruled that all children should receive education, by the churches if possible. Money was to be raised from local rates to make this possible and restrictions were now in force to prevent young children from being employed. By 1880 school attendance up to the age of ten years became compulsory, but we know from several sources that help with farming, potato picking and so on, kept many youngsters away from school. With the introduction of the Education Act and places for all children, it seems that 425 children were being educated in the parish, including Flushing.

In 1894 the Board of Education exerted greater demands and Mylor Bridge School was handed over to a board of managers. John Mitchell had retired in 1881 and Philip Ashton, who had married a local girl, Ellen, became the new headmaster of Mylor School. It seems likely from census returns that Ellen, an infant-school teacher, was one of John Mitchell's daughters. Philip Ashton was to continue until 1901 when his son John, who had been his assistant for 17 years, took over. John's son Noel also became a teacher, but not in Mylor Bridge.

It was now a National School with a committee of management elected in the same year. By then the school-leaving age had been raised to 12 and a certificate of work was required before a child could leave. By 1903, Mylor Bridge School and Enys School were combined by the County Education Committee. The following year, Enys School was closed by the authority and its furniture, maps, etc. given to Mylor Bridge School. The building which was Enys School no longer exists.

Memories of the Old School

A memory of Harry Moore's reads:

I remember the infants room at the top of the school reached by two flights of stairs and the gallery where we sat... At the back was a picture of Adam and Eve in the Garden of Eden, both in clothes made of leaves. Ugh! The school – damp smells – wet clothes – dark rooms!... I remember the school attendance officer, William Tong, who lived in the Elms at Tregatreath. He possessed a

small white terrier, which used to run along ahead of him, and we all blessed Shot, that was the dog's name.

Lieutenant Colonel Tremayne died in 1905 and his son, Captain William Tremayne, inherited the estate. From then on the influence of the Carclew estate became less as William spent more time away and in 1920 the estate was sold, although the Tremayne family continued to live there. Rose Rogers also wrote about the old school:

I started school at four years of age in the building now known as the Tremayne Hall. Our caretaker was Mrs Sara. When I first went to school, the boys wore navy blue Guernseys [pullovers]. The girls wore white pinafores.

In the early part of the twentieth century we see from the log-books of Mylor School that attendance continued to be seriously affected by illness. Influenza and whooping cough were common, with bouts of the more dangerous scarlet fever causing great disruption. On 9 December 1913, the County Medical Officer examined every child. The next entry in the log reads:

December 11th 1913. 18 cases – many others sick, many probably scarlet fever. The cases are so mild as to render recognition very difficult. 20 or 30 kept at home to avoid catching the fever. Telegram from District Office this afternoon closing the school for three weeks by order of the County Medical Officer.

It appears that boys also continued to be away from school, helping with agricultural work. Harvest time and potato picking or 'dropping' were the usual reasons. The weather also played its part: 'December 11th 1914. This morning, in consequence of bad weather, we have, out of 139 on books, present 54, sent home wet 4, leaving 50 or 35%.'

Despite many problems, the July Diocesan Report stated in 1915 that:

... the work was very well known indeed and the children took a great interest in it. They had also, as in other years, decorated the schoolroom with flowers on their own initiative. This does not imply a dread of the examination... The Headmaster is well carrying on the work so excellently done in the school for 44 years by his father. He himself has been at the school for 31 years as assistant and Head Teacher. Every effort should be made to preserve so excellent a school.

Cookery and carpentry classes started in Penryn around this time and the children had to walk to them. There were many occasions when children were reprimanded for arriving later than they should!

The stoves were a constant source of aggravation and there are frequent mentions of their annoying habit of smoking e.g. 'January 24, 1918. Classroom stoves again prove useless, filling the room with smoke.'

Many years later, George Hearle, a former pupil,

remembered these stoves were still causing problems, even in the 1950s:

There were no school dinners, but there was a Cornish range in the classroom, which helped heat the room and which also served to warm pasties brought to school for dinner. A blockage in the range filled the room with smoke.

The Fire of 1921

There are numerous entries concerning fire drills, with great emphasis on the number of minutes taken to evacuate the school. On several occasions they seem to have managed a complete fire drill in less than one minute, which is ironic when we remember the tragedy which followed:

June 12th: Fire broke out while I (headmaster) was at church. The greater part of the school building was destroyed together with much of the furniture and materials. The cause of the fire is unknown.

Although the fire was undoubtedly the most devastating event in the history of the school, it forced a decision to be made for a new school to be built. From a newspaper account at the time we read 'Mylor School Gutted'. It was estimated that £2,000 worth of damage had been done:

... in the almost entire demolition of the Church of England school. The outbreak was discovered about 7.15pm by Mr T Bunny who lives in an adjoining cottage. He gave the alarm and Penryn Fire Brigade was summoned. The whole of the villagers, including many women and children, turned out to help, but despite their endeavours, the fire gained ground rapidly.

At that time there was only one telephone in the village, at the Post Office. A call was made and the Penryn Fire Brigade arrived at 8p.m., the appliance having been pulled by hand for much of the way! A pair of horses were eventually provided to help and, with a plentiful supply of water pumped from the river, the fire was finally under control. The fire brigade left at 2a.m. By then the whole of the main building had been gutted, although the north-east wing built 13 years previously was saved. John Ashton was headmaster at that time, living in the adjoining house. He had been in the school an hour before and had no idea what had caused the outbreak. His house suffered considerable water damage and the roof had to be hacked away to prevent the fire spreading.

Rose Rogers, whose maiden name was Porter, was born at Rose Hill, Six Turnings, and lived there for 15 years. She was a pupil at the school at the time of the fire and recalled that she had taken a length of material to school that week for sewing lessons. She said:

I was more worried about losing the material than about the fire! It was a Sunday evening and there was a concert in the Methodist Chapel. The caretaker lived next to the school and someone called her out of the chapel. People were whispering to each other and they did not know what was happening. Mr Ashton was organist for the concert.

Sufficient furniture and books had been rescued to make it possible to reopen a temporary school. Harry Moore wrote:

The school was burned in the summer of 1921. By a singular coincidence, I was spending a holiday at the time in Mylor and together with another schoolmaster we rescued the registers and log-book, which were like the Bible in school in those days.

As a result of the fire, the infant school moved to the Sunday school room (the Tremayne Institute in 2004) and the rest to the Wesleyan Methodist premises.

Mylor School in 2004.

Mylor School, c.1928. Left to right, back row: *? Ferris, Donald Watson, Geoff Chellow, Alec Bennett, Cecil Andrew, Joe Lawry, Gerald ?;* middle: *Rose Winwood, Sybil Sweet, Grace Cundy, Eileen Pope, Mary Bray, Barbara Rogers, Marjorie Boswell, Vera Gray;* front: *Arthur Harry, George Hearle, Betty Collins, Ursula Mounce, Charlie Tresidder, Gerald Richards, Harold Ferris.*

The New School

In 1921 there was a national competition to design a perfect school and the winning design was chosen for two schools in the area, one in Gwinear and the other Mylor. An unusual feature was the covered play area which was to encourage healthy open-air play in all weathers. The new school was opened on 4 September 1924 by Canon Lewis, the rector of Truro. The architect, Mr Drewitt, was among those present. A few days later an entry in the log-book reads, 'Sept 11th. The new school building is evidently appreciated by the children, the attendance is very good.'

Captain Tremayne had agreed to hand over the old school building on condition that it should be re-built as a parish room. Once refurbished, it became the new Church Hall at Mylor. In 2004 it is known as the Tremayne Hall and the village hopes that future funds may preserve this lovely old building for generations to come.

The new school continued to flourish and the following year John Ashton retired after 31 years. The log says simply: 'June 10: My last day at school.' 'June 11: Commenced duty this morning, FW Johns.'

However, reports were not always good and after the July examinations the log records poor results:

July 20: The results are very unsatisfactory, except in Standard VII. Every standard is backward in arithmetic, spelling is very weak and there are few children capable of writing a simple piece of composition with reasonable accuracy.

Attendance continued to improve though and the log records the winning of an attendance shield. It is worth noting that on 5 October 1926 the shield went to St Mawes who beat St Mylor by 0.1 per cent! Apart from this one occasion the school had the highest attendance rate of all the schools in the district over a period of three years.

The school was inspected by HMI on 28 November 1928 and given a glowing report, which mentions the well-stocked gardens, bee-keeping, attentive children and a headmaster of 'much energy'. This tradition continued for many years. Gerald Tonkin, a pupil in the 1950s, remembers the school gardens:

Top class boys worked on the garden twice a week and there were competitions with other schools for the best garden. Girls generally did needlework when the boys did gardening.

In the log it says that 'Needlework is exceptionally well

taught; finished garments attractive and well-made.'

George Hearle recalls strict discipline and corporal punishment in the form of beatings with a sycamore stick. He describes himself as a lazy pupil who had trouble mastering the use of ink-wells and pens. Looking at the punishment book years later he was reminded that he was 'caned for dirty work'. Despite this he went on to gain a scholarship to Falmouth Grammar School and, in 1946, he returned as a teacher to the village school and remained there until 1953.

In the summer of 1935, a tragic accident occurred in which the headmaster, Francis Johns, drowned at Bedruthan Steps on the north Cornish coast. He was greatly missed by the whole community.

A temporary head was brought in until Gordon Gilbert was appointed the following November. Eric Gray remembers Mr Gilbert: 'He came from St Day and encouraged sport, building up a good football team, many of whom played for district teams.'

From then until the start of the Second World War there are accounts of numerous successes; the Trefusis Banner at the county music festival was won many times, attendance was good and an excellent HMI report mentions a headmaster who 'controls the school with energy, efficiency and sympathy.'

On 22 November 1937 40 children went to see HM King George VI who had come to visit Truro.

On a more mundane note, apparently the pump of the well remained troublesome. Looking ahead in the log-book it seems that mains water had not arrived at the school by July 1949 when 'the well appears to have run dry. Flow of water stopped while pumping into the canteen.' (The canteen was built in 1948.)

Wartime

In July 1939 the log-book records these words: 'Received instructions in case of National Emergency'. They were the first indication of the horrors to come. 'July 7th 1940: First air raid Falmouth'. Then came the fitting of gas masks, digging of air-raid shelters and the putting of wire-netting frames on the windows until:

May 8th 1941. Since Easter holidays raid alerts have become numerous. Gunfire has been frequent and with shells bursting over the village, rest is impossible. Several children are very tired in the mornings.

Gas-mask practices continued into October. The time needed to fit masks onto the heads of the children was reduced to five seconds. Five people died when bombs fell on cottages next to the Lemon Arms. 'November 13th: Air raid. Bombs on village. Casualties.' A car park has since taken the place of the demolished cottages.

The Education Committee decided to merge evacuated children with local schoolchildren so 27 evacuees were brought to the school from the Church Hall, but later that month, after several more air raids, some children returned to London. In January 1942 139 children were on the books, and only ten of them were evacuees. 'May 10th: Three air raid shelters being built on the premises.' These were placed above and below ground. Those above ground, according to Keith Avis, a former caretaker, were built with nine-inch-square concrete blocks and a roof one foot thick. They had an Elsan toilet at each end. The underground shelters had steps down into them and the earth was piled on top.

Mylor School, 1936, with teacher Miss Davis. Left to right, back row: *Richard Burns, Keith Menadue, Colin Coad, John Tregenza, Thelma Evans, Enid Tregenza, Ken Keast, Creswell Cundy;* second row: *Betty Cock, Winnie Keast, Elsie Rowe, ?, Joyce Hawke, Brenda Ferris, Christine Bishop, Betty Lawry, Peggy Bryant, Betty Hingston, Dorothy Watson;* front: *Archie Rollason, Dennis Rowe, Oswald Browning, Dorothy Ferris, Molly Hines, Pamela Tonkin, Bernard Rogers, Redvers Ferris, Tom Burley, John Rapson or Rogers.*

July 27th: War Agricultural Committee has said that the school should be closed for the last two weeks in September and the first three weeks of October to enable senior children to help the farmers in potato lifting.

This was a terrible time for all. Those who lived through it will understand all too clearly the following words written in the log by Gordon Gilbert, the headmaster:

Night after night children and parents were forced to their shelters, and the cries of little children, terrified of the explosions and falling debris. Then those awful nights (I cannot describe) which followed, still come before me.

Teachers arrived from London to help with evacuees and Mr C. Lanyon took over from Mr Gilbert in 1943 when he was appointed to St Day School. The school-leaving age was raised to 15 in 1944 when the Education Act was introduced.

The war finally ended and, in 1947, George Pyper replaced Mr Lanyon who moved to be a headmaster in Weston-Super-Mare. Mr Pyper recalls:

The school was a really happy place, even though we were often scared of the bees that swarmed around the hives at the bottom of the playground. Looking out of the windows we could see the fields of Gilbert's farm and watch the daily trudge of the cows, either before or after milking. Empire Day, 24 May, was always observed; the flag was flown and maypole dancing was performed by the children for parents and friends. The days of free milk being supplied to schools have long since passed, but the memory of those small bottles provided with straws will always linger on.

Normality had returned – but then came the notorious winter of 1947! 'Jan 30th: Very severe blizzard, snow several feet deep in places. 20 children present.' On a more cheerful note, in February an important technical achievement event took place: 'Feb 7th: BBC play Treasure Trove presented to pupils by Mr Tresize and the headmaster through the microphone and school wireless.'

More Recent Times

Some changes in teaching methods were taking place and a new scheme of work was operating in the school. It involved teachers specialising in their own subjects and 'centre of interest' lessons were included in the timetable. By September 1951, there were 135 children on role and it became necessary to use the

Mylor School, 1946/7. Left to right, back row: *Janette Ferris, Rex Collins, Ann Moore, Jean Collett, Doreen Bowden, Monica Rickard, Tommy Kevern, Michael Studd, Tom Collins, Brian Carlyon;* third row: *Brice Rowe, Joe Burley, June Vincent, Molly Hodges, Billy Palarm, Lillian Searle, Barry Carlyon, Sheila Gray, Harold Rollason, Robin Vinnicombe;* second row: *Cynthia Bishop, Joan Pellow, Audrey Studd, Elliott Nicholls, Betty Hodges, Teacher Mr Lanyon, Phyllis Loman, Keith Hodges, Patricia Lomax, Audrey Hawke, June Smith;* front: *Sheila Ferris, Corona Ferris, Pamela Goldsworthy, Marion Kendal, Josie Jones, Victor Addams, Lionel Hodges, Edith Hensman.*

dining-room as a classroom and a request was made for an extra teacher. Numbers fluctuated but by 1955 an HMI report states that there were 163 children between the ages of five and 15 in five classes with a headmaster, two assistant masters and two assistant mistresses. The school building was described as:

Very pleasant but inadequate by modern standards. To house an extra class, with numbers increasing beyond the capacity of the existing space, a large room in an adjacent Sunday School has been hired since last year.

From 1957, children of 11 and over transferred to secondary schools, which eased congestion at Mylor. The head teachers following George Pyper were Jeff Smith, who went on to be head of Archbishop Benson School in Truro, Alan Corwood and Chris Lea, the headmaster in 2004. The family of Rose Rogers has had connections with all of these teachers, as well as the Ashtons, Francis Johns and Gordon Gilbert before them. A great-grandson at the school in 2003 is the sixth generation of the family to go to school in Mylor Bridge.

Mrs Tresidder was a pupil at the school from 1966–72. In her time there was 'a garden to play in with climbing frames and a large garden plot where the swimming-pool is.' Other good memories from that time include the successes of the choir, sports days, football, rounders, television, certificates for good project work and excellent school meals cooked on the premises. But discipline was still severe with a sharp

smack on the hand with a ruler for bad behaviour, and this even included five-year-olds in the infant class.

A swimming-pool was built in 1975, during the headship of Jeff Smith, by Keith Avis and a group of volunteers after funds had been raised by the successful PTA of the time. Mr Avis attended to the maintenance of the pool, but the building work was done before his time as caretaker; he was at that time a member of the PTA. It was opened by David Penhaligon MP and on the occasion of the opening, Mr Penhaligon, Mr Smith and Mr Avis were all thrown into the pool! The pool itself cost about £1,000, but the total bill for heating etc. was around £2,000. Mr Avis recalled that after the pool was built it had been intended to roof it with a light plastic covering and examples in the area were considered. Unfortunately this did not meet with County Council approval. Changing facilities were added in the time of Alan Corwood's headship.

The new hall was started in September 1991 and finished in 1992. At the same time the old canteen and bomb shelter were demolished. Chris Lea, the head teacher at the time of writing, notes:

The old canteen, which had been built just after the war, was demolished after the building of the new hall. It had become unstable and suffered roof damage, particularly in the storms of 1990. Cracks in the building were constantly monitored and weather forecasts obtained by telephone from RNAS Culdrose when storms were expected and it had to be decided whether or not to use the building. It had been used for collective activities,

School sports on the playing field, c.1964. Leonie and Lorraine Rowe are with their school friends.

From left: *Sheila Ingram, Jeremy Turner and classmates enjoy an art class, 1964.*

Schoolchildren dancing round the maypole on May Fair day, c.1965.

Revd Conrad Sargisson says farewell from his red wheelbarrow cheered on by the children from Mylor School, May 1991. Left to right, standing: Tamsin Rees, Nicky Ferris, Simon James, Helen Tayol, Noelle Lawry, Darren Allen, Claire Lillie, Verity Lawry, Jenny Delderfield, Louise Scholbraid, Charmaine Brown, Marnie Kerslake, Jenna Davies; front: Andrew Bowers, Wayne Johns, Gareth Wills, Michael Elliot, Matthew Parnall.

A performance of Alice in Wonderland, *June 1988. Notice the open verandah at the back of the school.*

including assembly, lunches and indoor PE. Mrs Kathleen Dale, a prominent county councillor and member of the education committee, was instrumental in promoting the school's need with the authority and so the hall came about. It had been hoped that the weather vane from the Hawsa building would be fitted to the new hall but there were difficulties with this. It ended up on the roof of class three and the hall was fitted with a finial.

A large garden pond was made in 1994 and an ICT (Information and Communication Technology) room was built in 1998. Extra mobile classrooms called Elliots were again brought to the site and in January 2000 it became necessary to enclose the veranda to make additional space. At the time of writing this area is used as a library and work space. A violent storm in November 2000 damaged the roof of the chapel hall which meant that the class using it had to move into the school hall.

Awards

1990   Girls won the area netball tournament.
1991   Boys won the football tournament.
1991   Mylor school was voted the 'Greenest school in Carrick'.
1997   Girls won the netball tournament.
1997   The Barnabas award presented by Terry Waite.
2001   The boys won the local cricket tournament and the girls the Falmouth and Penryn netball tournament.
2002   The school won both local football and netball tournaments.

In March 2003 the school received a glowing report following an OFSTED inspection:

Mylor Bridge community is a very effective school. Standards are above average by the end of year six in most subjects and pupils are achieving well. Pupils achieve high standards in their personal development as their attitudes, behaviour and relationships are very good. The quality of teaching is very good overall. The school is very well led by the head teacher and key staff. Teamwork and the commitment to improvement among the staff are excellent. The school provides good value for money.

This well-established and successful school has come a long way since its New Row days. May it continue to prosper. It seems only right that a child should have the last word:

The School

I am nearly nine years old and in the time I have been at Mylor school there have been lots of changes. The verandah has been enclosed to make a brilliant art and craft space and we have had two temporary classrooms put in the playground. Soon we hope that the school will have new buildings including a new ICT suite. I am looking forward to that.

by Keiran Taylor, 2003

Mylor Pre-School

The pre-school was established in 1971 and provides friendly and professional care for 35 local children aged between two-and-a-half and school age. Play Leader, Jackie Thomas, and her dedicated team of assistants, plus daily help from a parent volunteer, run eight sessions every week, the mornings devoted to the older children and the afternoons tailored to the younger ones.

The pre-school offers a curriculum that prepares children for school entry, covering personal and social development, language and literacy, mathematics, general knowledge about the world, physical development and creativity, and the school has a wide range of toys and activities with which to nurture these skills.

September 2003 gave local children a further boost as the pre-school moved from the Ord-Statter Pavilion to the newly refurbished Methodist schoolroom in Comfort Road. It is a bright, convenient and well-equipped environment for all who use it, and parents and pupils alike are delighted with their new setting. And what of the future? There are plans afoot to create a play area from wasteland at the back of the building, so 2004 promises further investment in the next generation of the blossoming Mylor community.

Chapter 11

✤

Sport and Leisure

Sport in Mylor, Playing Fields, The Ord-Statter Pavilion, The Tremayne Institute, The Bowling Club, The Regatta, Sailing for the Blind, Rugby, Football, Cricket, Boxing, Wrestling, Mylor Bridge Table-Tennis Club, The Gardening Club, Mylor Women's Institute, Mylor Ladies' Choir, St Mylor Players, First Mylor Scouts, First Mylor Girl Guides, First Mylor Brownies, Floral Art Group, The Friends of St Mylor Church, Folk Dance Club, Yoga, Kernow Quilters.

Sport in Mylor

Over the years Mylor life has been enriched by a range of sporting and recreational activities. The fact that facilities have often been of a minimal standard has not deterred many enthusiastic volunteers who have put a great deal of effort into organising and running successful clubs and events. Being situated at the head of a tidal creek has ensured that water-based events have often had pride of place in the summer with yachting, rowing and swimming. Lime Kiln Quay, halfway down the creek, provided an excellent venue for the finish of the sailing, and the village quay for rowing and swimming.

Indoor facilities have been at a premium, but over the years the Tremayne Hall has been a focal point for a whole range of sports. The building of the Youth Centre in 1966 relieved the hall of some pressure, but the reclaiming of the waterlogged fields for the playing fields was most significant, as here was an area on which a wide range of games could be played and the annual sports and May Fair blossomed using the excellent facilities.

Playing Fields

Before 1930, a small area adjoining the bridge at Mylor known as the Promenade and owned by Mylor Parish Council, was used as a children's playing area and was furnished with swings. In 1931, the foreshore adjoining two of the fields was conveyed to the Parish Council by the Duchy of Cornwall and this was extended by a gift from Captain Tremayne.

Between 1946 and 1950, with encouragement from the National Playing Fields Association, the two fields were purchased from Colonel Trefusis for £100. Bruce Collier supervised the layout, drainage and grading of the fields and submitted plans to the King George V Memorial Fields Association for the proposed main entrance and gateway. The Parish Council decided that:

... the Playing Field Development Committee be delegated powers to do all that which is necessary in the making of contracts, purchasing of materials and carrying out of the work in connection with the future development of the Playing Field at Mylor Bridge. The work to be completed to the satisfaction necessary to obtain the grant of £450 from the King George V Memorial Fields Association.

Money was raised over the years by dances, vegetable shows and village carnivals. By 1952, the clerk was able to report that all major work had been completed by the volunteers and contractors, so that in May of that year a ceremonial opening of the King George V Playing Field was able to be carried out by Colonel Bolitho, Lord Lieutenant of Cornwall.

In succeeding years, a flagpole was added inside the main entrance, the playing field was extended by the purchase of the next two meadows, and a shelter was completed. In the 1960s the bridge was widened, a public convenience was sited near the entrance and the Ord-Statter Pavilion was built.

Much further work was done to improve the playing fields, a lot of it by volunteers. A stone retaining wall was built round the boundary facing Mylor Creek, a concrete slipway was constructed and tennis-courts and a children's play area were added. The area has been landscaped and planted and now has some fine trees.

The fields have been used for football and cricket matches, for sports days and May Fairs, for Mylor School games activities and by a wide variety of people for myriad different activities. We have a truly wonderful facility at the heart of the village, which can be enjoyed by all.

The Ord-Statter Pavilion

A significant development of the playing fields was driven by Colonel W.E. Ord-Statter, who lived on the creek side at Trelew. Retiring to Mylor after serving in the Army, he was a popular and respected man in the village and he took a great interest in all aspects of village life. The village had a marvellous outdoor facility for the youth, but he realised that a purpose-built indoor community area was also needed. He was driven by this vision and was given great support by Revd Frank Martin, who was chairman of both the Playing Field Committee and latterly the Youth Centre management.

Colonel Ord-Statter started the ball rolling with a generous donation and eventually, with other

Above: *Levelling the ground for the playing field alongside the creek, 1947.* **Left to right:** *Ken Nicholls, Harry Nicholls, Frank Curnow, Ben Sweet, Gordon Bennett, Nicholas Charles Rowe, Percy Sweet, Cardew Barnicoat, Elliot Rowe.*

Volunteers who helped to prepare the playing field: 1. Roy Crossley, 2. Cardew Barnicoat, 3. Joe Pellow, 4. David Rees, 5. Bennett Sweet, 6. Tom Rees, 7. Percy Sweet, 8. Bruce Collier, 9. Horace Prout, 10. Frank Curnow, 11. Percy Gray, 12. Jack Metters, 13. Arthur Ingram, 14. Harold Rollason, 15. Peter Hocking, 16. Philip Burley, 17. Michael Studd, 18. Billy Palarm, 19. Billy Keast, 20. Colin Rogers, 21. and 22. the Hodge brothers, Gerald and Lionel.

The swings on the playing field, 1952. Frank Curnow is pushing, with George Hearle (circled) behind on the left. On the swing, left to right: ?, ? Hodge, ? Moore, Jane Collier, Gerald Hodge, Dennis Moore.

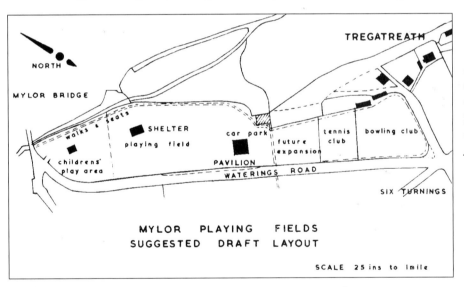

NORTH

MYLOR BRIDGE

TREGATREATH

walks & seats

SHELTER

playing field

childrens' play area

PAVILION

car park

future expansion

tennis club

bowling club

WATERINGS ROAD

SIX TURNINGS

MYLOR PLAYING FIELDS
SUGGESTED DRAFT LAYOUT

SCALE 25 ins to 1 mile

A map from the souvenir programme of the opening of the playing field in 1952, showing the suggested future layout.

The opening of the Ord-Statter Pavilion, 12 November 1966 by Lord Hunt CB DSO. Left to right: Cardew Barnicoat, Rodney Prout, George Green, Phyllis Martin, Revd Frank Martin, Lord Hunt, Alderman Kimberley Foster (Chairman of the County Council), Jon West (Youth Organiser), P. Varcoe (Chairman of the Youth Committee), Mrs Hooper, J.W. Hooper (Chairman of the Rural District Council), Kathleen Dale.

Colonel W.E. Ord-Statter, whose generous donation and enthusiasm enabled the first Youth Centre in Cornwall to be built in Mylor. He died in 1974.

donations, interest-free loans and grants from the Ministry of Education and Science, Cornwall County Council and the National Playing Fields Association, over £16,775 was raised to pay for the building. Many people gave freely of their time and expertise, none more so than Jon West, the County Youth Officer who lived in the village. Saturday 12 November 1966 saw the superb facility opened by Lord Hunt CB DSO, and it was appropriately named the Ord-Statter Pavilion. The actual building was on land made available by Mr Henry Trefusis and Mr R.M. James, which extended the area of the original playing fields. It was a gala day for the village with gymnasts from the Falmouth Youth Club, Falmouth's Drum Majorettes, Judo experts from St Ives and boxers from Falmouth YMCA all working out on the field. In addition there were canoe demonstrations on the creek and static displays in the Church Hall and Methodist schoolroom. The village glowed with pride at the facility, the first village youth centre in Cornwall. The array of distinguished guests were left in no doubt as to the importance the village centre would play in the life of the village and surrounding area. Initially the membership was limited to Mylor and Flushing boys and girls in the 14 to 20 age group.

The first Youth Leader was David Thomas, a former Mylor resident who had just returned to the area to take up a teaching post at Penryn County Secondary School. Under the watchful eye of the management committee, a programme of events was soon put in place and the centre became an extremely popular venue for the youth of the community.

Over the years, youth activities declined and other needs began to emerge, such as changing and hospitality facilities for visiting teams in various sports and a suitable meeting venue for other village organisations. So it was that the original designation of the building as a youth centre changed to that of a community facility under the general title of the Ord-Statter Pavilion. In recent times, the management committee has done considerable refurbishment, including a new heating system, and it has been used by groups as varied as the playgroup, the gardening club, cricket and football teams and many others. It has proved to be a valuable and much-needed asset for the village.

The Tremayne Institute

Thomas Tregossa was a Nonconformist vicar of Mylor, ejected in 1662, having been fined and gaoled several times. He founded Nonconformist chapels in Falmouth and Penryn and a meeting-house in Rose Hill. A larger church was built, now the Tremayne Institute, and the Rose Hill chapel became a cottage, now demolished. When this building was no longer required, Lieutenant Colonel Tremayne gave it as a mission church, hence the Tremayne Institute and Sunday School. Tommy Vincent remembers that 'on the third Sunday in the month, all the children [more than 100] walked in procession after Sunday School, with their teachers, up to All Saints Church in Bells Hill.'

The mission church, All Saints, was built in 1892, after which the old mission church became the Men's Institute and Snooker Club. It is a facility that has stood the test of time and has been a meeting-place for many years for all those interested in snooker, billiards, cards and general socialising. When Elliot Nicholls joined the Tremayne Institute in 1950, little did he imagine the large part he was to play in the activities of the club. As a member of the Falmouth and District Billiard League, the club has managed to raise snooker and billiard teams for over 50 years, during which time Elliott has served variously as president, chairman and treasurer. For all these years the club has run the institute successfully, raising funds to keep the tables up to the standards required by the league. The club consider themselves a 'contented bunch' and hope to continue to enjoy their evenings in this historic building for many years to come.

The Bowling Club

Community spirit was the driving-force in the formation and development of Mylor Bowling Club. The initial idea came from Tony Andrew and Rodney Prout during a discussion over a drink in the Lemon Arms! However, there were many difficulties with the proposal of creating a bowling-green on the

Laying the Bowling Club green with turfs from Falmouth Club, 1972.

Members of Mylor Bowling Club, c.1984 . Left to right, back row (gentlemen): *Rodney Prout, George Cole, M. Doidge, Reg Eva, Stuart Holmes, Gordon Rowe, Eric Wright, Arthur Harry, Jack Lane, Ken Keast, Brian Chambers, Mr Morrison;* middle (ladies): *Enid Wright, Margaret Askew, Mrs Gray, Connie Ougham;* front: *Nora Doidge, Barbara Rogers, Evelyn Coles, Trixie Lane, Ann Keast, Ruth Cooper.*

playing fields, so when Philip Pike offered a field in Passage Hill, this was gratefully accepted. After initial planning difficulties, a temporary building was erected and plans were made for the acquisition of a green.

Mr Pike, the first president, made a generous donation which ensured that the club was able to proceed when a well-kept green in Falmouth Docks became available in 1972, due to redevelopment. A turf cutter was hired and the immense task of lifting, transporting and laying more than 6,000 turfs was commenced. By August, the green was laid and the members carefully watched and tended it to ensure satisfactory growth.

Further work was done to complete the surroundings and the entrance. The green was officially opened on 27 May 1974 with Howard Bell, president of the Cornish Bowling Association, and many other dignitaries in attendance. The club membership has fluctuated over the years and there has been remedial work on the green and the clubhouse, but the club is highly regarded in bowling circles for its standard of play and hospitality to visiting teams. It is an important part of village life and a testimony to the vision and hard work of many people.

The Regatta

Mylor Village Regatta is a spectacular sight as the yachts move gracefully up the creek, desperately tacking as they seek every gust of wind.

In August 1892, the regatta was held in very fine weather and was witnessed by a large number of spectators. For fishing boats not exceeding 27 feet, the course was from the committee vessel, around HMS *Ganges* and back. In the challenge race for yawls, boats from the training ship also took part, but first were the Mylor men who were 'superior to HMS *Ganges*', according to a report in the *Falmouth Packet*.

In 1951, the tradition to finish the races at Lime Kiln Quay was reintroduced. When Rodney Corke's *Columbine* crossed the finishing line in Mylor Creek, it was the first time a yacht had received a winning gun there for over 25 years. During the evening there was a continuous procession of yachts of all descriptions filtering through the creek, with hundreds of spectators on both banks – a magnificent sight, the like of which is only possible in a narrow creek, with trees almost reaching the water.

After the racing, pasties, heavy cake and cream teas were the order of the day and excellent food is still provided by the ladies of the village for all those who have participated and officiated.

At one time the regatta was the highlight of the sailing calendar, topped off with a dance in the Tremayne Hall to the music of the Clavatones and the Arcadians. Events have moved on, but Mylor Regatta is still special to the village.

For many years, in conjunction with the sailing, the village also held a rowing regatta. The boats were

The finishing line for Mylor Regatta was for many years at Lime Kiln Quay. This picture was taken on 6 August 1957.

By 1987 the finishing line for the regatta was on the south side of the creek in front of The Owl's House.

based on the oyster punts, 15 feet long with a maximum four feet eight inch beam. Races consisted of such events as 'two oars', 'pair of paddles', 'two oars and two paddles' and 'three pairs of paddles'; all contested in different age groups. For many years Mylor was regarded as one of the leading clubs in the Cornwall Rowing Association regattas. A motor boat was used to tow the rowing-boats to the various venues. Most villages had boats and regattas were fiercely contested, with small amounts of prize money at stake as well as magnificent silver cups. The start and finish at Mylor were always from Mill Quay, which was also an excellent vantage point. The rowing turn was at the quarry, so the boats were constantly in view in the creek.

One of the highlights was the 'rowing and running' event, when each boat had a rower, using a pair of paddles, and a runner. Starting from the quay, the boats raced to Hooper's beach, now Tregatreath Boatyard, where the runners leapt from the boats to run back along Six Turnings and onto the quay, to be picked up by the boat and race to the finishing line. To keep the spectators amused there was usually a greasy pole and some swimming events for the children.

Sailing for the Blind

Of all the marine activities taking place from Mylor, one of the most rewarding is the Blind at Sea, which is Cornwall's sailing club for the blind. This club was formed in the early 1990s and has grown from strength to strength, catering for blind and visually impaired people of all ages. At the time of writing there are three 20-foot cruisers, painted in a distinctive bright yellow, with large black lettering – Blind at Sea – along the sides. There are several support craft and it is anticipated that there will be a new headquarters on the harbour complex by 2004. Membership is about 50, and the activities include river cruising, inshore exploration and racing in the Friday series at Mylor Yacht Club. The club is very proud that one member, representing the British Blind Racing Association, picked up a gold medal in a world series in Italy. However, the cost of this activity to the club is very high and they depend on donations and fund-raising by many dedicated volunteers.

Rugby

One of the sports in which Mylor men excelled was rugby, yet the village never fielded a team on a regular basis. In the late 1960s a XV comprised totally of Mylor men played a match against a Redruth XV at Redruth, borrowing shirts from the opposition. Practically all those who played that day were turning out on a regular basis for local clubs. Raymond George, of Falmouth and later Redruth, was an outstanding wing forward and played for Cornwall and Devon. His brother, Derek, was a wing three-quarter and played for many years at Falmouth with Lionel Hodges, who was a solid prop. A giant in his day, amongst the forwards, was John Blackburn, a Penryn player who also achieved representative honours with Cornwall and the Combined Counties.

Dave (Benji) Thomas, Penryn and Cornwall, coached the county for 20 years, the team winning at Twickenham in 1991 when over 40,000 Cornish people invaded London in their black and gold. It was a day to remember, with Dougie Pascoe, the local newsagent, leading a large contingent of Mylor people to the game. As a result, Dave was invited to become a Cornish Bard for services to Cornish rugby and adopted the name Map Melor, 'son of Mylor'. A lot of young men still play but the infrastructure is such that it would be impossible for the village to contemplate running a side.

Football

Over the years football has been an important aspect of village life, but the fortunes of the club have fluctuated as the supply of committed players has varied. Unlike some other sports, soccer has had an almost nomadic existence as the team have rarely been able to lay any permanent roots and play on just one pitch for any length of time. There have been pitches at the Bluff, Mylor Downs, Rose Hill, the playing fields and even at Penryn College but, sadly, none has become permanent.

Mylor School has been a great breeding-ground for promising players and, when it was an all-age school with pupils leaving at 15, many went straight into village teams. George Pyper, a former head teacher, was an outstanding player and he was followed by Roy Crossley who was also a keen and encouraging player. After the war, the club flourished and fielded two teams in the district league. Interest was high and Mylor's green shirts with black collars and cuffs became a prominent sight. In the 1948/9 season, the reserves won the Dallas Wake Cup and the following year the chiefs won the coveted Lockhart Cup.

In the following years the club competed for the Evan Smith Charity Cup and Colyer Shield and R. Crossley, K. Keast and E. Gray were selected for the district team. The club disbanded in 1956 but was re-formed a year later under Tangye Cox, Jack Passmore and Graham Jones and won the Dallas Wake Cup and shared the Barker Bowl with Constantine reserves. In the following season, Mylor won the Colyer Shield under skipper Johnny Rapson. They reached the final of the Lockhart Cup but were defeated 2–1 by Constantine. These were heady days and have rarely been equalled since.

The club has been re-formed several times since, but this has always meant starting in the lower divisions, which is discouraging for players, and lack of continuity meant that they lacked the vital band of willing volunteers who will do all the little jobs that are so necessary to keep a club going. Alas, there has been no team since 2002, but we still hope that enthusiastic volunteers will appear over the horizon, to re-form the club and attempt to recapture some of the glory of former years.

Cricket

Cricket is documented as early as 1847 at Carclew, but without a permanent base in Mylor there was little chance of forming a village team. In the 1930s, a team did play in a local league, half the players coming from Flushing. Mylor stalwarts included David Rees and Stowell Andrew. After the war, occasional twenty-over, away matches were played when enough keen players could be found.

In the 1990s, permission was obtained to use the playing field and a band of volunteers worked hard to prepare a wicket. With the field being fairly narrow, the pitch was aligned at an angle to avoid constantly hitting the ball into Waterings Road and the creek. Mylor entered the Cornish cricket league as a new club and there was a period of some success with the team being promoted several times.

With a good pitch and the Ord-Statter Pavilion for serving teas, it was an excellent set-up. The club was

Five members of the Thomas family in the Mylor Football Team, 1919/20. Left to right, back row: W. Thomas, Joe Thomas, A. Barnicoat, T. Barnicoat, T. Vincent; middle: J. Thomas, D. Rees, W. Toy, Ben Thomas; front: D. Tallack, B. Thomas, T. Rees.

Mylor Football Club Second Team, 1948/9, believed to be the first team from Mylor to win a cup for 40 years. Left to right, back row: Jack Passmore, R. Ferris, Trevor Doidge, Tom Rees, Bert Lawry, Ken Keast, Cardew Barnicoat; front: Jimmy Hodge, Ronnie Rapson, Joey Lawry, Joey Burleigh, Cyril Benney.

well run and enthusiasts such as Stuart Lawry, John Rose, David Jenkin and Cheryl Whiting worked hard behind the scenes. The future seemed assured and players were attracted from outside the village. But sadly, the club has been disbanded due to lack of sufficient support and players have drifted off to other clubs. It is hoped that after past periods of success, officials might be found to revive the club again.

Boxing

One of the most successful activities at the Youth Centre was the boxing, which had been at the suggestion of some of the male members. Frank Vinnicombe was the obvious choice to oversee this, as he had previous boxing experience in the Army. A large group was soon in training and a ring was erected in the main hall of the centre. Such was the expertise of the recruits that many were soon competing in county events and becoming champions at National Schools level. With space at a premium to hold competitions in the village, the Temperance Hall at Penryn was used to host home matches and they were always well supported. The fame of the club spread and Mylor boxers were invited to competitions all over the country, with Gilbert Ambrose being probably the most accomplished, winning a host of national titles. Eventually the club became so big that it moved to the premises of the National School at Penryn.

Wrestling

Boxing was not the only physical-contact sport practised in the village as many years earlier there was a wrestling club, which had been formed by the village sports club at the request of the young men of the village. The object of the sports club was to organise and get young people into sport, and they invited Mr W.T. Hooper from the County Wrestling Committee to give a talk on the objects of the Wrestling Association and also a demonstration of the principal hitches and throws. Adding weight to the formation of the club was the presence at the meeting of Colonel H.W.F. Trefusis and Revd G.C.E. Young, who agreed to be the president of the club. Around 40 members were present for a two-hour session after Mr Hooper had addressed the meeting, and he thought that there was some extremely promising talent as he saw them go through the various routines. With assiduous practice, he felt they would be able to challenge the villages around St Austell, who were at the heart of the sport.

Mylor Bridge Table-Tennis Club

In 1999, Ken Norcross and Frederick Habbe rediscovered their earlier love of table-tennis and began to play together in the Tremayne Hall, where they had found a table. Frederick put an entry in the *Mylor Stores Newsletter* asking whether anyone locally was interested in playing. Many people responded with varying degrees of experience and they were invited to come to the Tremayne Hall on Tuesday afternoons. As a result the Mylor Bridge Table-Tennis Club was formed at a meeting on 4 July 2000.

A committee was formed under the chairmanship of Ken Norcross, with Mary Hopkins as secretary, Ted Drake as treasurer, Bob Bridges – the most experienced player and umpire – as team captain and Frederick

Mylor Table-Tennis Club, 2003. Left to right: *Mary Hopkins, Jean-Paul Martinez, Alvin Heuston, John Carty, Denise Carty, John Northcroft, David Plumb, Michael Taylor, Andrew (visiting player).*

Habbe as Tremayne Hall representative. Mike Taylor had a good table available, which was bought for the club at a bargain price. The first AGM was held on 29 August when it was decided to enter two teams in the West Cornwall Table-Tennis League for the season starting in October 2000, Bob Bridges captaining the A team and Ken Norcross the B team. The club strip would be green shirts and black shorts, with refreshments kindly provided by Mylor Stores. It was agreed to set an annual subscription of £15, with players paying £2 per match and £1 per club session to cover the cost of team registration, hire of the hall and the cost of balls and nets.

Initial club funds were generated by Mary Hopkins and John Northcroft kindly hosting a very successful barbecue at their creekside home in August. A successful application was made for lottery money under the Awards for All scheme and the club received a grant of £2,400 for the purchase of two new tables and associated equipment.

The first season of league table-tennis was very successful, with the A team finishing top of the third division and the B team finishing third. The club celebrated with another barbecue at Mary and John's on 19 May 2001. At the second AGM, with further members interested in playing, it was decided to enter three teams, one in each division.

The club's second season was one of consolidation, with all three teams ending roughly mid-table in their respective divisions and everyone thoroughly enjoying the experience of playing at higher standards. Although no team achieved an award during the season, Alvin Heuston won the League Sportsman of the Year trophy. The club was now developing a social aspect and a very enjoyable Christmas party was held at the Lemon Arms. In April 2002 the club successfully hosted the League Pairs final at the Tremayne Hall.

The third AGM was held in August, at which it was agreed to enter four teams for the 2002/3 season, with Bob Bridges, Alvin Heuston, Mike Taylor and Cordelia Folland captaining the A, B, C and D teams respectively. The WCTT league committee decided that team A would play in division one, B in division two, with C and D being in division three. This turned out to be a very successful season with team A winning the 1st division. Alan Brobson and David Plumb won the League Pairs knockout competition and David Plumb was voted 'Most Improved Player'.

The Gardening Club

On the 16 September 1987 a meeting was held in the Parish Hall, called by Eunice Prince, to discuss the formation of a Garden Society in Mylor. A total of 45 people attended and Mrs Prince expressed her appreciation for the help she had received from the Horticultural Advisors at County Hall and from a number of local garden societies, particularly Carn Brea and Falmouth. At another meeting two weeks later, to which over 70 people came, Peter Davies was elected chairman, Eunice Prince secretary and Peter Jackson treasurer, the rest of the committee being Mrs S. Wills, Mrs E. Window, Mr J. Brown and Mr Whittingham.

Mylor Gardening Club on a visit to Trengwainton, near Penzance, 8 May 2000. The club is being shown around by the head gardener, Peter Horder, pictured in the centre with the moustache.

Left: *The Mylor Women's Institute present a village notice-board to the parish to mark its 80th birthday, September 2001.* Left to right, back: *Clara Cooper, Mary Young, Val Gale, Ann Langford, Liz Cock, Jenny Bramley;* front: *Ann Johnson, Mary Carling, Shena Harrison, Maureen Powell, Maisie Dunston, June Furlonger, Judy Cliff, Joan West, Pam Douglas, Rosemary Johnston.*

Right: *Darby and Joan Club on holiday in Paignton in 1963.*

Since then the club has become very popular in the village and now has over 100 members. Speakers are invited to monthly meetings from September to April, and outings take place in spring and early summer. The December meeting is always very special and well attended, perhaps partly due to the refreshments of wine and mince pies.

The talks are always very interesting and cover a wide range of gardening topics. In preparation for the visits to some of the beautiful gardens not too far away in Cornwall and Devon, head gardeners are invited to give a taste of the delights in store and to inform on the history and development of their particular garden. There have been talks on aspects of fruit and vegetable cultivation, and also on many species of garden flowers, shrubs and trees. The club has also been entertained with tales of travels to gardens further afield in Britain and abroad. Members have also entered flower shows and, in 1996, won the George Sowden Memorial Award at the Falmouth Spring Flower Show.

Meetings are held on the second Monday in the month in the Ord-Statter Pavilion and new members are always welcome.

Mylor Women's Institute

The Women's Institute started in Canada in 1897 and the first WI in Britain was formed in 1915. Mylor WI started in 1921 and in 2004 has 30 members.

Speakers offer a diverse selection of subjects from the arts to genealogy, and history to wildlife. There are films, slide shows, quizzes, demonstrations – a WI is not just 'Jam and Jerusalem'! There is of course entertainment – both home-made and imported. There are also parties, festivals and anniversaries to enjoy. A very special day was held in the 70th anniversary year when the WI invited all the women's

organisations in the village to their celebration tea and a good time was had by all. In 1987 the WI welcomed a party from Mylor in Australia. They had a Cornish cream tea with members and left the following day with St Piran's flag.

Members are proud to have produced several fascinating books over the years:

In 1971 a scrapbook of their golden jubilee year – many events reported and photographed in captivating detail.
The Hedgerow Book – *a record of a village hedge from March to October 1975 painstakingly described and sketched.*
A book describing the 75th anniversary celebrations in 1996.
The Millennium Diary of 2000 – *a social history to be preserved.*
The 2001 Birthday Book *celebrating the 80th anniversary.*

One of the strengths of Mylor WI is drama. There have been many notable productions, several of which have won prizes. Art and craft too have played their part – the lovely work of many excellent needlewomen is regularly displayed. Classes in the past have included basket making, crochet, lampshade making, toy making, dressmaking and painting.

Mylor WI has always supported the county and national federations. It has entered both county and national competitions, including the Royal Cornwall Show Competition, and prizes have been won. Over the years, members have attended many sporting activities arranged by the CFWI, including surfing, pony trekking, archery, cycling, tennis and hard-mat bowls.

Mylor WI has always been an integral part of the village community. It has supported the annual May Fair with a stall, raising a good sum of money for village organisations. The WI gave a new notice-board to the village to commemorate their 80th birthday. Members are also active in other village organisations including the flower club, the folk-dance club, the local history society, yoga groups and the Parish Council.

Mylor WI members live in one of Cornwall's prettiest villages and they are proud of their WI, knowing it to be warm, lively, active and supportive. Above all, it is a friendly and welcoming group of ladies.

Mylor Ladies' Choir

It was the tradition in the 1950s to go carol singing around Mylor Bridge during the week before Christmas. The conductor was the church organist, John Chalkley. One year, when the last carol was sung and lanterns doused, the singers made for the home of a hospitable soul who had laid on coffee and mince pies; a jolly time but sad, too, for the next carolling was far away. Someone said, 'It's a pity there isn't a Mylor Choir. We used to have one.' John Chalkley spoke up – he would be conductor if an accompanist could be found. Aileen Cole, organist of the Methodist church, volunteered and Mylor Ladies' Choir was born.

When John Chalkley left Mylor, by great good fortune a successor was found in Terry Burleigh, an experienced member of church and cathedral choirs and a well-known concert soloist. Pam Symons, organist at a neighbouring chapel, became accompanist. Many concert performances were given for charity at churches and chapels and carols were sung round the wards of Treliske Hospital at Christmas time. With excellent training by the musical director, the choir won several cups in the intermediate class of Cornish music festivals. It was a sad day when both Terry and Pam decided to retire.

For a time the choir was in limbo, then news was received that someone well experienced with choirs had come to live in the district, Bridget Westlake from Taunton. Having met and tested the choir, she agreed to become conductor/accompanist and at the time of writing everyone is happily preparing for future concerts.

St Mylor Players

A small body of very enthusiastic people met to form the St Mylor Players in April 1948, hoping to take over any balance and stage props held by the now-defunct village dramatic society. Officials elected at this meeting were Rodney Prout (chairman), Mr C. Keast (vice-chairman), Joyce Hawke (secretary), Mr J. Garvin (treasurer) and Mrs L. Patterson (producer), and 34 members were enrolled.

The first production, *Thin Partition*, took place in the Church Hall on Friday and Saturday 29 and 30 April 1949. The play, written by T.F.L. Cary, was a great success and the following letter was sent from the author:

Dear Sir, I am writing to congratulate you on what I hear was a most sympathetic production of my play Thin Partition. I think you had great courage in putting on a play with a tragic ending – would that all amateurs had that pluck. Sincerely yours, T.F.L. Cary.

From this time the St Mylor Players went from strength to strength producing plays, variety shows and even pantomimes with a cast of about 80, until 1996 when the last production took place in the Tremayne Hall.

First Mylor Scouts

The first Scout group was inaugurated in March 1922 with John Vincent as leader, and since then Scouting has continued with very few breaks and continues to thrive. The original group met in a hut on the Trefusis estate and then in Church Road. Later, they moved into the Youth Centre on the playing fields until the Scout hut, at the far end of the fields, was acquired in 1981.

At the time of writing they have three sections under the leadership of Peter Bray. There are Cub Scouts, aged between eight and ten, under assistant Cub Scout leader Amy Matthews; Scouts aged between 10 and 14, under assistant Scout leader Nigel Hocking, and Explorer Scouts (formerly Venture Scouts) between 14 and 18, run by Scout leader Tony Garvin.

They meet on Tuesday evenings and have a full programme of activities, including camps, pig roasts, survival weeks and a current project clearing footpaths and bridleways. They have been represented regularly at the World Jamboree and have achieved the considerable distinction of having six Queen's Scouts appointed in the last 12 years.

First Mylor Girl Guides

The Girl Guide Company was inaugurated in September 1938 and met in the Vicarage barn on Mondays at 6p.m. Mrs Wagner, the vicar's wife, and her daughter ran the company with some assistance from Mrs Milner who lived at Govel Goth acting as Commissioner. Ena Coombes was the captain with Miss Wagner as lieutenant, the former travelling some distance each week from her home in Cadgwith in her Austin Seven car with her Army rucksack containing the paraphernalia for the meeting. The discipline and training was strict, inclusive of the Baden-Powell principles of Guiding, which was eagerly awaited each Monday.

The Second World War started a year later with all

Mylor Ladies Choir, 2000. Left to right, back row: *Daphne Train, Doreen Baksche, Betty Curnow, Jean Symons, Prue Evans, Shena Harrison, Gil Stephenson, Ginny McDonald, Jean Marsden, Jenny Dunlop, Maureen Powell;* third row: *Hazel Carruthers, Gill Wherry, Sheila Wellman, Sheila Braddon, Marleen Horne, Olive Ware, Hilary Jefford, Naomi Joslin, Maureen Walkey, Pam Cornish, Irene Gardner, Margaritha Wrekens;* second row: *Barbara Patterson, Margaret Simpson, Glenys Robinson, Sally Collett, Joan Shelbourne, Joan West, Dot Trouton, Phyllis Harvey, Ruth Shingles, Margaret Stables;* front: *Len Simpson (president), Doreen Brier (chairman), Terry Burleigh (musical director), Pam Symons (accompanist), Eileen Humphrey (secretary).*

Mylor Players present their first production in April 1949, Thin Partition *by T.F.L. Cary.* Left to right: *May Garvin, Herbert Rogers, Margaret Roscorla, Arthur Harry, Eileen Prout, Rodney Prout, John Garvin, Nan Williams, Basil Webb, Marjorie Pyper, Roy Crossley, Mary Rollason.*

the officers except Mrs Wagner joining the Forces. Miss Wagner returned after a short absence and took over as captain with Susan Dorrien-Smith as a very young lieutenant. The girls worked hard for the war effort, making camouflage nets for military hardware, collecting empty medicine bottles, Red Cross subscriptions (one penny per week) and for missionaries. The patrols alternately took turns to prepare tea in the Church Hall for the ladies of the village using their sewing machines to make pyjamas, knitted articles and bandages for the troops. On some Sundays there were church parades where the girls were complimented on the precision of their drills, having been instructed by a locally stationed Army officer.

In January 1982 Christine Askew and Sally Hearle were presented with their Queen's Guide Certificates by the late David Penhaligon MP. Invited guests were Ena Coombes, Alice Tovey, Peggy Crossley (former Guide and Brownie Guiders), Miss Terry, District Commissioner and Bernice Gay and Gill Stevenson, Guiders.

In January 1982 Christine Askew and Sally Hearle were presented with their Queen's Guide Certificates by David Penhaligon MP.

First Mylor Brownies

A Brownie pack was established during the Second World War by Bernice Curnow, later followed by a Miss Durant for a short while.

A new Mylor pack was formed in 1946 under the leadership of Peggy Crossley as Brown Owl. Since its inception, it has had a full pack of 24 girls aged from seven to ten years old. Mrs Crossley then left the district and Alice Tovey became the new Brown Owl. The pack used to meet at the school yard with just the veranda for shelter during the winter months. The girls used to take part not only in the Mylor unit but joining with others in the district and division for Brownie revels and competitions. Eventually, Lillian Hearle became the Brown Owl and used the Tremayne Hall as a more suitable venue.

The uniform has changed considerably over the years. Gone are the brown dress and yellow tie and their place taken by culottes, and since by tee-shirts and trousers. In 2004 the Guider is Miss Susan Prout

with the help of Sue Askew, Helen Hughes and Laura Hitchman. At the time of writing the weekly meetings are held at the Scout hut with the highlight of the year being the Pack Holiday.

Floral Art Group

Mylor and District Floral Art Society has been running since the 1970s. The aims of the club are to promote the beauty of flowers and foliage and to learn the art of arrangement through demonstrations, workshops and exhibitions. It is an extremely friendly club and members who enter the monthly competitions and annual exhibition find that they learn and improve their ideas for design, the use of colour and texture and mechanics, whilst those members who come just to enjoy the skills of the demonstrators find that they gain new ideas, concepts and hints to experiment with in their own homes.

At each meeting visitors and new members are assured of a warm welcome and the chance to win one of the demonstration set pieces in the monthly raffle. There is a sales table and a plant-sale table with plenty of people to offer advice. Tea and coffee are also enjoyed in very convivial company.

The Friends of St Mylor Church

The Friends of St Mylor Church dates back to the early 1970s but by 1986 had almost ceased to be active. In March 1987 the Church of St Mylor was seriously in need of a new roof, so to help to raise funds for this large expense the vicar, Revd Conrad Sargisson, called a meeting of interested parishioners in the Tremayne Hall with a view to re-activating the Friends. A new committee was formed and set about organising a programme of fund-raising events and also social events to bring the parish together as a community.

In due course the church was successfully re-roofed, and although the group no longer organises so many events, they have succeeded in keeping the Friends active with regular fund-raising events to assist the church-fabric fund and with purely social events to maintain the social life of the parish. The most successful fund-raising event has always been the annual Christmas market where there are normally about a dozen stalls selling cakes, gifts, plants, books, etc. The group also has frequent coffee mornings and other such events.

On the social side the Friends organise a parish lunch every winter and a harvest supper or lunch each autumn and have also enjoyed visits to various places of interest such as the earth station at Goonhilly, the Copeland collection at Trelissick and boat trips up the River Fal. For several years the Friends have enjoyed an evening in the spring at the Country Skittles establishment at Townshend near Hayle. It is not necessary to be a churchgoer to join the Friends,

Kernow Quilters presenting cheques to Macmillan Nurses and Air Ambulance representatives, 2000. Left to right, standing: *Julia Smith, Peggy Beadle, Carole Monk, Nina Taylor, Macmillan Nurses' representative (receiving cheque), Maureen Webber, Shirley Crook, Anne Gearon, Air Ambulance representative (receiving cheque), Pat Riley, Deidre Sibthorpe, Chris Drummond, Barbara Farmer, Pam Annear;* sitting: *Lois Brown, Pat Dwyer, Chris Gurney.*

Mylor Merrymakers, c.1969. What a graceful sight! Left to right: *Jack Lane, Bill Sparkes, Tony Andrew, Reg Sowden.*

Folk-Dance Club, garden party, 2002. Left to right: *Wendy Atherton, Patience Searle, Lynn Allerton, Norman Baker, Pat Hugh, Doreen Christmas, Marion Ashford, Ruth Akesley, Mary Young, Mary Baker.*

but only to have a strong desire to see the lovely historic old church maintained, preserved and used so that it will still be there for future generations.

Folk-Dance Club

The club meets twice a month in the afternoon and in 2004 opened its nineteenth year in the same venue, Tremayne Hall. There are founder members who travel from as far as Helston and Mawnan Smith, and their Thursday afternoon sessions give much pleasure and exercise in friendly company. With a short break for refreshments and a lucky number prize, everyone participates. Though not taking the dancing too seriously, a good standard is encouraged by the caller, John Searle, ably assisted by his wife Patience.

Holiday-makers and members of other local clubs attend, such as Truro and Gweek. The afternoon sessions are convenient for dancers who wish not to turn out in the evenings, especially in the winter. One may attend with friends or without a partner. The club slogan is 'you are never alone in a square'. Although most of the dances are English folk-dances, some American-style squares are also included. Two favourite dances, composed by Pat Shaw, are 'The Waters of Holland' and 'Levi Jackson's Rag'.

Yoga

The yoga class at Mylor Bridge School has been running for over four years and continues to be well supported by people in the area. The class is open to all who wish to develop the practice of yoga, integrating postures, movement and breath, and to explore the use of relaxation and breathing techniques to develop mental focus and relax both body and mind.

Yoga helps you take care of yourself physically and it is an ideal form of exercise that can keep you strong, flexible, energetic and relaxed. It can be a mental discipline too; one designed to develop concentration, improve mental clarity and instil greater calm and awareness. Yoga's gentle approach to exercise can be easily adapted to the individual's needs and is a perfect warm up, or cool down, for other forms of exercise.

Kernow Quilters

Kernow Quilters are a group of women meeting fortnightly at the Ord-Statter Hall in Mylor. The group was formed in 1985 by about eight ladies, at that time mostly living in the Helston area. They met in each others homes, all sharing a love of patchwork and quilting to develop ideas and skills. Over the years the group grew to its present restricted membership of about 25 people enjoying each other's company and knowledge. An exhibition is held bi-annually where members' work is displayed and a quilt made by the group is raffled in aid of local charities.

Chapter 12

The War Years

The First World War, The Second World War Begins, Air Raids, Living with Shortages, Carrick Roads, The Year 1943, Camps for Refugees and Troops, Mylor War Memorial.

The First World War

It took some time for the village to respond to the demands of the war, as this excerpt from a local newspaper indicates:

Mylor Parish Council was criticised for not supporting the Air Raid Precaution Service. Volunteers were slow to come forward in Mylor and Flushing as ARP firemen and there were calls for fire-fighting appliances in the villages.

Another cutting from a local newspaper dated 3 September 1915 reads:

Authorities in Cornwall issued notices warning visitors to the area not to take photographs anywhere along the coast. If caught their cameras and plates would be destroyed.

However, it was not long before local boys were corresponding from the Front, as another newspaper cutting demonstrates (DCLI stands for Duke of Cornwall's Light Infantry):

Sergt Philip Passmore, son of Mrs E.P. Kevern of New Row, Mylor, who is in the second DCLI at the Front, has written the following lines whilst in the trenches:

'Verses from the trenches' by Sergt P. Passmore.

You sit and read the papers, re 'Football at the Front',
One thinks we're on a picnic, or perhaps some other stunt,
One hardly seems to realise that this is not a game,
But a very serious business, to protect our country's name.
One sees the 'cream of England' go marching down the street,
It stirs one's very heart-strings to hear the tramp of feet,
Yet few of you yet understand that those who now pass by
Are, for your country's honour, going out to fight or die.

'What a glorious time they'll have,' 'a picnic' you might say,
One often hears remarks like this passed, almost every day.
But what a difference one does find whilst waiting for the fray,
If you heard the shrapnel bursting I wonder what you'd say.

We sit or stand in trenches, with mud up to our knees,
And perhaps a little water, we wait for it to freeze.

We hear a bullet whizzing, like a motor in a race,
We peep out through our loop-hole, yet seldom see a face.

We hear reports from some big guns, perhaps some miles away,
The shell bursts somewhere near us and "makes a hole" you say.
Perhaps it may, or it may not, it does create a smell,
But if you actually smelt the fumes, you'd say its near to ----.

Could I with pen or pencil depict the dreadful scene,
Of war and all its horrors, and lots of other things,
Well, I would gladly do it to stop this awful strife,
And have the world at peace again, and save perhaps many a life.
Roll on when it's over, and, we plough the raging main
Back to dear old England, to see our friends again.
There's many a spot and many a place, retained in memory,
But few like dear old Mylor, though mud up to my knee.

Sergt Passmore went to the Front in December, and has seen some hard fighting in Flanders. He is now on his way home, however, having been wounded. The following postcard was received from him last week: 'Dear M. – do not write until you hear further. Am wounded slightly and on my way down. Nothing to worry over, simply a flesh wound. – yours etc. Phil.'

Apart from the terrible losses recorded on the war memorial and the need to manage with shortages by growing more food locally, the First World War impinged fairly little on everyday village life. It was all going on a long way away and could only be followed days or even weeks later in newspaper

'Your country needs you'. Villagers gather during the First World War. The speaker is possibly Captain William Tremayne.

reports and letters from the Front.

In 1920, Philip Passmore's younger brother William purchased a house in New Row, believed to be the one in which his mother had lived. At the start of the Second World War, William was working at Falmouth Docks. He was recalled to the Royal Navy and joined HMS *Adventure*, a 7,000-ton minelayer, as a chief engine room artificer. On 13 November 1939 this ship was in contact with a magnetic mine off the *Tongue* light vessel and became one of the first victims of the German use of this device in the Thames Estuary. Twelve crew were killed and 35 wounded – sadly, William was one of those who died and he is buried in the family grave in Mylor churchyard.

CPO Edwin Porter served in the Royal Navy during the First World War and died in June 1918. He is believed to have been buried in Simonstown, South Africa. Always known as Happy Sam, this picture was taken outside the cottages at the end of New Row, where his family lived. His nephew Fred Ingram still lives in New Row.

The Second World War Begins

At 11a.m. on Sunday 3 September 1939, England declared war on Germany. The influence of the First World War on Mylor may have been rather distant but the beginning of hostilities in 1939 was no less remote to begin with. In *Portrait of a Village* Eric Gray writes:

The 'Dig for Victory' campaign started immediately, lawns were dug up and vegetables grown in place of flowers. We were given identity cards and gas masks that smelt all rubbery and seemed similar to being anaesthetised with gas in the dentist's chair. We all became accustomed to buying food on ration

Merchant ships laid up in Mylor Pool in the 1930s due to the Depression.

books and clothing on coupons, never suspecting this mode of life would go on for more than ten years. Many cars were laid up throughout the duration of the war, and for the others, petrol coupons were issued that severely restricted the distance one could travel, even car lights had to be masked and driving at night consequently became more difficult. Sign posts and road signs were removed to prevent them from assisting invading forces. We found ourselves in an unaccustomed world of darkness. Lights no longer lit up our roads, shutters were fitted to windows and heavy blackout curtains hung in our homes. We dug air raid shelters in our gardens, ours was damp and miserable and we were glad we only had to spend a few nights in such cramped conditions. Later, steel shelters were issued that could be fixed indoors, a real luxury in comparison. Church bells stopped ringing and would only ring in future to alert us that an invasion was taking place. Air raid wardens were appointed to ensure the blackout rules and regulations were strictly observed. Horace Prout served the village in this position and having an irritable cough, one always knew when he was on patrol. 'Put out that light' was the common shout should anyone contravene regulations.

Later, there were monthly gas-mask drills outside Miss Tresize's shop, which is Mylor Stores at the time of writing.

Eileen Prout was the wartime district nurse for the village and she remembers:

On one occasion a manoeuvre was to take place. Flushing was to invade Mylor, or vice versa – I'm not sure which. This confrontation was to take place at Devils Roost. Dr Herwald being in attendance, I was to be called upon in an emergency – and one arose! A Home Guard member lacerated his inner thigh muscle whilst climbing over a barbed wire fence at the entrance to Trefusis. Whilst rendering first aid, an over-enthusiastic Home Guard officer let off a tear gas canister. Terror struck! Did I put on my gas mask first, or help my patient with his? How could I arrest the bleeding and get a mask on with just a light from a small torch? A voice called out of the darkness 'PUT OUT THAT LIGHT'. Every time I lent over the

patient my tin hat slipped down my nose; somehow I never got my helmet to stay put – I seemed to have the wrong-shaped head!

Many children were evacuated to distant parts of the country from London and other south-eastern target areas. James Thomas remembers sharing his home with one evacuee:

We went down to the church for our allocation and were presented with brother and sister called 'Evans' who did not wish to be parted. We only had room for one body so Mrs Moore, who lived in the adjoining house, agreed to take the girl if we could accommodate the boy, hence 'Jimmy Evans' joined the Thomas family. He was a poor little scrap with only one kidney. His family lived in the East End of London and we came to understand that Jimmy's main treat of the day used to be a meat pie from the back door of the local public house. We had a stock cupboard containing blackcurrant puree and honey, and what with the produce of the garden and plenty of butter milk from Mrs Moore, whose husband ran the small holding with two cows and some pigs on the land behind Mylor police station, Jimmy rapidly fleshed out into a healthy little boy. We were provided with a camp bed and army blankets from the state for his accommodation. Out of one of the surplus blankets my mother and her sister made winter coats for themselves. The blankets were grey with a red stripe at each end and made up into quite stylish garments. One afternoon a barrage balloon came down on a farm near Bissom and soon all the village population sported silvery shopping bags! Waste not, want not.

Air Raids

In *Memories and Gardens*, Marion Howard Spring recalled the following:

So here we were at Hoopers Hill, with our gas masks, identity cards and ration books. Howard joined the Home Guard and was a liaison officer between them and the regulars – the Worcesters were stationed quite close to our bungalow, just by the Mylor Jetty. One day I saw an aeroplane over our raspberry cage with little puffs of smoke all round it and that was the first of our German visitors. After that they came often, in ones, twos or threes, dropping bombs here and there – nuisance raids they were called. If they came close we would go into our concrete cellar, where we should be safe from anything but a direct hit. It was very tiring and nerve-racking and one day, when the siren had gone for the fifth time, I said out loud in the hearing of a neighbour of ours: 'I can't stand it!' Then he went for me hammer and tongs and said I had jolly well got to stand it like everybody else. That did me a lot of good and I learned to control my words and my face, but my heart always fluttered when I heard the bombs whistling down. The coolness of those around me helped considerably. I used to say to Mrs Ashwin: 'Now you must not go home until the All Clear

THE RURAL DISTRICT COUNCIL OF TRURO.

COULTER HANCOCK,
SOLICITOR,
CLERK TO THE COUNCIL.

TELEPHONE 81.

12 Princes Street,
Truro,

20th November, *1941.*

Mr. H. R. Prout,
Air Raid Warden,
MYLOR.

Dear Sir,

Air Raid Damage.

I am directed by the Council to convey to you an expression of their appreciation for the excellent services rendered *and Mrs Prout* by you/on the occasion of the Air Raid at Mylor on the 13th instant. The Council consider that you did a splendid job of work.

Yours faithfully,

Letter of thanks from Truro Council sent to Mr Harold Prout, Mylor's Air-Raid Warden.

has sounded' and she would answer: 'Oh, it's all right. I'll just keep under the trees.'

Mylor's own air-raid alarm was a Great Dane belonging to Mr Rollason at the abattoir opposite All Saints Church. It started barking a full ten minutes before the planes arrived! However, it could not prevent the loss of life when in 1941 a stick of bombs fell on New Row. Alex Hamilton died in a cottage halfway along on north side, where the first bomb fell. The second fell on Nos 1 and 2 (the houses have since been renumbered). Mr and Mrs Bird died instantly as did Marion Rickard. Her mother died later.

At No. 15, opposite the Hamiltons, the lamp on the table did not shatter nor did the windows when the bomb dropped, as the blast went over the roof. The family stood in the doorway looking up at the plane and then dived under the table and stairs – there was no time to reach the Anderson shelter. A bucket chain was formed by people to put out the fires. Many residents were re-housed, among them the Bettinsons, Richards, Franklins and Collins.

The ARP warden slept in a hut in New Row and the pump, a big Dennis fire-engine, was kept in a galvanised shed beside the oak tree by the bridge, where the public toilets are now. Most of the shelters that were built were of the Morrison pattern rather than Anderson shelters.

Living with Shortages

James Thomas recalls:

Uncle kept ferrets and went rabbiting for stews and pies. They helped themselves to the outside rows of crops and the farmer, Mr Dale, turned a blind eye. Everything was food and fuel oriented and when we went playing in Carclew Woods, where there had been a sawmill, we always returned home dragging a branch for the fire or bark to fire the copper in the wash-house. Farm labourers were in the Forces so school closed for a week at harvest time so the children could help get in the cereal crops. As payment, they were allowed to glean the fields for grain for the chickens that every family seemed to have. They were also given a share of the rabbits that were caught as they ran out of the standing corn in front of the mower. I learned how to gut and skin rabbits at quite an early age.

Marion Howard Spring writes:

I joined the Women's Institute and listened to lectures on all sorts of dodges to make our meagre rations go round. I also bought a dozen Rhode Island Reds and fed them on all sorts of unlikely odds and ends which we boiled up and mixed with their ration of bran, or whatever it was. Rude people called it shop sweepings! Anyhow, they were splendid hens and behaved in a most patriotic way. I was able to give three eggs a day to an invalid who lived up the creek and who was unable to eat normal food. Each autumn after the harvest we used to go over the stubble and glean every bit of corn we could find, and I grew sunflowers, as my Rhode Island Reds loved the seeds.

It was was also reported in the *Falmouth Packet* that 'Mrs Burdett, a resident of Mylor aged 103 has been granted three priority eggs per week, but this was not to be treated as a precedent.' There was a big campaign to increase food production and a grant of two pounds per acre was offered for grassland to be ploughed and sown with wheat, potatoes, oats, barley and corn. In Mylor, butter-making classes were held at the Institute. People were encouraged to keep a pig or a few hens and farmers were urged to keep their machinery in full use, ploughing by night and day. During the course of the war, the national harvest was more than doubled. Adults were issued with ration cards and later there were points for bread, coupons for clothing and permits for this and that. There were never-ending forms to be filled in – all in triplicate. Each household was supposed to criss-cross their windows with brown sticky tape to prevent flying glass fragments during air raids.

During the war the Vinnicombe family lived at 11, Lemon Hill, the house next to the pump. Frank's mother sold fish in front of the house and Frank recalls that:

I came home on leave in 1941. Dad must have been out fishing the next day and there were queues right down to New Row. Word got around that 'George got fish, look out!' Everything was rationed. Dad used to bring the fish up to the house, but he only brought enough to look after the locals.

Carrick Roads

Mylor Creek flows into Carrick Roads, the large body of water forming the estuary of the Fal and Truro rivers, with Mylor Churchtown and the Dockyard on the south side of its mouth.

The Free French had a centre of operations at Mylor Dockyard, then owned by the Admiralty. Later, it became a secret base for shipping agents to France. Locals clearly remember four or five French fishing boats that used to come alongside and then disappear for periods of time before reappearing. Free French fighters were supplied with their documents prior to being sailed across the Channel to Brittany and French sailors were frequently put ashore. There was intense rivalry between the Free French at Mylor and the SIS (Secret Intelligence Service) organised in Falmouth and the SOE (Special Operations Executive) working from the Helford River.

The Treneer family, who farmed by the harbour, had a number of servicemen billeted in their farm sheds and on the hill behind. They remember the Frenchmen and how in a very few months there were few snails left in the area!

A sail store on the jetty (Mylor Yacht Club in 2004), owned by George Corke, became a mortuary for bodies from vessels sunk or burnt out. The Americans built another jetty and slipway at the entrance to the harbour for the repair of damaged small ships and landing-craft. David Spring of Mylor particularly remembers a ship which sank off Penarrow Point, the headland just south of Mylor Harbour. It was loaded with cotton and burned fiercely for days.

As a footnote to the use of Mylor Dockyard for small-boat repair by the Americans, the *Western Morning News* carried the following report on 23 October 2003:

A Royal Navy bomb squad from Plymouth was yesterday called to Mylor Yacht Harbour, near Falmouth, after shipwrights cutting the keel from an old 44ft wooden motor sailing vessel discovered what appeared to be shell casings that had been used as ballast. The harbour's winter lay-up area in a valley was cordoned off by police while the casings were inspected and declared safe. The harbour, a naval dockyard in the nineteenth century, was used as a base in 1944 by American boat maintenance crews in the run-up to the D-day landings in Normandy.

The Year 1943

A big agricultural show was held at Canara Farm by permission of Mr A. Hammill in 1943. A particularly large entry of horses in a wide variety of classes, as well as a cattle show and comic-dog competition, not to mention a sports event, ensured a good profit and

more than £100 was raised for the RSPCA fund for Russian horses and the Red Cross fund in aid of Cornish prisoners of war. Major Maurice Petherick MP opened the show and, as a cavalry officer in the First World War, spoke movingly of the need for support for the large number of horses employed by the Russian army which had to undergo great hardships. One of the villagers remembers:

That year we had a memorable Christmas in Mylor, what with the Americans stationed nearby and also the Green Howards Regiment. Sweets and chocolate were in abundance and the children of the village never had so much to eat. Dances were held in the village hall. A miniature 'Glenn Miller' band played and all the mothers went, along with kids, teenagers, grans and granddads.

The local girls were well catered for – we had a lot of opposition, we lads! There was competition also from the Dutch Cadet School at Enys, who were reported to have excellent manners. One American soldier, a dispatch rider, rode a Harley Davidson round the village, impressing all the girls and gaining admiration from the village lads.

The Americans had so much but were very generous. However, all the black soldiers were camped separately at Perranwell. Some of the white soldiers came from the southern states and still detested the blacks and this was the first time villagers had realised how deep was this hatred.

Camps for Refugees and Troops

Cornwall has welcomed a wide variety of refugees over the years, but the decade from 1937 to 1947 produced a big influx. First there were exiles from the Spanish civil war and from communist Russia, then there were Jewish people from Germany and the low countries, and Ukrainians and Poles followed. Many of them provided agricultural labour.

There were also prisoners of war. Camps were established, particularly on the road from the Bluff to Restronguet Barton at the top of the village, near the American and British military camps and the anti-aircraft battery. Mains water had been laid on to the American camp at the Clump and the British camp at Restronguet.

After the war, prisoners of war were repatriated, but many displaced persons remained and established a church in one of the Nissen huts. It was beautifully decorated by the men who lived there and a Roman Catholic priest from Falmouth used to visit regularly to hold services. Some non-Catholics were made welcome at Mylor Methodist Church. Some of the men still live in the area – Dmitro Szewczuk (known to his English friends as Jim) and his wife Valentina were eventually able to move into a small cottage in the village. Dmitro had learnt English in the camp and became one of its natural leaders, helping many others to meet villagers and obtain work locally. Mr Ted Stewart, now naturalised British, recalls that there were about 110 men and he acted as interpreter for the warders. There were about ten huts, a recreation hall, administrative buildings and a kitchen. When the camp finally closed they built a cross eight feet high, on the site of the old guard house, in gratitude and as a symbol of the faith that had sustained them. Bryan Budgen translated the inscription for a man named Rimec to chisel: 'This symbol of faith in God was erected by Ukrainians who, escaping from Russian communism, found refuge in England, 1948.'

Above: The church at the old Army camp at Restronguet created by the Ukrainians who escaped the Russian communists, June 1948.

Left: The Ukrainian cross at Restronguet.

Below: Inscription on the Ukrainian cross Restronguet.

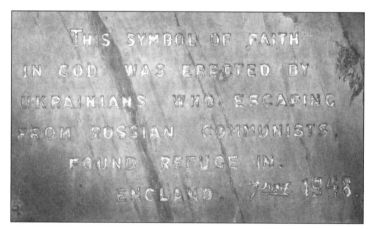

Left: *Fishing boats at Mylor Dockyard in April 1949 which had been used as minesweepers during the Second World War.*

(REPRODUCED BY KIND PERMISSION OF THE NATIONAL MARITIME MUSEUM, GREENWICH)

Below: *The naval guardhouse and store on the end of the quay early in the 1930s.*

Grids at Mylor Dockyard used for the maintenance of small naval vessels, c.1960.

Welcome Home parade for returning servicemen in 1945. Nicholas Charles Rowe is pictured with his car.

The war memorial outside St Mylor Church, dedicated to those who lost their lives in the two world wars.

They shall not grow old, as we that are left grow old;
Age shall not weary them, nor the years condemn.
At the going down of the sun and in the morning
We will remember them.

Laurence Binyon 1869–1943

Mylor War Memorial:

In Memory of the Parishioners who fell in the Great War 1914–1919

Pte A.E. Blackler DCLI
2 Lt H.F.W. Chamberlin DCLI
2 Lt J.B. Chamberlin RAF
Lt D.M. Coles NF
Dvr W. Doidge RE
Pte S. Gay RB
Pte A.H. Gilbert SLI
Pte H.G. Hankins DCLI
L/C Sgt F. Lovell RBR
Aptce T.E.L. Olivey Merchant Service
ERA C.W. Rees RN
Rfn S. Rees KR RC
Lt J.V. Rogers 78 Canadians
Pte R.M. Tallack WR
Ldg Str S.J. Toy RN
Pte T.C. Walley RBR
PO E. Porter RN
AB A.D.R. Pearce Merchant Service

Roll of Honour 1939–1945

Barnicoat J. Sgt RE
Burley E.C. St 1st Cl. RN
Bunny F. S/Sgt RA
Cundy J. Spr RE
Dorrien-Smith G.R. Capt. Buffs - para
Dorrien-Smith H.A. Lt DCLI - para
Ferris R.C. Str RN
Ferris G. AB RN
Hingston R. Str 1st Cl. RN
Lawry G.M. PO RAF
Passmore W. Chf ERA RN
Pike R. Sub Lt FAA
Pearce N. ERA RN
Prout W. CPO RN
Richards K. ERA RN
Rogers D. Pte KR
Vincent C. Pte QRR
Wilmot G. PO RN
Chamberlin G.H. Ft Sgt RAF
Trevena W.R. CPO RN

Mylor Parish Civilians Killed by Enemy Action

Bird C.	40
Bird O.	36
Brusey P.	34
Hamilton A.	12
Rickard B.	28
Rickard M.	8
Tallack L.	38

Chapter 13

Miscellany

'Gather ye the fragments that are left that nothing be lost'
is the motto of the federation of Old Cornwall Societies

The Carol Choir, Transport, 'Figgy Duff', Tea Treats at Carclew, Frank Curnow, Revd Richard Parker, Mylor Christmas Lights, Dorothy's Story, Feast Days and Ancient Customs, Reminiscences of Mary Young, Cornovi Cottage, Vera Moore's Memories, Reminiscences of Becky Bunny, The Old Post Office, School Chums Meet.

The Carol Choir

Some years before his death, Mr Harry Moore made some notes about the Mylor he remembered as a boy. He came from a family with generations of local associations and he was blessed with a retentive memory. Of the carol choir he recorded:

There were between 40 and 50 in the choir. One of my uncles was the choirmaster and two of my uncles were also instrumentalists in it. One played a flute and another a cornet. The one who was choirmaster played sometimes the flute and also the euphonium. I was the youngest member and played the flute. There were four Moores and three Tallacks who were instrumentalists. Another old celebrity was Harry Connor who gave out the words of the carols after the whole choir 'struck sound', that is they sounded the chords of the four parts. We practised in Penhall's barn at Cogos at the end of Comfort Road. Another famous character in the choir was Albert Rowe (Bill's father). He had a fine bass voice

and I can still hear him pouring out 'The gates of brass before Him bow, the iron fetters yield.' One of the anthems was the well-remembered 'Second Chapter of Luke' with solos and fugues and instrumental accompaniment. 'And suddenly and suddenly' etc. I remember my uncle saying 'Stop! It is not suddently, suddenly is the word.'

On Christmas Eve, the choir journeyed to Falmouth, opened the programme at Market Strand and then toured the town, singing outside the hotels and reaching Mylor at about midnight. At 7a.m. on Christmas morning, the choir sang in the village, then went to Mylor Churchtown, singing en route, then around Trefusis to Flushing and back to Mylor to eat Christmas dinner. After dinner we went to Restronguet and, of course, a call at the Pandora for refreshment. Then to Carclew, where, after singing in front of the house, the choir was entertained to supper in the servants' hall, beer, beef, pudding, cake, mince pies, etc. From there we went to Broads Lane and on to Enys. At Enys the same ritual prevailed and then we returned to Mylor just in time for another lot of

Mylor Male Voice Choir in the 1930s. Left to right, back row: *Charles Rawling, C. Thomas, Vincent, Gray, ?, ?, Barnicoat, Rowe, Symons, Hooper, Cole;* middle: *Vincent, Welch, Curnow, Thomas, Thomas, ? , Bunny, Evans, Doidge, Tresize, Rees, F. Porter;* front: *Rickard, Johns, Johns, R. Hawke, Pearl Frost (pianist), Mr Lester (choirmaster), F. Tresise, B. Brewer, R. Rawling, P. Rogers.*

Programme for a Christmas Concert held in the Mission School on Boxing Day 1895.

refreshments before 10 o'clock. My uncle and I always went to Miss Elizabeth John's house, and had supper with Harry Connor and then, like Pepys, to bed.

Transport

Rose Rogers recorded memories of early transport in the village:

Mr Porter ran a Jersey car from Mylor to Flushing to catch the boat to and from Falmouth. He also had a cab for weddings and to take people to and from the railway station. Leonard Gilbert came home from the 1914–18 war and he too had a cab that he kept in a shed where the entrance to the playing field is now.

When villagers went on outings they sometimes hired Randle and Ferris's Jersey cars from Penryn. Sometimes when they came to the hills they had to disembark and walk!

After the 1914–18 war, Captain Paul of Flushing ran a bus from Mylor to Flushing. Johnny Harcourt ran the first bus to Falmouth (fare 9 pence in old money). Then came a Mr Johns from Praa Sands and he kept his bus at Rose Hill Farm.

George Hearle recalls that, from the 1930s on, Prout's garage, which was opposite the blacksmith's cottage, not only sold petrol from a pump but ran a reliable taxi service, sold household goods and hardware, and charged accumulators for the old-style radio sets. Eventually, there was a bus service provided by George's father, Mr Hearle, and then finally Western National. James Thomas remembers:

Mrs Hearle was the widow of the gentleman who inaugurated the service. At the end of the war in Europe, she acquired a continental charabanc in return for a bus that had been commandeered at the start of the war. It was painted olive green and entered the village under tow! We were impressed as children because it had a tail fin and all the instruments were lettered in German. I think that it was also left-hand drive. The bus was eventually refurbished, painted white and became the flagship of the Hearle's fleet for several years. The Western National buses were never maintained to the condition of the Hearle's. I remember several occasions when the bus was unable to climb Truro Hill out of Penryn with its passengers on board and we would all have to disembark, and sometimes lend a shoulder to assist its progress! This was always achieved with good humour and much friendly banter but, in retrospect, was not a lot of fun in bad weather.

Virtually every Saturday we would make a trip to Penryn. To keep costs down, it was usual to walk into Penryn via Rose Hill and Bissom, using one of the buses for the return trip. I remember once, during the winter of 1947, having to make both journeys on foot because of the severity of the snow. No wheeled transport could move and at the bottom of Bissom Hill we were literally knee-deep in snow in the middle of the road. In places it was difficult to determine where the hedges were because of the drifting. Thank God no one got stranded or lost! On the rare occasions that we needed to go to Falmouth, we walked over the hill to Flushing and caught the ferry to the Prince of Wales pier. After attending to our business, we caught the bus back. The ferry charge was one old penny each way and so made economic sense.

Snow, certainly a very unusual sight in this sheltered valley, is seen here on St Valentine's Day 1994.

'Figgy Duff'

Caroline Perkins remembered Mr Porter who drove the horse bus, cab and sometimes the brake for outings. Often the coal cart was cleaned up to take passengers to Flushing. She recalled when the Post Office was in the middle of the village, and stables for horses were on the site of the present Post Office. She could remember coal barges arriving at Lime Kiln Quay delivering coal to Mr Barnicoat who ran the coal business there. The village barber arrived twice a week to cut the men's hair. She recalled great fun on regatta days; roundabouts, swings and all the fun of the fair; there were stalls selling fruit, cockles, mussels and limpets on Mill Quay. Feast Week, she remembered, was always the nearest Sunday to 25 October, when they used to eat cheek of pork (pig's head) and figgy duff (plum pudding).

Tea Treats at Carclew

A member of Mylor Darby and Joan Club recalls the tea treats at Carclew. First the children would be walked round the gardens in crocodile. Then, they would have tea, the Carclew staff waiting on them. The saffron bun was sometimes too big to eat at one go, so the remains were wrapped in a handkerchief and taken home. Afterwards, there would be games. House guests at the mansion would come out on to a balcony and dangle bags of nuts on a line for the children to catch in their teeth.

This lady also remembers the concern of Mrs Tremayne for the poor of the parish. In about 1900, she appointed a Mrs Pearce, who lived on Mill Quay, to collect money weekly for a paying-in club. Lengths of shirting and curtain material would then be bought by the bolt wholesale for the use of the members.

Frank Curnow

Mr Frank Curnow began work in 1912 as a pantry boy at the Vicarage. When there were guests to stay he cleaned the boots and shoes – sometimes as many as 24 pairs! Later he went to work at Perran Foundry and this was his work for 50 years. In 1946 he took over the care of the churchyard. Mr Curnow lived in Mylor all his life and was an authority on the history of the village. In the King George V Playing Field a plaque reads: 'This children's Playing Area is a memorial to Frank Curnow, who devoted a lifetime of Service to Mylor (1898–1973).'

Frank, born in 1898, was Mylor's sexton and gravedigger and died in 1973. He recorded his memories of the ploughing up of the common land at Mylor Downs:

Looking from Carclew Lodge one sees that the hedge-banks of the four converging roads are built of handy-size spar stones. These were ploughed up by horse and oxen, and children were paid a penny for each bucket of stones picked up behind the plough.

Frank Curnow, 1898–1973.

These small stones, the size of a child's hand, can be seen at the crossroads today. There must have been many injuries sustained by workers on the land in those early days. Herbert Rogers recalls the rough and ready medical care on hand. His father had been working with his grandfather chopping turnips, when his father chopped off his left forefinger. It hung off, held only by the skin, but when asked later if he had gone to see the doctor, he replied, 'No. My father cut two sticks from the hedge for splints, bound up the finger with twist tobacco and I've felt no discomfort from that day to this.'

Revd Richard Parker

In the time of Richard Parker, incumbent from 1898–1924, confirmations were truly outstanding events. Wagonettes, more usually transporting straw, were hired from Mr Porter in Church Road and the candidates, their families and friends set out for Falmouth Parish Church. The small children rode all the way but the big ones had to get out and walk up the hills. After the service, a special tea was arranged in a Falmouth restaurant and the party would then walk back to the Flushing ferry and so home.

Mylor Christmas Lights

In September 1988, Tony Andrew called a public meeting to explore the possibilities of erecting Christmas lights in Mylor. The meeting was well attended and a committee was formed. Various fund-raising events were arranged and generous donations received from local organisations, which enabled the first strings of lights to be purchased. In December of that year about 500 lights were erected and there was the first switching-on ceremony and carol service. Falmouth Temple Salvation Army Band played and nobody could have envisaged the number of people who attended. The success of that first evening was a huge thrill for everyone who had worked so hard. At the time of writing, that was 15 years ago, and since then Mylor Christmas lights have gone from strength to strength. Many strings of lights have been added, together with set pieces including a working boat, a star which shines from the top of the village and can be seen for miles around, and a beautiful illuminated crib.

Switch-on night for the Christmas lights, 1 December 2003, was enjoyed by a large crowd from near and far.

The caravan which inspired Bill and Maggie Sparkes to move to Mylor in 1952.

Throughout it all, there has been a relentless programme of fund-raising, to maintain existing lights and provide new ones as they are subject to extreme weather conditions. The street market, held in the Lemon Arms car park every August, and the Christmas raffle are the principal sources of revenue, plus jumble sales, and an Easter-egg raffle held in the Lemon Arms.

The switching-on ceremony is the culmination of the effort throughout the year. There is a large Christmas tree in the Lemon Arms car park, as well as Father Christmas in his sleigh, the Pendennis Brass Band play carols, and Nankersey Male Choir lead the singing together with a children's choir. Each child is given a small present and a light stick to wave around which add greatly to the gaiety and colour. The crowds get larger every year and a feature of this special evening is a social gathering in the Tremayne Hall where everyone is invited to tea and mince pies.

The Christmas lights have made a big impact on Mylor and beyond. It is evident, from the support received, how much they are appreciated. A tribute in verse was found on the village notice-board. It was later found that it was written by Maureen Harmer who lives in Devon at the time of writing and is married to John Brown, once chairman of Mylor Parish Council.

Dorothy's Story

After the Second World War, an increasing number of city-folk saw an opportunity to move to the country, be near the sea and live a fuller life. In 1952, two such people were my parents, Bill and Maggie Sparkes. They were lucky enough to see an advertisement for a caravan on a smallholding of about three acres in Mylor. The caravan had been horse-drawn to a site off Comfort Road where there was a pigsty, a chicken house, no water except from the village pump and no electricity. It meant leaving behind all mod-cons and starting from scratch but they decided to make it work, and Mylor was to become their home.

After a lot of hard work and determination, the caravan was transformed and the land was producing enough to keep their heads above water. They joined in with various village activities: i.e. Women's Fellowship, Mylor Players, Women's Institute, Darby and Joan, Art Club, and they were accepted by the locals, making many life-long friends. After 30 years of the good life, the land my parents had was developed and became the lower part of Willow Close. Altogether, they enjoyed 40 years in these lovely surroundings, living in Willow Close themselves after the changes had been made.

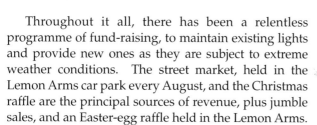

Come all, and climb up Lemon Hill
Past Comfort up to Passage.
The lights of Mylor call us still,
In voices sweet but never shrill,
To gaze with wonder, look our fill
And dig our hands deep in our purse
For those whose Christmas might be worse
Than either yours or mine.

The village men have worked for days
To string the coloured baubles
Across the street, as in a maze,
So everyone can come and gaze
As myriad lights become ablaze,
In contrast to the blackest pitch,
As Mrs Collins throws the switch
And Mylor shines once more.

Throughout the village windows bright
Will tell the Christmas story
In colour, tinsel, pattern, light;
And folks will come from miles that night
To sing, to give, to share the sight
Of people happy, filled with joy,
Remembering the baby boy
Who once was born for us.

And children's posters bid us seek
All that is best in Mylor;
The lights reflected in the creek,
All those delights of which I speak,
They will be here through Christmas week,
Pointing us to the oxen's stall.
See the most precious gift of all,
Jesus the Infant King.

Bill Sparkes and his daughter, Dorothy, soon settled into the rural way of life. They are pictured here c.1970.

Bill Sparkes as Grandad in the Tremayne Hall, c.1970. The children were, left to right, standing at the back: Nicola Rogers, Marcia Cavill, Claire Laity, Teresa Hodge; the rest: Linda Knight, Jo Vinnicombe, Lila Parsons, Anna Tonkin, Sue Ferris, Linda Curnow, Margaret Laity, ?, Vivien Hearle, Michelle Parsons, Sue Cavill, Catherine Vinnicombe.

Feast Days and Ancient Customs

In common with other parishes in the old days, Mylor celebrated its feast day. The original date was 28 August but, following the reformation, this was changed to October, when all available farm labour was no longer required on the land. Many feast days have ceased to be observed but St Mylor Feast was revived in 1974 with an exhibition of Mylor's past and a display of the art and craftwork, which are so much a part of Mylor present.

There were also customs that went back into the remote past, one curious one observed in Mylor being the election of a Mock Mayor. Robert Hunt, a writer who for some years lived in Flushing, tells us about this ceremony in his *Popular Romances of the West of England or the Drolls, Traditions and Superstitions of Cornwall*, published in 1865. On a particular day in September, when the hazelnuts were ripe, Nutting Day was kept. A rabble of Penryn men went into the country to gather nuts and returned in the evening carrying hazel boughs, shouting and making a great noise of a rude, rough, wild and riotous nature. Meanwhile, the journeymen tailors of the town went to Mylor and chose the wittiest of their number to be Mayor of Mylor for the day. Borne on the shoulders of four stalwart men, the Mayor was carried from his good town of Mylor to his ancient borough of Penryn, led by bodyguards, torch-bearers and two town sergeants in official gowns and cocked hats, each carrying a large cabbage in lieu of a mace. A band met them and played them into the town where, before the Town Hall, the Mayor presented an excellent burlesque of the speeches of parliamentary candidates. The procession moved on to each of the great number of public houses in the town at that time, where all were liberally supplied with ale. The night was then devoted to drinking, the populace carrying torches, throwing fireballs and discharging rockets. A huge bonfire burned on the Green until dawn broke.

It is said that this custom was a survival of an ancient ceremony of some significance. A revival of religion in the Penryn district was responsible for the event falling into abeyance.

A familiar sight was Lizzie Sherdy (1820–1905), one of the many pedlars who walked the countryside with a large basket of goodies – some say penny dips for the children to buy, some say doll's eyes, faces and hair and others butter and eggs – perhaps it depended upon the occasion and season. Her real name was Elizabeth Dunstan and she was born near Chacewater. She always wore a heavy plaid shawl and white apron. One night, she and her husband had a row and, in fury, he started smashing her china. In revenge, she made him a pasty which contained some of the broken pieces. Thereafter she was known as Lizzie Sherdy! (DRAWING BY PETER CLARK, 2004)

Reminiscences of Mary Young

The Revd Gilbert Young, his wife and his daughter, Mary, moved into Mylor Vicarage from Trevone in 1924. Mary, educated by her parents, has many clear memories of those early days – of the general strike, when a daily bulletin was displayed on the Vicarage gate, of the first wireless in the district being installed in the Vicarage and mains electricity the following year. The household comprised the vicar, Mrs Young and Mary, Canon Young, the vicar's father and Miss Molle, the vicar's aunt. The staff consisted of a gardener, two general staff (cook and housemaid), a boot and knife boy and a gardener's boy.

Gilbert Young was not only a very popular parish priest but also a good sportsman, entering into all the sporting occasions, being an especially keen member of the tennis club. He drove a strange old car, in the back window of which was the notice, 'It is better to be late in this world than early in the next.'

Canon Young, Mary's grandfather, was living in the Vicarage in retirement but was called upon from time to time to perform delicate commissions. One of these assignments was concerned with the case of Florence Maybrick of Liverpool, who was accused, convicted and sentenced to death for the murder of her arsenic-addicted husband. Due to public outcry, the sentence was commuted to life imprisonment, but she had already served a number of years. It was desirable that the release be low key and Canon Young was consulted. Mrs Maybrick had been sent to the Convent of the Epiphany in St Agnes and there the Canon visited her in the utmost secrecy. Not even his family knew of the plan. But the press had an inkling and descended in force upon the Vicarage, pestering Mrs Young. 'Would you kindly remove yourselves,' she said, 'since you are frightening the servants.' When Mrs Maybrick was considered fit to travel, she was taken to Truro station, where, on the bridge, Canon Young handed her a ticket for Dover. Not a word was exchanged. The journalists, however, were hot on the trail, forcing the Canon and his charge to miss their train on which yet more of the press were waiting. The pair took a

A parish occasion in the Vicarage garden, c.1927. Left to right, seated: Miss Molle, Miss Trefusis, Lady M. Trefusis, Bishop Frere, Revd Parker, Colonel H. Trefusis, Revd G. Young (vicar), Mr Johns (schoolmaster), Mrs C. Thomas, Mrs Burley, Mr Burley; children: Maud Porter, Billy Roberts, Rene Cundy, Jim Cundy, Donald Bond, Sylvia Cundy; among those at the back are: Mr Ashton (headmaster), H. Rowe, Miss D. Roberts, L. Rowe, Jack Curnow, C. Thomas, Miss Daniel, Miss Doble, Miss Tillman, Miss Hingston, J. Barnicoat, Miss J. Stevens, R. Prout, E. Beaton, R. de Vere Stacpoole, K. Beaton, Mr Rawling, W. Thomas, C. Bunny, Miss May Olivey, Benjy Thomas, F. Tresise (churchwarden), J. Cole, Mrs C. Thomas, Miss M. Young, Miss Alice Evans.

Revd 'Gibby' Young assists a friend into a boat, 1915.

It is believed that Cornovi Cottage was built c.1790.

later train, changing to another en route and travelling in different coaches. From Dover, Mrs Maybrick was escorted across the Channel to France, there to be re-united with members of her family.

Mrs Young was a sensitive person, who could see more than most people. One very warm summer's day, she called her daughter to her side and pointed through an upstairs window at what seemed to be a beautiful city with a castle, towers and gardens rising above the far side of Restronguet Creek. This could have been the mysterious Fata Morgana some-times seen by sailors in the straights between Italy and Sicily; a mirage which is due to reflections occurring on the surfaces of the layers of air at different temperatures.

On another occasion, Mrs Young awoke to see a pretty lady dressed in white standing at the foot of her bed. The figure moved towards the door and out onto the landing, there to descend the stairs and disappear. Some time later, Mrs Young was taking tea with friends in Flushing. An album of photographs was produced, some showing groups of local people taken in earlier times. 'Who is this lady?' asked Mrs Young, pointing to an attractive face, 'I'm sure I recognise her.' 'That is Mrs Hoblyn, wife of the Revd Hoblyn, who was vicar here early in the last century,' was the reply.

Cornovi Cottage

Number 41 Lemon Hill is a cob-and-stone cottage which was probably thatched when it was built in around 1790 as part of the Carclew estate and appears on the Ordnance Survey maps for the village of Mylor in 1808. The tithe map of 1840 shows that the house plan had been extended.

Cast-iron handrails project down the granite steps from the front door. These rails and some of the twisted newels were probably made by the local blacksmith, who sweated them into the granite with molten lead.

In 1900, James H. Tresise leased the property from Lieutenant Colonel A. Tremayne for a period of 60 years at £2.10s. per annum, and the house was finally sold into private hands in 1961. Since 1983 much of the character of the house has been restored and the dining-room has been converted to business purposes. Dealing mainly with weddings, it is from here that Sandra Redwood runs Cornovi Creations which hires and sells Cornish tartan kilted outfits to people from all over the world. The Cornish Hunting Tartan was designed in this house in 1983.

Vera Moore's Memories

I was born in 1920 and the Christmases I remember are of all the family getting together, and the log fire in the grate. It all started a week before Christmas, when we would go out carol singing at people's doors. Sometimes we would get asked in for a mince pie. Then we bought coloured papers and, as children, would glue them together to form

a chain. Our Christmas tree would be cut which would be holly, and my Mum and Dad would decorate it after we had gone to bed on Christmas Eve to be a surprise for us in the morning. We didn't go to town very often, so it was a highlight to catch the afternoon bus on Christmas Eve to look at the shops. We were given some money first to buy a present for ourselves – I usually bought a book. My Dad's brother and family lived in Falmouth so we would go up to them for a meal, go out singing carols and come home on a later bus. All my grandparents lived in Mylor, so after we had looked at our presents on Christmas Day, we would all go up to our maternal grandparents for the day. All our aunts, uncles and cousins would be there. I remember we always had roast beef for dinner, and after that, while everything was cleared away, the children would go up to the bedroom which was very large, and play with balloons. After our tea, we would all play games together.

On Boxing Day, we would go to our paternal grand-parents, who lived in the village. All our cousins would be there as well, so we had a good time together. We always had turkey for dinner on that day, which was a luxury in those days. In the afternoon we would go outside to hear the wassailers, as we called them, who would come each year and sing outside the Lemon Arms. After the days of Christmas were past, we would all go to each other's houses on different days for a party. When I was growing up we didn't have much money, but we were very happy. Wherever you were born, you found work and rented a cottage. So families stayed together more. It is good to reminisce about the Christmases you remember.

Reminiscences of Becky Bunny

Mrs Becky Bunny (née Rawling) lived in Mylor all her life. At first, with her three brothers and two sisters, the family lived in Mill Cottage. This still stands above Mill Quay. Burchells Fair used to come regu-larly to Mill Quay, an occasion enjoyed especially by the children of the village with hoopla and swing boats. Along the lane were standings – stalls selling nougat, toffee, sticks of liquorice and white and pink strips of coconut. The recreation-ground had not been drained then and it was still a marshy area.

Regatta days were enjoyed too. There were rowing races as well as sailing. A long pole was secured to the quay jutting out over the water. This was the slippery pole on which opponents fought each other with pillows until one, or both, fell off into the water. What hilarity and excitement that must have aroused, along with the comic singing competition. The evening concluded with a dance in the church hall.

In those days Becky's uncle, Saul Brown, kept the village grocery shop, now Mylor Stores. This was when the leat flowed behind New Row (now the Leats car park), under the bridge and beside the carpenter's shop (now the butchers), and along what is Tremayne Close at the time of writing. Becky went to school in Tremayne Hall when it was a

Gran Becca in the early 1900s. She was the great-grandmother of Yvonne Andrew who still lives in the village in 2004.

church school. Miss Sara taught the infants, Miss Davies Standard 1, Miss Lucy Gray 2, Mr Bennie Lee 3, with Mr Ashton as the headmaster.

Mrs Rawling's mother, Mrs Tregenza, known as Gran Becca, lived with the family. Mr Rawling worked in the garden at Greatwood. His children would take it in turns, even in the short lunch-hour, to take a pasty or sometimes a small roast to their father, walking up over the fields to Greatwood and eating their own lunch on the way.

In those days Greatwood was owned by Mr Bond. He lived alone except for the cook, Daisy Foot and her sister, Agnes, who was housemaid. Mr Crewes was the butler and chauffeur. Mr Rawling left to serve in the First World War, after which he worked on the council-house project on Old Hill, Falmouth. He was, however, asked to return to Greatwood as the gardener. The family, who were by now living at 41 Lemon Hill, Cornovi Cottage, moved up to a cottage in the grounds of Greatwood in the 1920s. Here they continued to live a very happy life. Aunts, uncles, cousins and friends were constant visitors. These included Rose Rogers and Pat and Herbie Rogers. British tankers were laid up in the Carrick Roads in front of Greatwood and the Rawling family would entertain the captains and their wives and the sailors as guests. When old Mr Bond died, Greatwood was bought by Mr Dorrien-Smith. He originated from the Isles of Scilly and created a flower and bulb farm. Mr Rawling continued to work until he and Mrs Rawling retired to Passage Hill.

This picture of Lemon Hill, taken in 1905, shows Ash Villa completed and the terrace of three cottages next door under construction.

Great Gran Buzza, pictured c.1890, was mother to Gran Becca.

Becky worked in the house owned by Mrs Johns in Rose Hill and assisted in the market garden by bunching the flowers grown there – daffodils, violets and gladioli. Here it was that she met her husband, John. They were married in 1955 and started life together at No. 25 Lemon Hill, where Becky lived for the rest of her life and where Yvonne, their daughter grew up. In the house is a beautifully decorated Cornish range. In earlier days, when working on Rose Hill, Becky had to blacklead a similar stove every Friday morning – an arduous, dirty task – earning just one shilling a day.

Minnie May's great-grandfather owned the water-mill situated with a few cottages behind the quay, where the corn was ground to flour. He also owned one of the three grocery stores in Mylor and the terrace of three cottages, Nos 24–26 Lemon Hill, the middle one being Becky's home.

The Old Post Office

The Old Post Office, of Georgian style, was probably built sometime before 1840, when it is shown on the tithe map. Solidly constructed of stone with a slate roof, an interesting feature is its overlapping eaves, which are not normally found locally.

In 1883 it was leased by Arthur Tremayne to Edward Hankin for 14 years at £15 per annum. Edward Hankin's daughter, Hannah, ran the Post Office until her marriage in 1918, when William Tremayne leased the property to William James Rees, the local blacksmith, who then moved in with his family. It is difficult to imagine how the Rees family fitted in as they had 15 children.

Dorothy Rees, William's daughter, ran the Post Office for seven years. In 1940 the property was sold to Mrs Dunstan, a widow from Flushing, who continued to run the Post Office. In 1957 the property was sold as a private house and the Post Office moved to where it is at the time of writing. Peter and Joan Davis bought it in 1983.

There have been many alterations to the inside of the house, but the window-seat, which people sat on whilst awaiting their turn at the counter, is still there. It is now much appreciated by the family dog who enjoys sitting on it to watch passing people on Lemon Hill.

School Chums Meet

A few years ago, four friends, all in their nineties, met up at a Network meeting in Mylor. Elsie Gregory and Dorothy Congdon used to go to Flushing School together. It was lovely to see them chatting to Ivy Collins and Rose Rogers, who used to attend the school in Mylor.

School was very different in those days. The girls, and even some of the little boys, wore pinafores to keep their clothes clean, and they wore ankle boots which laced up, over long socks or stockings. They sat at long wooden desks most of the time, learning to read, write beautifully, spell and do sums. Learning tables was done by rote. Ivy remembers living in a thatched cottage at the bottom of Rose Hill on the Enys estate. It was here that she and her four brothers and sister were born. Her grandmother lived with the family and when her sight began to fail, Ivy and her younger sister could earn a halfpenny by threading all the needles in her flannel sewing case, so that they were ready for grandmother to use.

Encouraged by her father, Ivy took the Mylor scholarship when she was 11 years old. To her surprise, she passed the examination, enabling her to attend Falmouth County High School. There were no buses so every day she had to walk to Flushing and take the ferry across to Falmouth, the fare being a halfpenny, and then walk up the steep hill.

Ivy's father was the Parish Clerk. One of her brothers died in the First World War when he was only 18 years old and two of her brothers became farmers at Rose Hill and Feock, the other a butcher. While they were still children, the family moved to Rose Hill Farm House.

Above: *The Old Post Office built in the early 1800s.*

Right: *Mylor Bridge postmark, 10 August 1910.*

The cast of a play entitled **The Lacemakers** *which was taken from village to village, riding in a haycart, c.1913. In the centre is Henrietta Hankins, at one time Mylor's postmistress, and front left is Dorothy Rees, one of the blacksmith's daughters.*

Above: *The Mylor Band outside the Vicarage, c.1900.*
Left to right: Tom Moore, Will Copeland, Dick Moore,
Annie May, John Tallack, Walter Kevern, Mabel Martin,
Mr Law, Phoebe Scantlebury, Eb Moore, and the Revd
Parker, who was a keen musician and started the band.

Right: *Carnival float, 1950s. Left to right, on the float:*
Phyllis Rees, Eileen Tallack, Edna Studd, Edna Ingram,
Florrie Goldsworthy, Bill Rowe, Ivy Collins; in front:
Ursula Turner, Minna Rollason.

Mylor Carnival, 1957, featuring Mylor Steam Laundry. Left to right: Kenny Keast, Terry Heard, ? Blackmore,
and Tony Andrew with the black face.

Chapter 14

The Future

Mylor Parish Council, The Tremayne Hall, Hopes for the Future.

Mylor Parish Council

Mylor Parish Council came into existence together with all other Parish Councils in the land on 4 December 1894. It is elected every four years when the number of candidates exceeds 13, otherwise those who apply fill the vacancies. At the time of writing the last election was in May 2003. Monthly meetings of the council are held alternately at Mylor Parish Hall and the Flushing Club Room on the first Monday in the month in accordance with standing orders, and parishioners are welcome to attend as spectators.

The Parish Council are custodian trustees of the King George V Playing Field from the bridge to Tregatreath, the Ord-Statter Pavilion and the Scout hut. The Tremayne Hall is on lease. The council own the clock tower, the Leats car park, the Parish Hall and Mill Quay; they also own the Sands car park and Bowling

Mylor Parish Council, 1894. Left to right, back row: *Mr Stephens of Crownick Farm, Mylor; W. Rowe of Tregew Farm, Flushing; Michael Moore, shopkeeper; W.H. Tong, registrar of births and deaths, Flushing; John Cloak, a retired merchant and JP, Flushing; W. Beer, a Flushing baker; Revd Francis Forbes-Savage, vicar of St Peter's, Flushing;* front: *Richard Dunstan, Pellow (Porloe) Farm, Mylor; Edwin Barnicoat, Mylor builder; Dr D.V. Davis of Flushing; William Rundle of Dowstall Farm, Mylor; Mr Daniel, Parc Vean, Mylor; W. Geach, farmer, Mylor dockyard, Halwyn; W. Bird, farmer, Tregew Farm. Mr John Cloak sounded a colourful character. It is reported that 'when presiding in court in Penryn, if a man was charged with being drunk and disorderly he would proclaim 'scandalous' and send him down for ten days. He not only wore lavender coloured spats and gloves, but also a choker collar and used a black ebony stick, walking the village streets as if on parade.' Revd Francis Forbes-Savage later became a canon and was very interested in local history.*

Parish Council of 1948 taken at Lawncliffe Hotel, Flushing. Left to right, back row: H. Moore, B. Edney, F. Spear, C. Barnicoat, G. Hearle, C. Wilkes, W. Dadda, G. Pyper, R. Prout; front: H.R. Prout, G. Bennett, M. Orchard, E. Gray, (parish clerk), A. Ingram.

Mylor Parish Council, 1994. Left to right, back row: D. Burley, B. Collier, M. Burden, A. Stevenson, E.J. Strike, D. Laity, J. Frapwell (clerk); front: C. Hadley, A. Langford, A.N. Andrew (chairman), E. James, M. Berryman, S. Curnow.

Green at Flushing and all six parish pumps. The lawn-type cemetery is owned and administered by the Parish Council who are responsible for its maintenance and charges and the war memorials at Mylor and Flushing are also in the ownership of the Parish Council.

All planning applications within the parish are submitted for the observations of the council, but final decisions are taken by the District Council. The maintenance of public footpaths is the responsibility of the Parish Council in partnership with the County Council. Most of the street lights are the responsibility of the Parish Council.

Mylor Parish Paths maps were published for sale by the Parish Council in 1997 and have since been updated. They have proved very successful and are for sale at £1 each in various shops in the villages.

The Tremayne Hall

At the time of writing the Tremayne Hall is in urgent need of renovation. It is a Grade II listed building and the management committee are working hard to obtain the necessary funding.

The history of Mylor's Tremayne Hall began in 1827, when the increasing numbers of paupers forced local overseers and guardians to do something more than placing them in rented houses, which had been their practice. By 1817, Mylor's population was 1,897 and one person in 20 depended upon relief – sad effects of the Industrial Revolution, bad harvests and the Napoleonic Wars. The administrators then rented a piece of land in the centre of the village and their books stated that:

The sum of £13 is paid to Bartholomew Laurence for one-ninth part of an acre in one of his fields near and upon the mill leat for the term of 13 years or during the whole term he may be entitled to it, whereon to erect the proposed poorhouse.

The sum of £200 was borrowed to set the plan in motion, which had to be done quickly because repayment was required within five years. All was speedily done and for £6 Mr O'Brien superintended the work of Mr Wm Pearce, as his £109.1s. tender had been accepted.

Completion came none too soon apparently, for by 1830 a special meeting was called 'to take into consideration the appointing a governor over the poorhouse and to enlarge the building.' Next, Mr Barbary drew plans for two rooms for the governor and dining accommodation for approximately 40 inmates, but not till 1833 was it agreed 'to take the field adjoining the poorhouse to rent of Bartw. Laurence at £8 per annum with leave to build on as much thereof as may be necessary.'

Work then proceeded, the carpenter receiving £98.18s.10d. and the mason £81.7s.10d. More paupers required more furniture, so 24 bedsteads, bed ties and other bedding were ordered and another committee was appointed to order food and draw up menus such as:

Saturday:	*Broth and vegetables*
Monday:	*Peas, 1 oz of beef suet to each man*
Wednesday:	*Fish or rice milk.*

On broth days one pound of extra bread was allocated to those older than ten. In an effort to recoup some of their expenditure, the overseers sent truckloads of children to cotton and woollen mills, but in 1834 parliament passed the Poor Law Amendment, which altered matters by recommending the setting up of schools within the workhouses. Over the next few years there were fewer paupers and people began to realise the importance of education. Sir Charles Lemon, the wealthy and compassionate owner of Carclew, was one of these and offered to buy part of the poorhouse for a private school. Eventually, however, in 1850 the whole building was sold to him for £75 and he and his heirs maintained it privately until 1894 when it became a National School.

When a fire damaged part of the building in 1921, a new school was built in Comfort Road, although the original workhouse remains. The schoolmasters' living quarters are privately owned and are still known as Old School House. The extensions have become the Tremayne Hall, once pride of the village, thanks to another benefactor, Mr Jack Holt, who bequeathed thousands of pounds for the restoration of the old building. He left detailed instructions for the work, which included repairs to the clock in the campanile tower and handsome wrought-iron gates to complete the twentieth-century look. On 28 October 1978, Mrs J. Tremayne opened those memorial gates to a very different future to that envisaged by the workhouse overseers more than a century earlier.

Hopes for the Future

A refurbished and modernised Tremayne Hall, with some additional accommodation and facilities for the disabled, should have an exciting and important part to play in the life of the community. Well into the future, it would continue to provide the essential meeting-place which must exist at the heart of any village, particularly one as large as Mylor.

The many organisations currently using the hall should find the improved premises and facilities more comfortable and as a result would be expected to gain added membership for their individual groups or clubs. Others who have given up use of the hall because of past discomfort should return to this upgraded venue.

Improvements to the floors, heating, lighting and toilets should make the hall attractive as a venue for people of all ages. The changes to the layout and additional accommodation would generate an increase in the range of activities being undertaken and thus the number of people in the area able to share in the benefits.

Left: *Official opening of the wrought-iron gates to the Tremayne Hall, 28 October 1978. They were a legacy from Jack Holt. Left to right: Mrs Eileen Prout, Mrs Ruth Andrew, Mr Rodney Prout (chairman of Mylor Parish Council), Mrs Joan Tremayne, Mr Tony Andrew (chairman of the Tremayne Hall Management Committee).*

Below: *Celebration meal for the opening of the gates, in the Tremayne Hall.*

The British Legion children's party, held to celebrate the opening of the Church Hall, 23 April 1925. Originally the poorhouse, it was used as the village school from 1850 until it was burnt down in 1921. It was rebuilt and known as the Church Hall for many years. The tall man standing at the back right of the picture is Sgt Major Hurrell of the Seven Stars Inn, Flushing.

Model of the proposed renovations and alterations to the Tremayne Hall, made to plans passed by Carrick District Council.

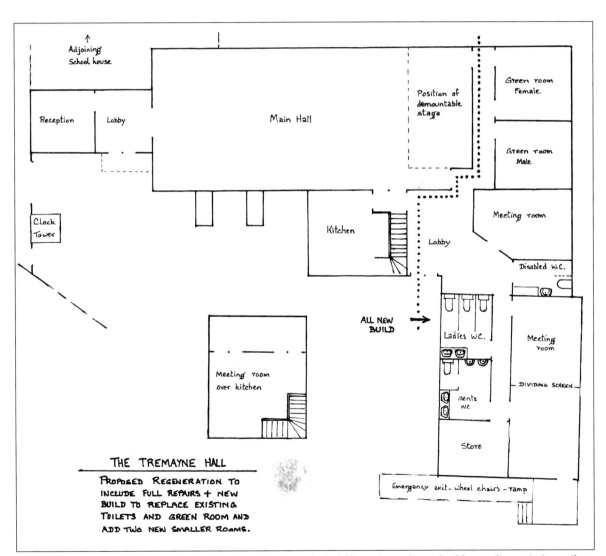

Tremayne Hall plan showing proposed regeneration to include full repairs and new build to replace existing toilets, green room and add two smaller rooms.

By removing the stage the length of the main hall would be increased. Space behind the baselines of the badminton court would thus be greater and the level-floor access into green rooms behind the present stage area would allow chairs and tables to be tidied away easily into those rooms. A demountable stage is a planned part of the improved premises and when a show or concert takes place, chairs would be moved into the main hall, thus freeing up the green rooms for use by the artists.

Although parties, wedding receptions, concerts etc. have taken place in the past, such usage should increase considerably. A drama group is expected to be formed and once again residents will have the pleasure of local theatre. In addition small, regional, touring theatre companies are likely to show an interest in the venue. Extra activities will most likely include carpet bowls in the large hall. Also committee meetings, exhibitions, coffee mornings, lectures, classes such as IT, WEA courses and possibly a lunch club for the older population, could all make use of the two new rooms. A local archive might also be set up, making use of the material supplied for this book.

With the Leats car park close by, the hall would be assured of a thriving future with multiple simultaneous bookings boosting income to the point where employment of someone to act as caretaker and oversee the premises becomes a real possibility. The hall will continue to be managed by a committee operating under the rules of the Charity Commissioners and elected annually by the community, with a responsibility to maintain and run the premises and to manage its finances efficiently, so that costs are met but letting charges are kept to acceptable levels.

The listed Tremayne Hall, standing in a conservation area at the heart of the village, dates back to the nineteenth century and for much of that time has served the population well. Regenerated, it should be doing so for many years to come. However, all this will only happen with the support and involvement of everyone in the parish.

Celtic Blessing

May the road rise to meet you,
May the wind be always at your back,
May the sun shine warm upon your face,
The rains fall soft upon your fields
And until we meet again
May God hold you in the hollow of His hand.

Subscribers

'Rosilian', Flushing, Cornwall

Lt Col and Mrs A.R. Adams

Bunnie Adams, Mylor Bridge, Cornwall

John and Karen Adams, Mylor, Cornwall

Patricia Ainsley, Mylor, Cornwall

Suzanne and Jeffery Askew,

A.J. (Buzz) Banks, Carclew, Mylor

David Barnicoat, Lanner, Cornwall

Mary Beattie (née Rollason), Mabe, Cornwall

Peter Bettison, born Mylor 1921

Pamela Bird, Mylor Churchtown

Gillian Blackler, Mylor Bridge, Cornwall

Mr Jonathan G. Bomford, Mylor Churchtown, Cornwall

Mrs Marion A. Bomford, Mylor Churchtown, Cornwall

Alan and Celia Boughton (née Rowe)

Mrs Clare Bradley, Mylor, Cornwall

Helen Brown (née Thomas), Sevenoaks, Kent

Dr I.M.C. and Mrs S.J. Brown, Truro, Cornwall

John and Mo Brown, Chillaton, Devon

Tom Brown, Mylor Bridge

Sarah J. Bull, Mylor Bridge, Cornwall

K.J. Burrow, Bucks Cross, Devon

Jean Calvert

Ruth Chamberlain (née George)

Irene T.B. Champion, Mylor

John Charnock, Mylor Bridge, Cornwall

Stella Charnock, Mylor, Cornwall

William Charnock, New York

Mr H. and Mrs. D. Christmas

Penny A. Chuter O.B.E., Mylor, Cornwall

Major Bruce Collier, Mylor, Cornwall

John and Felicity Collins, Mylor

Mr and Mrs Michael Corfield, Lymington, Hampshire

Anne Craig, Mylor, Cornwall

The Criddle Family, Mylor

Alistair Crombie, Falmouth, Cornwall

Ian Crombie, Bromley, Kent

Kate Crombie, Old School House, Mylor Bridge

Mr P.A. and Mrs M. Crump, and Master J.W. Crump, Creek Cottage, Mylor

Miss T.L. Cuff, Manea, Cambridgeshire

M.A. Curnow, Mylor, Cornwall

M.D. Curnow, Mylor, Cornwall

Vyvyan Curnow (née Williams)

M. D'Alessandro, Mylor, Cornwall

Dan and Juliet, Ripon, North Yorkshire

John and Joyce Darbyshire, Mylor, Cornwall

Barbara Darling, Chatsworth, California

Joan Davis, Mylor Bridge

John and Nola Davis, Geelong, Vic., Australia

Mr Tony Deacon, Mylor, Cornwall

Audrey Dean, Mylor, Cornwall

Caroline De Esposiso (née George)

The Delbridge Family, Mylor and Sussex

Dorrit and Barbara, Mylor Bridge

Marion Drabble, Mylor, Cornwall

The Duncan Family, Mylor, Cornwall

Clive Eich, Luxulyan, Cornwall

Bob and Sarah Epps, Mylor, Cornwall

Falmouth Local History and Research Group

D.C.S. and B. Farmer, Mylor, Cornwall

Mrs Eileen Ferris, Mylor, Cornwall

Michael Fleming, Mylor, Cornwall

Nick and Helen Fletcher, Chytreth, Mylor Harbour

Graham and Cordelia Folland, Restronguet, Mylor

Kenwyn George

Thelma and Peter Gilson, Falmouth

Eric P. Gray, Horsham, West Sussex

Peter and Katie Gray, Bristol

Mr and Mrs Simon Gray, Lymington, Hampshire

Sue Griffin, Wiltshire

Emma Grundy, Mylor Bridge, Cornwall

L.T. Gwynn, Lee-on-Solent, Hampshire

Mr Kenneth C. Hall, Mylor, Cornwall

Keith and Aldyth Hambly-Staite, Feock, Truro

Mrs Shena E. Harrison, Mylor

Mr and Mrs Percy Harvey,

Charles E. Hatfield, Mylor Bridge

Thelma L. Heard, Mylor, Cornwall

Mr D.M. Hearle, Mousehole

Mr G.M. Hearle, Vellanvounder, Mylor

Mr J.A. Hearle, Falmouth

Miss Sally R. Hearle, Texas, USA

Mr T.E. Hearle, Falmouth

Mrs Tamsin Hearle Banks, Carclew, Mylor

T. Hockett, Enfield, Middlesex

Dr Kaspar Hocking, Constantine, Cornwall

Betty Hodges, Mylor, Cornwall

Howard B. Hodges, Mylor, Cornwall

Victoria Fay Hodges, Mylor, Cornwall

W.H. Hodges, St Mawes, Cornwall

Mr and Mrs S.F. Honey

Susanne E. Humphreys, Mylor Bridge, Cornwall

Marvin Johns, Tasmania, Australia

Ray Jones

Ray and Margaret Jones

Wendy Jones, Mylor, Cornwall

Pat, Nicholas and Timothy Juett, Beach Cottage

Vice Admiral Sir James and Lady Jungius, Mylor

Colin Keast, Stevenage, Hertfordshire

Tony Keast, Stevenage, Hertfordshire

Dr and Mrs S.R.A. Kelly, Cambridge

Mary Kerr, Mylor Bridge, Cornwall

The Killick Family, Mylor, Cornwall

Paula M. Kirk, Toronto, Canada

Laura Anne Kneebone, St Buryan

Sid and Pam Leadbetter, Mylor, Cornwall

Bunny Lewis, Mylor, Cornwall

P.G. Lobb J.P., Ponsanooth

R.P. Lobb M.A., Vet. M.B., M.R.C.V.S., Mylor

Malcolm J. Lockhart, Mylor, Cornwall

George F. Marshall

Mike and Gill Marshman, Mylor, Cornwall

Mary Martin, Mylor Bridge, Cornwall

Matt and Kate, Labrador, Queensland, Australia

Minnie May, Mylor, Cornwall

Malcolm McCarthy, Padstow

Rob and Al Menary, Hillside, Mylor

Sarah M. Merabet, Mylor, Cornwall

Mr R.K. Merrifield, London

Mr T.D. Merrifield

Richard and Dorli Milsom

Kim Mooney, Mylor, Cornwall

❖ SUBSCRIBERS ❖

Patricia Mooney (née Truscott), Restronguet, Cornwall

Mrs A. Moore, Mylor, Cornwall

Mr Bart Moore, Mylor, Cornwall

Basil Moore, Newton Abbot, Devon

Mr E.T. Moore, Truro, Cornwall

Robin and Celia Moore, Mylor

Tom Moore, Washington, USA

V. Moore, Mylor, Cornwall

Robert and Charmaine Morgan, Mylor Bridge, Falmouth, Cornwall (October 2004)

Angela Murphy

Mylor Local History Group

Mylor Yacht Harbour Ltd

Daphne Neale, Carclew

Jennifer Nicholls (née George)

Ken Norcross, Mylor, Cornwall

Hugh Olivey, Cromer, Australia

Palarm

Mr Rowland Palmer, Willow Close, Mylor Bridge

William Dean Parker, Mylor Bridge

Mrs B.A. Pearce, Mylor, Cornwall

Miss Carol and Mr Tony Pearce, Mylor

Rosemary Pearson (née Rowse)

Kathryn Pelletier (née George)

Matthew Julian Penryn, Cornwall

Melissa, Merven, Daniel, Rebekah and Matthew Pereira, Mylor

Christopher Perkins, Mylor Churchtown

The Revd Canon Dr Anthony Phillips

Mrs Mary Pilkington, Brightlingsea, Essex

Bob Pitt, Vienna, Austria

Lynne Pitt, St Austell, Cornwall

Mike Pitt, Georgia, USA

Roger and Laura Plumb, Mylor Bridge, Cornwall

Mark and Sandy Polglase, Mylor, Cornwall

Meriel Polglase, Bissoe, Cornwall

Patrick and Pen Polglase and Family, Albion House, Mylor, Cornwall

Maureen Powell, Mylor Bridge

Jack Samson Prout, Mylor Bridge, Cornwall

Susan M. Prout

Anne Rafferty, Mevagissey, Cornwall

Julia Redwood, London

Sandra Redwood, Mylor Bridge, Cornwall

Jean Reed (née McWilliam)

Joan Rees Heard, Falmouth

Shirley Richards, Porkellis

Charles and Christine Robinson, Mylor

Barbara H. Rogers (née Moore), Mylor

Nancy Doreen Rollason, Mylor, Cornwall

Albery Rowe, Limekiln, Mylor Creek

Mrs Elsie Lillian Olive Rowe,

Marcus F. Rowe, Mylor, Cornwall

Peter Rowe, Alford, Lincolnshire

Stuart and Janet Rowe, Mylor and Buckinghamshire

Tamsin Saphir (née George)

Terence and Joan Shelbourne, Mylor Bridge, Cornwall

James Siddall, Skipton, North Yorkshire

Len and Margaret Simpson, Mylor, Cornwall

Mavis June Slade

Anthony W. Smith, Mylor Bridge, Cornwall

Zoe and Bill Spikins, Mylor Bridge, Cornwall

Mr and Mrs M.H. Stevenson, Mylor, Cornwall

Michael Studd, Mylor, Cornwall

Brian and Isabel Taber, Mylor Bridge

David Thomas, Penryn, Cornwall

Lisa Timmins, Mylor, Cornwall

Elaine Trathen (née Rogers)

Margaret Tregilges (née Newman),

Jerry Turner, Mylor, Cornwall

Mr Alan Vaudrey, formerly of Passage Hill, Mylor

June Vincent, Mylor, Cornwall

Tom and Gwen Viveash, Penarrow Cottage, Mylor

John F.W. Walling, Newton Abbot, Devon

Cyril and Jackie Wardill, Amasue, Mylor Yacht Harbour

O.R. Ware, Mylor, Cornwall

Peter J.A. Watson, Restronguet

Christina West, Mylor, Cornwall

Mrs Joan West, Mylor Bridge

Katherine M. Wheatley

Dorothy White, Mylor, Cornwall

Claire Marie Whiting, Mylor

C.N. Wiblin, Shrewton, Wiltshire

Gavin Wilson

Janette Wilson

Fred and Julie Wing, Sunningdale, Mylor

Mike and Cathy Winn, New Row, Mylor Bridge

David and Joan Wyper, Mylor

Gordon and Alison York, Crowborough, East Sussex

Mary Young, Mylor, Cornwall

There are now over 120 titles in the Community History Series.

For a full listing of these and other Halsgrove publications, please visit www.halsgrove.co.uk or telephone 01884 243 242.